HALLMARK TOURIST EVENTS

HALLMARK TOURIST EVENTS
Impacts, Management and Planning

Colin Michael Hall

Belhaven Press
London

Co-published in the Americas by Halsted Press, an imprint of John Wiley & Sons, Inc., New York

Belhaven Press
(a division of Pinter Publishers)
25 Floral Street, Covent Garden, London WC2E 9DS, United Kingdom

First published in 1992

Co-published in the Americas by Halsted Press, an imprint of John Wiley & Sons, Inc., 605 Third
Avenue, New York, NY 10158-0012, USA

C. M. Hall is hereby identified as the author of this work as provided under Section 77 of the
Copyright, Designs and Patents Act, 1988.

British Library Cataloguing in Publication Data

A CIP catalogue record for this book is available from the British Library

ISBN 1 85293 147 7

Library of Congress Cataloging-in-Publication Data

Hall, C. M. (C. Michael)
  Hallmark tourist events: impacts, management, and planning /
Colin Michael Hall.
    p.   cm.
  Includes bibliographical references and indexes.
  ISBN 1-85293-147-7 (Belhaven). ISBN 0-470-21929-7 (Halstead)
    1. Sports and tourist trade. 2. Leisure industry. 3. Festivals.
I. Title.
G155. A1H345 1992
338.4'791–dc20
                                                            92-28308
                                                              CIP

ISBN 0-470-21929-7 (in the Americas only)

Typeset by Koinonia Ltd, Manchester
Printed and bound in Great Britain by Biddles Ltd., Guildford and King's Lynn

For the Wandering Islands and One of the Best Ones

Contents

Figures

Tables

Preface

Our lives are full of events. Events are those things out of the everyday which punctuate, mark, and identify collective and individual social realities. Hallmark tourist events are significant in the development, experiences and lives of communities, travellers and cities. On either a one-off or cyclical basis they mark moments of celebration, spectacle and performance which can have a dramatic effect on those who directly or indirectly experience them. However, the primary focus of this book is not the tourist. Tourism presents to the student a phenomenon of a complementary nature, requiring that attention be given to the relationships and spaces *between* the host and guest. It is impossible to understand one without the other. Indeed, one of the great problems of much of the research on event tourism is that it has only focused on the travel market and the nature of the economic, commercial and promotional benefits that are being sought. The social and political dimensions of events have, until recently, been much neglected.

Australia and New Zealand, which have placed much emphasis on events in their tourism promotion and development strategy, have provided an excellent base to become aware of the various dimensions of hallmark tourist events. The present book has its origins in research that was conducted on the America's Cup in Western Australia from 1985 onward. Originally, interest in event tourism and its associated impacts was a sideline interest of my Ph.D. research on heritage management in Australia. However, thanks to a fortuitous meeting with John Selwood of the University of Winnipeg who was examining the role of the America's Cup on urban development, a minor interest in the impacts of the Cup on the potential World Heritage status of the West End of Fremantle evolved into a long-term study of Cup-related effects and, more generally, the role of events in tourism development.

The study of event tourism was further pushed along by media and 'expert' reaction to a paper that John and I gave in New Zealand in January of 1987 (Hall and Selwood, 1987). A small paragraph in the paper which noted the potential effects of the Cup on crime and prostitution was seized on by the media and local 'experts' and we suddenly found we were temporary celebrities. Undoubtedly, the experience gave us a salutory lesson in the politics of event research with the 'boosters' or 'insider's' view of the local expert standing in marked contrast to the perspective of John and myself, concerned as we were that the negative aspects of the event should be publicly discussed. Indeed, our comments were regarded as somewhat sacrilegious, as we had dared to profane the received view of government, business, and those who had conducted the official research on the effects of the event, by questioning the idea that the America's Cup *must* be of great short- and long-term benefit to the State and to Fremantle.

Since the America's Cup I have had the fortune to witness first hand many other events and bids in Australia and New Zealand, including the 1988 Brisbane Expo, the Australian bicentennial, the Melbourne bid for the 1996 Olympic Games, the

Sydney bid for the 2000 Olympic Games, the Eastern Creek raceway debacle in Sydney, and the 1990 Commonwealth Games in Auckland. Much of my experience with these events has found its way into the present book, along with North American, European, Asian and South American examples of event tourism. From these experiences, and as the book indicates, I believe that events can present great opportunities to meet economic and social objectives. However, unless events are operated and developed in a consultative and participatory manner with the community in which they are hosted, and for which the benefits of hosting should be, then the use of events to achieve sustainable forms of tourism development will be extremely limited.

Many people have helped provide the stimulus for researching and writing Hallmark Tourist Events. The work that I have conducted with John Selwood (America's Cup, crime and prostitution), Heather Zeppel (arts, cultural and heritage tourism), and David Tweed (provision of quality in service industries) has been extremely enjoyable and valuable to the development of my understanding of event tourism and quality management. Geoff Syme and Blair Nancarrow provided great encouragement and opportunities in the study of event tourism for which I am truly grateful. Steve Britton, Dick Butler, Jenny Craik, Ian Elliot, Bill Faulkner, Paul Foley, Don Getz, Harry Hiller, Keith Hollinshead, Geoff Kearsley, Lee Nichols, Kris Olds, Eric Pawson, Doug Pearce, Linda Richter, Brent Ritchie, Maurice Roche, Dennis Rumley, Brian Shaw, Ivan Surridge, Geoff Wall, Jim Walmsley and John Warhurst, have all contributed, either through discussion or through the provision of material, to the writing of the book, although the interpretation of their thoughts and research is, of course, my own.

For their 'infrastructural' and moral support during the writing of this book I would like to thank: Ross Annels, Mariella Bates, Nicole Beasley, Claire Campbell, Graham Castledine, Judy Cooper, Dave Crag, Anne-Louise Crotty, Carley Finn, Steve Hapgood, John Jenkins, Jenny Kinny, Simon MacArthur, Jacqui Pinkava, David Press, Penny Spoelder, Margot Sweeny and Josette Wells in Australia; Robert Kaspar in Austria; Bruce Cockburn and Doug Marshall in Canada; Ingrid van Aalst, Chris Daly, Bill Hanning, Nik Horn, Jeanette Manahi, Ian Mitchell, Tony Molloy and Pip Richardson in New Zealand; Clive Gregson and Christine Collister in the United Kingdom; and Steve Mark in the United States. Intellectual and physical nourishment has been supplied by my fellow members of 'The Basement', Mithras, and the staff of Options at Massey University. Financial assistance for research on hallmark events has been gratefully received from the University of New England Internal Research Fund and the Massey University Research Fund, while I wish to make a special acknowledgement of the Canadian Studies Award made possible by the generosity of Canadian Airlines International which enabled me to travel to Ontario, Alberta and British Columbia in order to study cultural events.

Emma Willson provided invaluable comments and enormous help in the preparation of the final draft, while the institutional support and assistance provided by Brian and Delyse Springett at the New Zealand Natural Heritage Foundation, Linda Coop, Janet Toogood, Linda Macnamara, Stephanie Pearson and Tony Vitalis of the Department of Management Systems, Massey University, has been much appreciated. I would like to give a sincere note of thanks to Iain Stevenson, Jane Evans and everyone at Belhaven for their seemingly endless support and professionalism. Finally, I wish to thank Treve for just being there and, hopefully, understanding what it all means.

C. Michael Hall,

Massey University and New Zealand Natural Heritage Foundation, Palmerston North, New Zealand

1 Introduction: Defining Hallmark Events

Whether festivals are good medicine for the soul, a glue that galvanizes communities together, or a tourist attraction that generates all sorts of economic benefits, the fact remains that very little research documents this phenomenon. Anthropologists and historians have made some efforts, but leisure sciences have not yet found festivals and events as a fertile ground for research. (Cousineau, 1991, p.1)

Hallmark events are the image builders of modern tourism. Since the commencement of commercial travel in the mid-nineteenth century, short-term staged attractions or hallmark events have been a primary means by which to place or keep tourism destinations on the tourist map. Despite their undoubted significance, relatively little academic attention has been paid, until recently, to their management, marketing, planning and impacts. However, 'increasingly, events are being viewed as an integral part of tourism development and marketing plans. Although the majority of events have probably arisen for non-tourist reasons ...there is clearly a trend to exploit them for tourism and to create new events deliberately as tourist attractions' (Getz, 1989b, p.125).

Hallmark events, otherwise referred to as mega or special events are major fairs, festivals, expositions, and cultural and sporting events which are held on either a regular or a one-off basis. Hallmark events have assumed a key role in international, national and regional tourism marketing strategies. Their primary function being to provide the host community with an opportunity to secure high prominence in the tourism market place. Hallmark events are also extremely significant not just for their immediate tourism component but because they may leave behind legacies which will impact on the host community far more widely than the immediate period in which the event actually took place. Examples are large-scale public expenditure, the construction of facilities and infrastructure, and the redevelopment of urban areas that have been regarded as requiring 'renewal'. However, the study of hallmark events is fraught with definitional, methodological and theoretical problems which reflect the many research directions that exist within the study of tourism.

The purpose of this introductory chapter is to clarify the definition and analysis of hallmark events and to highlight the significance of events as tourist phenomenon. This discussion will be expanded to highlight the need for an analysis of hallmark event development which emphasises the need to examine events from a variety of contexts and at a number of levels. The chapter will also stress the need for events to be seen as one component of an overall tourism development process.

Defining Hallmark Events

The standard definition of hallmark events is that provided by Ritchie (1984, p.2) who defined such events as

> Major one-time or recurring events of limited duration, developed primarily to enhance the awareness, appeal and profitability of a tourism destination in the short and/or long term. Such events rely for their success on uniqueness, status, or timely significance to create interest and attract attention.

A primary function of the hallmark tourist event is to provide the host community with an opportunity to secure a position of prominence in the tourism market for a short, well defined, period of time (Ritchie and Beliveau, 1974; Buck, 1977; Della Bitta, Loudon, Booth and Weeks, 1977; Ritchie, 1984, Hall and Selwood, 1987). For example, the 16-day 1988 Calgary Winter Olympics attracted 134,000 out-of-town spectators and generated an estimated Can$158 million in visitor spending on accommodation, food and beverage, retail, entertainment and transportation in Calgary (Kolsun, 1988). The hallmark event is therefore different in its appeal from the attractions normally promoted by the tourist industry as it is not a continuous or seasonal phenomenon. Indeed, in many cases the hallmark event is a strategic response to the problems that seasonal variations in demand pose for the tourist industry (Ritchie and Beliveau, 1974).

One of the major problems involved in defining, and hence analysing, short-term, staged tourist attractions is that of scale (Davidson and Schaffer, 1980). Ritchie (1984, p.2), understood hallmark events to be major events which have an 'ability to focus national and international attention on the destination...'. Similarly, Burns and Mules (1986, pp.6–7) noted the importance of scale in 'special events', '...sometimes called a 'Hallmark' event...' which are 'events that are expected to generate large external benefits, or where the external benefits are so widely distributed and the event costs are so substantial that they are funded, either partially or wholly, with public monies'. Burns and Mules (1986, p.7) identified four key characteristics of special events:

1. The major demand generated by the Special Event is, for the most part, not the demand for the event itself but demand for a range of related services – typically accommodation, food, transport and entertainment.
2. This demand is condensed into a relatively short period of time, from a single day to a few weeks and, as services cannot be produced ahead of time and stored, this leads to the typical 'peaking' problems experienced in the main service industries mentioned.
3. 'Peaking' influences both the level and the distribution of benefits received.
4. The net impact of redirecting local funds towards Special Events is relatively small;

the major benefits arise from the attraction of new funds from outside the region by way of the export of goods and services, especially services.

Of particular importance in the identification of special events is the large outlay of public monies which may be associated not only with the hosting but also with the bidding for such events. 'Most commonly a city wanting to upgrade its infrastructure or its political image will use a large-scale event as a tool to generate funds from higher levels of government and corporations' (Bonnemaison, 1990, p.25). Indeed, the majority of hallmark events have substantial government involvement, whether it be a national, state or local level, with the amount of government financial assistance increasing in relation to the size and marketing scale of the event.

An alternative definition of special events has been adopted by Getz (1989b, 1991a) and Badmin, Coombs and Rayner (1988, p.106) who argue that special events are activities which occur outside the regular routine of an organisation: 'Special events can vary in size and importance through the whole spectrum from childrens parties to international events and all the consequent organisational factors'. According to Getz (1991a, p.44): 'A special event is a onetime or infrequently occurring event outside the normal program or activities of the sponsoring or organizing body. To the customer, a special event is an opportunity for a leisure, social or cultural experience outside the normal range of choices or beyond everyday experience'. Similarly, the Canadian Government Office of Tourism (1982, p.3) stated that while the term 'festival' and 'special event' were used synonymously, 'the primary difference between the two is that festivals are usually held annually, while special events are often one-time only observances'. In contrast, Tourism South Australia (1990a, p.2) argued that it was 'simply too vague to define festivals as recurring events and special events as one-time occasions' and defined a festival and event in terms of the nature of the public. For a festival, 'the public are participants of the experience', while for a special event 'the public are spectators to the experience'.

Ritchie and Hu's (1987) categorisation of a 'mega-event' corresponds to Ritchie's (1984) earlier definition of hallmark events, while the 1987 Congress of the Association Internationale d'Experts Scientifiques du Tourisme resolved that mega-events could be defined in three different ways: 1 by volume (1 million visits), by a money measure (Can$500 million, DM 750 million, FFr 2,500 million), and in psychological terms (by reputation: 'Must see', '*Muss miterlebt werden*', '*Il faut absolument voir*') (Marris, 1987, p.3). Nevertheless, substantial difficulties in the definition of mega-events still remain (Jafari, 1988; Witt, 1988). Ritchie and Hu (1987) argued that mega-events and mega-attractions posed similar problems for tourism development. However, while they may have certain common characteristics, such as large visitor numbers in relation to the size of the event or attraction, there are also fundamental differences which will have significant implications for the analysis of their impacts.

The key difference between an event and an attraction is the period of time over which they impact on the host community or region. Events, by their definition, are of a transitory nature whereas attractions will generally tend to draw visitors for a longer, more sustained, period of time. It is the short time frame in which events operate that distinguishes the hallmark event from other tourist attractions and which therefore demand the appropriate temporal and spatial specifiers in their analysis and management. Bonnemaison (1990, p.25) has gone so far as to argue that 'cyclical events, such as markets, fairs and festivals – temporary urbanism – appear and disappear like apparitions or television images, visible when on and invisible when off'. Nevertheless, as this book will illustrate, hallmark events may leave long term architectural, economic, social and political legacies well beyond the immediate period of the event.

The majority of researchers have tended to view hallmark events as major, large scale, events. However, several studies (Heenan, 1978; Shepherd, 1982; Getz, 1984; Hall, 1989a) have identified short-term staged events, such as carnivals, festivals and fetes, in small towns and villages as hallmark events. Such events may be of significant economic and social importance. Indeed, events may not only serve to attract tourists but may also assist in the development or maintenance of community or regional identity (Getz and Frisby 1987, 1988; Hall 1989a, b). An additional perspective on the definition of hallmark events is provided by Sparrow (1989) who argued that events could be identified according to the manner in which events were 'won' by the host community. According to Sparrow, two distinct types of hallmark events could be distinguished: indigenous, which are 'those events which the host community bid for, and therefore had a discretionary input'. These in the main could be planned for from the outset; and adventitious, 'those which came about or were thrust upon a host community by accident. For these in the main, there was possibly little discretionary input and planning was mostly undertaken "on the run"' (1989, p.251).

The term 'hallmark event' therefore cannot be confined to the large scale events that generally occur within cities and major towns. Community festivals and local celebrations can be described as hallmark events in relation to their regional, local, and cultural significance. Such an observation is not to re-define the notion of a hallmark event, rather it is to note the importance of the economic, marketing, socio-cultural, and spatial context within which hallmark events take place (Hall, 1989d). According to Tourism South Australia (1990a, p.2):

> Festivals are a celebration of something the local community wishes to share and which involves the public as participants in the experience.
> Festivals must have as a prime objective a maximum amount of people participation, which must be an experience that is different from or broader than day-to-day living. It is not necessary to extent that hands-on experience by more than one day, though it is often economically desirable.

The role of festivals as events has also been stressed in the work of Getz (1991a). According to Getz (1991a, p. 39), 'Event tourism is concerned with the roles that festivals and special events can play in destination development and the maximization of an event's attractiveness to tourists'. A festival, 'a public celebration of some happening, fact, or concept' (Wilson and Udall, 1982, p.3), 'is an event, a social phenomenon, encountered in virtually all human cultures' (Falassi, 1987, p.1) which has five key elements:

1. A sacred or profane time of celebration, marked by special observances.
2. The annual celebration of a notable person or event, or the harvest of an important product.
3. A cultural event consisting of a series of performances of works in the fine arts, often devoted to a single artist or genre.
4. A fair.
5. Generic gaiety, conviviality, cheerfulness. (Falassi, 1987, p.2)

Festivals are intimately related to the maintenance and celebration of community values. Falassi, (1987,p. 2) says:

Both the social function and the symbolic meaning of the festival are closely related to a series of overt values that the community recognizes as essential to its ideology and worldview, to its social identity, its historical continuity, and to its physical survival, which is ultimately what festival celebrates.

The expression 'hallmark event' therefore applies to a wide range of events, including festivals and fairs, which exhibit a broad range of economic, physical and social impacts at various scales (Olds, 1988; Hall, 1989a, d) (Table 1.1). Mega-events, such as World Fairs and Expositions, the World Soccer Cup final, or the Olympic Games, are events which are expressly targeted at the international tourism market and may be suitably described as 'mega' by virtue of their size in terms of attendance, target market, level of public financial involvement, political effects, extent of television coverage, construction of facilities, and impact on economic and social fabric of the host community. Similarly, special sporting events, such as the America's Cup (Hall and Selwood, 1987, 1989), Commonwealth Games, or the Adelaide Grand Prix (Burns et al., 1986), are substantially international in their market orientation. Undoubtedly, domestic tourists are attracted to these events in significant numbers. It is the international dimension in the promotion of these short-term tourist attractions which leads to the large scale impacts which have come to be most associated with the hosting of hallmark events. However, as noted above, regional, local and community events are also hallmark events relative to their potential economic, organisational and social impacts on smaller communities.

Perspectives on the Analysis of Hallmark Events

The majority of studies of hallmark events are primarily economic in orientation. As Jafari (1988, p.273) noted: 'One cannot help but wonder when tourism research will graduate from the bounds of economics and marketing to amplify the subject in its fullest dimensions'. If researchers are to provide a systematic account of event tourism then it is vital that they become aware of the widest possible implications of events for host communities. In addition, research should also attempt to answer the questions of why, for what, and for whom, are these events held? Governments and private industry generally hold that hallmark events, as with tourism, are 'a good thing', otherwise why would they be held? But as Coppock (1977, p.1.1) observed:

Table 1.1   Characteristics of hallmark events

Market	Major level of public financial involvement	Organisation and leadership	Examples	Associated descriptions of hallmark event
International	National	Establishment of special event authorities by central government	Olympic Games, World Fairs, Australian bicentennial	Mega-event, special event
International/ national	National/regional	Coordination between various government levels, often using Inter-governmental committees. Leadership role shared between central and regional government	Grand Prix, America's Cup, Commonwealth Games, New Zealand sesquitennial	Special event
National/ limited international	National/regional	Limited local involvement, leadership role shared by regional and central government	Touring international art exhibitions, Festival of the Pacific	
National/ regional	National/regional	Consultative government role only	Coast-to-Coast Race, agricultural expositions	
Regional/ limited national	Regional/local	Major role for regional tourism bodies, local business and government	Arts and cultural festivals such as the Festival of Adelaide	
Regional/ local	Local	Leadership and organisation provided from within host community	Blyth Festival, Shaw Festival Wellesley Apple and Butter Festival	Sometimes referred to as community events
Local (event designed for local consumption)	Minimal local government expenditure, social rather than economic considerations	Local control	Community fetes and celebrations	Community events

Source: After Hall, 1989d, p.265

Good for whom?… Not only is it inevitable that the residents of an area will gain unequally from tourism (if indeed they gain at all) and probable that the interests of some will actually be harmed, but it may well be that a substantial proportion does not wish to see any development of tourism.

There are no accepted criteria for the analysis of hallmark events. Perhaps not surprisingly research on hallmark events has tended to follow established lines of tourism research. For instance, Ritchie's (1984) and Ritchie and Hu's (1987) reviews of the conceptual and research issues involved in the assessment of the impacts of hallmark events is akin to Getz's (1977, 1991a) proposals for the study of the impact of tourism on host populations. Similarly, the questions posed in Mathieson and Wall's (1982) review of the economic, physical and social impacts of tourism can be equally applied to hallmark events. A summary of the factors identified by Getz (1977) and Ritchie (1984) are presented in Table 1.2.

Ritchie (1984) proposed a classification of the types of impact which need to be assessed for particular hallmark events. Six types of impact were identified, these being economic, tourism/commercial, physical, sociocultural, psychological and political. For each of the types of impact Ritchie (1984) recorded the nature of the variables to be measured and associated problems in data collection and interpretation. Despite the value of Ritchie's work, he himself noted that it was only a beginning, and concluded that there was a need for a 'more comprehensive' approach 'to the assessment of the impact of hallmark events' than that currently employed in most situations (1984, p.11).

Despite the broad range of topics identified by Ritchie (1984), the study of hallmark tourist events has usually occurred within an economic or marketing oriented framework (Perdue, Coughlin and Valerius, 1988). This is possibly a reflection of Bodewes (1981, p.37) argument that tourism research 'is usually viewed as an application of established disciplines, because it does not possess sufficient doctrine to be classified as a full-fledged academic discipline'. Nevertheless, several studies have now been conducted within a multi-disciplinary framework which seeks to combine elements of adjunct disciplines such as economics, commerce and marketing (see Burns, Hatch and Mules, 1986). However, Leiper (1981, p.71) claimed that a multi-disciplinary base has become an impediment to tourism research and has argued that 'while different disciplines will always have specialized contributions to make to the study of tourism, a need exists for a different approach to form the central ground'. An inter-disciplinary approach integrates concepts and ideas from different disciplines or fields within the one approach. Similarly, Jafari (1977, p.8) believed the inter-disciplinary approach to be 'more expedient, productive and meaningful'.

The study of the 1985 Adelaide Grand Prix by the Centre for South Australian Economic Studies (Burns, Hatch and Mules, 1986) represented one of the first attempts to provide a thorough analysis of the impact of a special event. Burns and Mules (1986, p.9) argued that a framework of analysis was needed that established the nature of the benefits and costs involved; indicated how they may be measured after the event, using multipliers where appropriate; and, knowing this, allowed reasonable estimates to be made before the event. The Adelaide study went a long way towards achieving these objectives. Similarly, the OLYMPULSE series of studies conducted on the 1988 Calgary Winter Olympics to monitor residents' awareness, knowledge and perception of a number of factors related to the Games, retained a traditional 'value-free' outlook with emphasis being placed on the quantifiable impacts of the event (Ritchie 1984; Ritchie and Aitken, 1984, 1985;

Table 1.2 The analysis of the possible impacts of hallmark events on host communities

Type of impact	Positive	Negative
Economic	•increased expenditures; •creation of employment; •increase in labour supply; and •increase in standard of living.	•price increases during event; •real estate speculation; •failure to attract tourists; •better alternative investments; •inadequate capital; and •inadequate estimation of costs of event.
Tourism/commercial	•increased awareness of the region as a travel/tourism destination; •increased knowledge concerning the potential for investment and commercial activity in the region; •creation of new accommodation and tourist attractions; and •increase in accessibility.	•acquisition of a poor reputation as a result of inadequate facilities, improper practices or inflated prices; and •negative reactions from existing enterprises due to the possibility of new competition for local manpower and government assistance.
Physical/environmental	•construction of new facilities; •improvement of local infrastructure; and •preservation of heritage.	•ecological damage; •changes in natural processes; •architectural pollution; •destruction of heritage; and •overcrowding.
Social/cultural	•increase in permanent level of local interest and participation in types of activity associated with event; and •strengthening of regional values and traditions.	•commercialisation of activities which may be of a personal or private nature; •modification of nature of event or activity to accommodate tourism; •potential increase in crime; •changes in community structure; and •social dislocation.
Psychological	•increased local pride and community spirit; and •increased awareness of non-local perceptions.	•tendency toward defensive attitudes concerning host region; •culture shock; and •misunderstandings leading to varying degrees of host/visitor hostility.
Political/administrative	•enhanced international recognition of region and values; and •development of skills among planners.	•economic exploitation of local population to satisfy ambitions of political elite; •distortion of true nature of event to reflect elite values; •failure to cope; •inability to achieve aims; •increase in administrative costs; •use of event to legitimate unpopular decisions; and •legitimation of ideology and socio-cultural reality.

Sources: Adapted from Getz, 1977; Ritchie, 1984; and Hall, 1989a

Ritchie and Lyons, 1987, 1990). Both studies, although extremely valuable in their own right, ignored important aspects of the political economy of such events (Hall, 1989c).

Perhaps in response to the excess of economic analysis a number of studies of the social impacts of hallmark events have emerged in recent years. Of particular interest are the studies of World Fairs and Expositions (Benedict, 1983; Rydell, 1984; Hall, 1988a; Ley and Olds, 1988; Olds, 1988) and the America's Cup (Cowie, 1986; Shaw, 1985, 1986; Centre for Applied and Business Research, 1987; Hall, 1987; Hall and Selwood, 1987, 1989). Indeed, along with the 1988 Calgary Winter Olympics (Ritchie and Smith, 1991; Ritchie and Lyons, 1990), the America's Cup has probably been one of the most analysed hallmark events to date. However, it is valuable to note that the broad analysis of government financed studies (Centre for Applied and Business Research, 1987) produced markedly different conclusions about the benefits of the event to those which specifically examined externalities such as crime and homelessness (Hall and Selwood, 1989).

Getz and Frisby (1988) have evaluated management effectiveness as part of a survey of community-run festivals in Ontario (1987). Related to the community research of Getz and Frisby is the sociological analysis of festivals and cultural performance (Duvignaud, 1976; Lavenda, 1980; Manning, 1983a). Anthropological and sociological critiques have provided the basis for several studies of the political dimension of hallmark events (Ley and Olds, 1988; Hall, 1989c), yet this area of study has received only limited attention. Nevertheless, an understanding of the political and administrative processes associated with the hosting of events would appear to be crucial to their success:

> In their quest for viability and legitimacy, enlightened investors and community leaders must balance local and outside needs and interests... if the constructive impact of tourism is to be realized, collaborate approaches between diverse stakeholder groups will be needed. To survive and prosper in the decades ahead, tourism must develop some multiple constituencies. (Heenan, 1978, p.32)

The present work seeks to unite a variety of perspectives on the nature and development of hallmark events. Every discipline provides its own perspective or 'bounded rationality' on the multiple meanings which hallmark events have to offer. To bring to mind the words of Morgan (1986, p.339), 'the most fundamental problems that we face stem from the fact that the complexity and sophistication of our thinking do not match the complexity and sophistication of the realities with which we have to deal'. As the next section will illustrate, any meaningful attempt to understand and manage event tourism will require the analyst to develop a framework which assists in grasping 'the multiple meanings of situations and to confront and manage contradiction and paradox, rather than to pretend they do not exist' (Morgan, 1986, p.339).

A Framework for the Analysis of Hallmark Events

Perhaps the most fundamental question which needs to be asked in the examination of hallmark events is that of for what and for who are the events being held? Such a question is not purely academic, it is the starting point for the measurement of the success of any event. While classic rational organisational planning techniques such as management by objectives (MBO) are now matched by a battery of other approaches to optimal management of resources, the setting of objectives raises fundamental questions about the characteristics, nature, and functions of events. The formal and informal objectives by which an event is held have their origin in the amalgam of the individuals, organisations and values which are involved in the hosting of an event (Hall, 1989c). Therefore any framework for the analysis of hallmark events should be able to account for the involvement of individuals and organisations in hallmark events, the effectiveness of organisational functions and structures, and the values which events may represent.

The present book proposes a framework of analysis which sees events developing from and impacting on the socio-economic environment of the region, culture and nation within which the event is being held (Figure 1.1). Within this framework events are simultaneously a function of their socio-economic environment, and an influence on it. Broadly, the socio-economic environment constitutes the external environment which will influence the dynamics of the internal environment of event organisation, and within which event organisation and management will operate.

The socio-economic environment can be divided into four sections:

1. nature and significance;
2. economic dimensions;
3. social dimensions; and
4. political dimensions.

These aspects of events which are dealt with as separate chapters. The meanings and significance of events may change over time. Events are not static. The meaning of events will shift in accordance with both changes in society and changes in the event itself. For instance, carnival in Latin and South America has shifted from a means of protest to a celebration of hedonism (Lavenda, 1980). However, the nature and significance of events is entwined with the economic, social and political dimensions of events and these three aspects deserve individual analysis.

The perceived economic benefits of events often provide the official justification for hosting events. However, the answers which emerge in any economic study of the impacts of an event will be dependent on the framework of analysis. Therefore, not only do the results of any costs and benefits allocated to an event require thorough examination, but also the methods by which such details of economic impacts were derived.

Economic analysis of events provides one aspect of why events are held and the effects that they have on a region. However, while many of the economic impacts of events are quite tangible many of the social effects are not. The social dimension of events is particularly significant when one considers that many events have their origins in community celebrations and festivals. Indeed, the success of many community based events should not be measured on profit alone. Events may provide a means for the social expression of place, faith and culture. As Stansfield (1991, p.352) noted: 'People do take pride in promulgating the special identities of their home towns or regions and surely not entirely for reasons of avarice'. Alternatively, events may be imposed on communities by elites and alter the social environment of the host and the nature of place. For instance, while Getz (1991a, pp.16–17) perceives the Baltimore City Fair as a good example of urban regeneration and renewal, other commentators, most notably Harvey (1988, 1990), have argued that the Fair and the associated development of leisure space has altered the nature of place and space to represent a substantially different set of socioeconomic values: 'The present carnival mask of the Inner Harbor redevelopment conceals a long history of struggle over this space' (Harvey, 1990, p.421).

Governments and elites play a critical role in the formulation and development

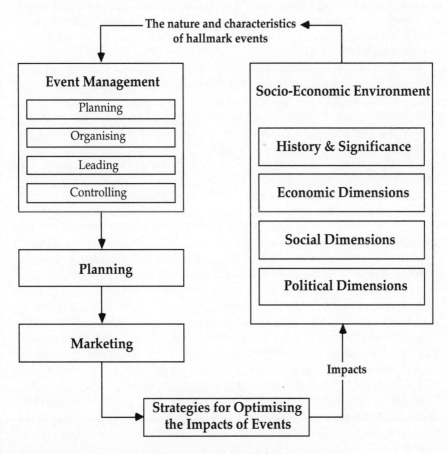

Figure 1.1 A framework for the analysis of hallmark tourist events

of modern-day, large-scale tourist events, such as the Olympic Games and World Fairs. For instance, Richter (1989, p.125) has commented: 'High profile sports events, international forums, and the like produce marginal doses of prestige intently sought by governments that feel neglected or underrated by world opinion'. Therefore, the hosting of hallmark events also necessitates an examination of the political nature of events and the means by which events also impinge on the political process at both the macro- (ideology and values) and the micro-political (political careers and structures) level.

The sum of the above four dimensions (historical, economic, social and political) which comprise the socio-economic environment helps explain the nature and characteristics of the values which any event represents. However, at the organisational and individual level, analysis of events is more concerned with managerial processes, planning, and marketing.

Much of the discussion on event 'management' fails to consider the insights that management and organisational theory can bring to the analysis of events. The responsibilities of event management can be divided up into the planning, organising, leading (directing), and controlling functions. These functions are then used as a basis to illustrate the role that management has in meeting the various objectives which cities, organisations and governments have in the hosting of events (Chapter 6).

The planning function deserves special emphasis (Chapter 7) because, in the context of event planning, it refers to both the strategic planning process by which objectives are designed and implemented and the physical planning process which lends shape to the development of infrastructure and purpose-built facilities. Clearly these processes are, or should be, entwined. However, the quality of the planning process will be dependent on the objectives which the event is designed to meet, the agreement of stakeholders to the achievement of those objectives, and the broader participation of the host community in planning for the event. Indeed, in the case of host community involvement in events, planning becomes a strategic process which seeks to optimise returns for all parties affected by the hosting of the event. Therefore, planning becomes a mechanism not only for ensuring the success of an immediate event but also for events that may be held in the future.

Given the role that planning has in the development of events it becomes essential that the objectives of events are translated to the required audience. Therefore, attention needs to be given to the role of marketing in not only promoting an event but also the image that marketing provides for the host community and how this affects the socio-economic environment. From this perspective, marketing is seen as the creation and offering of values for the purpose of achieving a desired response (Kotler, 1972). However, in so doing, unintended responses may also emerge.

The final component in the proposed framework of analysis for hallmark events is the strategies for optimising the impacts of hallmark events. This brings us back to the first point made in this section. For what and for who are hallmark events held? This is no easy question. The answer will depend on the perspective of the analyst. Nevertheless, in the seeking of a strategy or selection of strategies we must consider what resources are being optimised and for who are the returns being made. From the point of view of the present study, the effects of the hosting of hallmark events need to be considered from the perspectives of all the stakeholders, but especially the local community which is faced with the most direct economic, social and political impacts of event tourism, a consideration which is further developed in the next section.

Events Within the Tourism Development Process

Tourism is an extremely complex phenomenon with a multitude of economic, social and environmental impacts. However, with the perception of tourism as a 'smokeless industry' and a panacea for economic malaise and unemployment, the full range of impacts of tourism development has often failed to be appreciated by either government or the private sector (Hall, 1991). As Butler (1990, p.40) noted, there exists:

IGNORANCE of dimensions, nature, power of tourism;
LACK OF ABILITY to determine level of sustainable development, i.e., capacity;
LACK OF ABILITY to manage tourism and control the development;
LACK OF APPRECIATION that tourism does cause impacts, is an industry, and can not easily be reversed;
LACK OF APPRECIATION that tourism is dynamic, and causes change as well as responds to change;
LACK OF AGREEMENT over levels of development, over control, over direction of tourism.

The above six factors apply equally as well to event tourism. Therefore, as Pearce (1989, p.292) observes 'tourist development in the future must be better planned, more professionally managed and set in a broader context of development'. Dutton and Hall (1989) have argued that the application of the ideas behind sustainable development to tourism can offer a basis for maintaining the long-term growth of tourism. However, such an approach can only be achievable if attention is also given to the social context within which development occurs. A sustainable approach to tourism is concerned with tourism, including the hosting of tourist events and festivals, being the appropriate form of development for the economic, social and physical resources of a region in a manner which conserves the social and physical environment and promotes the long-term goals of the community. The approach contains several essential components (Hall, 1991, p.13):

1. Tourism development cannot be measured solely in economic terms. Social and environmental development are interdependent with, and equally as important to, economic development.
2. Tourism development must ensure the maintenance and conservation of ecological processes and the physical environment.
3. Tourism development must ensure the maintenance of social processes and the social environment.
4. Tourism development requires full public participation and community involve-

ment. Indeed, the most appropriate form of tourism development for some communities may well be no tourism development.

5. Tourism development must ensure the conservation of the uniqueness and integrity of the destination whether it be at a local or national scale.

6. Tourism is but one of a range of mechanisms that may be appropriate for the economic development of particular regions.

'There is a growing tendency to see events as the sparks needed to light a community fire' (Bonnemaison, 1990, p.31). Event tourism, with its emphasis on communities, provides a ready-made basis for the development of a sustainable approach towards tourism. As Getz and Frisby (1988) observed, a community development perspective implies a number of factors: the development of public participation in municipal activities; the creation of self-reliant actions and values; and improvements in the social (parks, community halls) and physical (sewage, roads, public transport) infrastructure.

The amount of local involvement and the dominant level of government in the planning of hallmark events would appear to be crucial to deriving the maximum benefit from hosting an event for the host community. The more an event is seen by the impacted public as emerging from the local community, rather than being imposed on them, the greater will be that community's acceptance of the event. However, the international dimension of many events will often mean that national and regional governments will assume responsibility for the event's planning. Indeed, because of the interests that impact upon upper levels of government, local concerns may well be lost in the search for the national or regional good with special legislation often being enacted to minimise disturbance to the hosting of an event (Hall, 1989b, c) (see Chapter 5 on the political dimension of hallmark events).

The loss of local involvement in the planning process is not the only consequence of an increase in the size of an event. The size and duration of the event will tend to correlate with the scale of impact. For instance, the facilities and surrounding infrastructure established for the hosting of special or mega-events will be a major influence on long-term land use, and possibly the social structure, of the core event area. This is especially the case where an event is used to rejuvenate inner-city areas often occupied by lower socio-economic groups, as in the cases of World Fairs such as the 1986 Vancouver Expo and the 1988 Brisbane Expo (Olds, 1988; Hall, 1988a) (See Chapter Four on the social dimensions of hallmark events). Nevertheless, as will be stressed throughout this book, the adoption of a sustainable approach towards tourism, emphasising the role that communities have to play in holding and legitimising events, will dictate the level of success in hosting events and festivals.

Summary

The study of hallmark events is a relatively new area of tourism research marked by significant differences between researchers in definition, method and theory.

Nevertheless, the importance attached to events within national and regional tourism marketing strategies emphasises the urgency for research to be conducted before, during, and after the event. Moreover, as commentators such as Heenan (1978) and Jafari (1988) have observed, there is clearly a need to go beyond conventional economic analysis to examine the social and physical impacts of such events. Furthermore, I would whole-heartedly support Dovey's (1989, p.73) arguments that our lack of rigour in the prediction of the effects of hallmark events 'should not be biased in favour of the measurable or the marketable, and against the intangibles of everyday life or the views of the powerless'.

This chapter has provided a comparison of the various definitions of staged tourist events and their characteristics. It has noted the relationship between the size of an event, the major level of public financial involvement, organisation and leadership and the economic and social impacts of the event on the host community. In addition, it has noted some of the directions which have been taken in the analysis of hallmark events and which will be drawn upon in the following chapters. It would be unrealistic to expect that researchers will reach accord on a single framework for the analysis of hallmark events. Event research, however, is increasingly paying attention to the impacts of events on the host community in comparison with the traditional emphasis on the nature of the tourist product and the perceived potential economic benefits of hosting hallmark events. It should also be noted that tourists and host communities alike are becoming concerned with the negative aspects of tourism and tourism development.

The first part introduces the reader to the definition, methods of analysis, and nature of event tourism. The present chapter has outlined some of the definitional and methodological problems in examining hallmark events. Chapter 2 provides a historical perspective on hallmark events through an examination of the development of events as a mechanism for providing appropriate images for destinations and their role as tourist attractions. The first two chapters therefore provide the reader with a better understanding of the context within which the analysis and management of contemporary hallmark events occurs.

The second major section of the book examines the socio-economic framework within which events are staged, and their various impacts. Chapter 3 illustrates the significant economic role that events play in local, regional and national economies. Indeed, as the chapter discusses, the perceived economic benefits of event tourism typically provides the rationale for which to stage or bid for events. Nevertheless, the economic benefits of hallmark events are not clear-cut and substantial questions remain about their economic analysis as well as their potential costs for sections of the host community. Chapter 4 emphasises that events occur within, and may stem from, particular social and cultural contexts. The hosting of events may impact society and culture. Indeed, over time the meaning of events, such as carnivals, may change for the societies involved. Chapter 5 reviews the political nature of events. It is argued that events are essentially political in nature at both the macro- and micro-political level. Events may serve to promote certain interests while shutting out others. However, as the chapter notes, research into the political implications of events is not only of academic interest but may also assist in improving their planning and management.

The third section examines the means by which events may be managed and the benefits of hosting events maximised to the host community. Chapter 6 provides a framework for event management which identifies the importance of the organisation, leadership, and planning functions as elements of successful management. Chapter 7 focuses on planning at both the operational and strategic levels, while Chapter 8 details the roles that marketing plays in meeting the objectives of event staging and planning.

The final section, Chapter 9, discusses the variety of issues that need to be considered in event research. This chapter emphasises that a more systematic approach to event analysis and management is required if the potential economic and social benefits of events are to maximised for both host and guest.

Hallmark events will long continue to be a mainstay of tourism promotion and development. The task of event planners and tourism researchers is to assist in maximising the benefits of hosting events while minimising the undesirable costs to the host community. This will ensure the success one of the major reasons for conducting hallmark events – the creation of a sustained and viable tourist industry in the host community.

2 The Nature and Significance of Hallmark Events

Not so long ago, when the human species was part of the land, cyclical natural phenomena were subjects for celebration. In cities, where we almost have succeeded in our pursuit to ignore the seasons, cyclical events are taking a new significance. They are the opportunity to break the seemingly endless continuum of time. Not only do they allow us to reconnect with mythical and natural time, festivals are also strong social and political statements and, in many cases, they mean big business. (Cousineau, 1991, p.1)

This chapter details the growth of event tourism in recent years and provides an overview of the nature and economic and social significance of hallmark events. It provides a categorisation of hallmark events and discusses the contribution that events and festivals can make to host communities as a means to achieve a number of objectives including: community development, promotion, attracting investment and tourists, and economic development and employment generation.

The Significance of Hallmark Events

Events are increasingly becoming an essential component of local, regional, and national tourism promotion (Wilson and Udall, 1982; Chick, 1983; Mitchell and Wall, 1986; Bos, H., van der Kamp, and Zom, 1987; Frisby and Getz, 1989). However, in addition to the potential of hallmark events to attract tourists and enhance destination awareness and profitability, events may also be held for other purposes, such as to attract investment and to assist in the redevelopment of run-down urban areas. 'Events present the opportunity to participate in a collective experience which is distinct from everyday life' (Getz, 1989b, p.127). According to Armstrong (1986, p.11) the hosting of international events is 'intended to enhance local esteem, both nationally and internationally. Most often they are meant to attract tourists. They provide an opportunity to display local skills and cultural attitudes, to improve the reputation of a city beyond its boundaries and to demonstrate civic pride and the ability to mobilize resources'.

Evidence suggests that there has been a dramatic growth in the number of events staged in recent years throughout the Western world (Janiskee, 1980; Law,

1985; Tuppen, 1985; Getz and Frisby, 1988). Gunn (1988, p.259) argued that 'probably the fastest growing form of visitor activity is festivals and events'. In the case of rural and small town festivals in the United States, Janiskee (1979, p.1) observed:

> Some are simple affairs staged for the local citizenry in the spirit of a community gathering. Most, however, are designed to attract urban daytrippers by the many thousands in the interest of visitor industry. In this effort they have become so successful that they can no longer be regarded as a mere footnote to American rural recreation.

A number of reasons can be suggested for the apparent growth in events:

1. a desire of regions, cities and communities to put themselves on the tourist map through positive imaging;
2. a 'keep-up-with-the-Jones' or 'follow-the-leader' effect by which one community or city seeks to emulate the success of another's event or festival;
3. the use of tourism by government as a means of economic development thereby encouraging the creation of events through funding mechanisms, sponsorship, and cooperative marketing campaigns;
4. the increasing segmentation and specialisation within the tourism market;
5. the availability of government grants for sports, arts and culture;
6. the use of the profile and image created by events to attract investment;
7. the wish of communities and cities to celebrate themselves, promote civic pride, and/ or overcome adverse circumstances; and
8. the changing nature of leisure activity in western society.

'Modern leisure is a certain kind of time spent in a certain kind of way. The time is that which lies outside the demands of work, direct social obligations and the routine activities of social maintenance; the use of this time, though socially determined, is characterised by a high degree of personal freedom and choice' (Bailey 1987, p.6). In recent years there has been a growing demand for short duration, meaningful leisure activities that are easily accessible, have a flexible time component, and satisfy a number of leisure motivations. Therefore, 'partially in response to this demand, municipal culture and recreation personnel, event managers, and special interest groups have developed a wide variety of special events or festivals' (Robinson and Noël, 1991, p.78).

The large growth in the development of new events and festivals, especially at a time when traditional fairs and events are in decline, may lie in changing leisure preferences and work patterns. In their study of community-run festivals in Ontario, Getz and Frisby (1987, p.11) observed:

> Direct links with an agricultural heritage are now absent for most urban Canadians, so traditional fairs with their agricultural themes and old-fashioned entertainments are perhaps alien and boring. At the same time, there is a nostalgic interest in quaint small-towns and heritage-oriented events. Add to this the emergence of multiculturalism as [a] fact of Canadian life and the easily documented growth in 'high' cultural pursuits, and there exists great scope for a proliferation of festivals and events of all kinds.

Table 2.1   Themes, events and attractions reported by respondents to a
survey of community-run festivals in Ontario, Canada (number of
mentions, n=58)

Main Themes	No.	Events and Attractions	No.
Music	21	Contests	37
Food	18	Food	34
Culture	17	Music/concerts	26
Recreation	17	Displays/exhibitions	25
Entertainment	9	Dancing	21
History	6	Theatre	19
Creative Arts	4	Sports	19
Education	2	Kids' activities	19
Other	7	Parade	14
		Arts/crafts	14
		Beauty contest	12
		Sale/flea market	7
		Raffle/lottery	7
		Recreation	7
		Gambling	6
		Races	5
		Tours	4

Source: Getz and Frisby, 1987, p.21

Events may also meet a number of other diverse needs. For example, in the case
of the 1988 Brisbane International Exposition, Queensland, Australia, Carroll and
Donohue (1991, p.130) argued, that the initiators of the event, 'saw the need to
attract the greatest degree of support for what was an inherently risky project. One
of the methods used to develop such support was to claim the widest possible
variety of purposes, so as to attract the broadest coalition of support'. Therefore,
the Brisbane Expo was not only a celebration of 200 years of European settlement
in Australia but also an opportunity to redevelop the South Bank of Brisbane,
attract overseas and interstate investment to Queensland, construct new infrastructure, and generally promote a positive image of Brisbane and Queensland to the
rest of Australia and the world.

Events may also be a response to social problems. For example, in the early
1970s, after a series of attacks by the Red Brigades, evening street life in Italy was
on the wane. In response, the Mayor of Rome organised a festival to take over the
'city of the night' as a means of re-establishing the traditional street life of the city.
The success of the events was so great that they have now become a part of the city
calendar and have helped to establish and sustain a friendly and safe image for
Rome. Similarly, in San Francisco the creation of the Haight Street Fair in 1977 by
City Supervisor Harvey Milk not only helped to raise funds for a communal
kitchen for the homeless but has also contributed to the revival of the Haight-
Ashbury district without displacing the homeless (Bonnemaison, 1990). The
diversity of themes used to promote events and rationales for hosting events is
evidenced from the range of attractions reported by respondents to the Getz and
Frisby survey of community-run festivals in Ontario (Table 2.1).

The almost instinctive celebration of anniversaries (Camacho, 1979) in the modern era is most likely a reflection of humankind's need for social drama through ritual and cultural performance. A social drama is a cultural form with 'a limited area of transparency in the otherwise opaque surface of regular, uneventful life' (Turner, 1957, p.92). According to Turner (1974, 1982, 1984) social dramas can be detected at all levels of scale and complexity within society and is universal to all cultures, although it may be culturally elaborated in different ways in different societies. From this perspective, therefore, events are occasions which allow the sharing of systems of symbols and meanings within a culture. Similarly, Singer (1959) popularised the notion of 'cultural performance' by which the cultural content of tradition is carried by specific cultural media, such as festivals and plays, in a manner that is related to the social organisation of that culture.

One of the most neglected aspects of the social study of rituals and perform-ances is caused by the concentration on the central acts and the participants while tending to ignore others who have gathered for the event. As Kapferer (1984, p.202) observed, 'The presence of guests and spectators is often regarded as marginal to the major aims of the rite'. However, 'spectators' are not detached onlookers, and instead should be regarded as integral to both the ritual processes of religious and certain cultural celebration, such as carnival, and other events such as sports meetings and spectacles, political conventions, and World Fairs and exposi-tions (Da Matta, 1977, 1984; Kapferer, 1979; Gusfield and Michalowicz, 1984; MacAloon, 1984a; Ley and Olds, 1988). Through their attendance at social dramas and cultural performances, pilgrims and tourists may undergo transforma-tions in individual understanding and sustain particular ways of ordering social reality (a point discussed in further detail in Chapter Five on the politics of hallmark events):

> This structuring of the gathering creates the conditions for a further empowering of the meaningful and experiential possibilities of ritual act and symbol. In addition, it establishes conditions for the transformation of context. Thus the bringing of those hitherto kept apart from much of the central action into relations that engage them more immediately within it facilitates the transformation of the symbolic ordering and the meaning of the... world. (Kapferer, 1984, p.203)

The shaping of social reality through the hosting of events has been associated, in particular, with the conduct of spectacles. In this sense, a spectacle is a dynamic social form, 'demanding movement, action, change, and exchange on the part of the human actors who are center stage, and the spectators must be excited in turn' (MacAloon, 1984a, p.244). Such spectacles, of which the Olympic Games and the World Fairs are the most notable, are seen by several commentators as being the epitome of manufactured imagery which serves to confuse the public as to what is real and what is not (Boorstin, 1973; Debord, 1973; Ley and Olds, 1988).

The Olympic Games is regarded by MacAloon (1984a, p.245) as the 'spectacle par excellence' within which the needs of spectators, including both visitors to the host city and the television viewing audience, are 'often predominant in organiza-tional matters'. Indeed, the ritualistic characteristic of the modern-day Olympic spectacle is a fundamental characteristic of the Olympic movement (MacAloon, 1978, 1981). As Coubertin, the founder of the modern Games wrote in 1910, 'the crowd has a part to play, a part of consecration' (1967, p.32). Nevertheless, the Games have shifted in a social dramatic form from the original notion of a 'festival of human unity' to the present-day 'more-is-better' ethos of the spectacle, often to the consternation of Olympic officials (MacAloon, 1984a).

A Categorisation of Hallmark Tourist Events

Hallmark tourist events can be classified in a number of ways (Ritchie, 1984). Table 2.2 presents a categorisation of hallmark events according to their religious, cultural, commercial, sporting and political emphasis. The following section discusses the social and economic importance of hallmark events in the light of Table 2.2. Undoubtedly, the significance of events will depend on the perspective of the viewer: organiser, host community, economic stakeholder or visitor. An attempt is made in the discussion to highlight both Western and non-Western attitudes towards the hosting of events. As Friedmann (1990) indicated, many non-Western cultures have a different way of approaching events with long-standing traditions that are based in religious or cultural values. By examining such events we can gain insights into the ways in which we manage such events in Western society, particularly when cultural and folkloric values have assumed such a major role in the development of events in many communities.

Religious and Sacred Events

Religious and sacred events and festivals have long provided the traditional basis for travel to events. From the time of the ancient Greeks and Romans, religious festivals and holidays have promoted travel to sacred sites. Muslims have sought to meet the prescriptions of their faith by journeying to Mecca at the time of the Haj. The visits of the Pope to members of the Catholic Church outside of western Europe has also sparked substantial interest in the visited countries with many modern-day pilgrims travelling to attend the Pope's masses. For example, during the Pope's 1984 visit to Edmonton, Canada, over 100,000 people lined the motorcade route while about 150,000 people attended the mass (Preshing, 1986). Significant numbers of Americans were attracted across the border specifically to see the Pope or attend a mass (McDougall, 1986).

Religious events are perhaps the most obvious examples of cultural performance and social drama which have been discussed above. However, it must be stressed that the meaning of such performances are critical to both the performers and the audience. As Singer (1959, p.xiii) noted:

> Indians, and perhaps all peoples, think of their culture as encapsulated in such discrete performances, which they can exhibit to outsiders as well as to themselves. For the outsider these can conveniently be taken as the most concrete observable units of the cultural structure, for each performance has a definitely limited time span, a beginning

Table 2.2 A classification of hallmark tourist events

Classification	Examples and locations
Religious and sacred events	The Haj (Mecca) Blessing of the Fleet Christmas in the Holy Land (Bethlehem and Jerusalem) Papal tours RamLila
Cultural events	
Carnivals and festivals	Mardi Gras (Rio de Janiero) Spoletto Festival (Spoletto and Melbourne) Gay and Lesbian Mardi Gras (Sydney) Festival of the Pacific Oktoberfest (Munich, Waterloo) British Royal Weddings (London)
Historical milestones	United States Bicentennary (1977) Australian Bicentennary (1988) 500th Anniversary of the Sailing of Columbus (1992)
Commercial events	World and International Expositions Royal Agricultural Show (Sydney)
Sports events	Olympic Games (Summer and Winter) Commonwealth Games Pan-American Games World Cup Athletics World Cup Rugby (United Kingdom and France, 1991) World Cup Cricket (Australia and New Zealand, 1991) Australian Football League Grand Final (Melbourne) National Football League (NFL) Superbowl Baseball World Series Football Association (FA) Cup Final (Wembley) The America's Cup (Fremantle 1987, San Diego 1991) Formula 1 Grand Prix racing Melbourne Cup (Melbourne)
Political events	Party conventions International Monetary Fund/World Bank conferences Visits by the British Monarchy

and end, an organized program of activity, a set of performers, an audience, and a place and occasion of performance.

The RamLila at Ramnagar Religious events have retained their significance in Indian life. Near the end of the monsoon season performances of the RamLila, the story of the life and deeds of the popular Hindu deity Ram, are held throughout India. The sacred city of Ramnagar across the Ganges River from Benares holds a RamLila which 'is famous for its length, its spectacular staging, and its religious feeling' (Bonnemaison and Macy, 1990, p.3) and attracts between 40,000 and 100,000 visitors per night for the period of the thirty-one-evening festival.

According to Bonnemaison and Macy (1990) a 'temporary urban fabric' is overlain annually on the permanent structure of the town in order to accommodate the more than forty sites in the town that provide staging points for the story of Ram. The sites host combinations of stages, tents, platforms, props and effigies. In addition, the town acquires temporary restaurants, parking lots and special bus services in order to accommodate the influx of pilgrims.

Each site in the RamLila has a prescribed setting in the town. 'Certain land-marks were chosen, others were especially built to be the settings of this story. Places chosen for their "good fit" to the text have, year after year, acquired significance so that they eventually adopt the name they use during the RamLila, even when the festival is over'. Physical space becomes a mirror of the mental map that pilgrims recreate as they walk from one site to another in the footsteps of Ram's travels through the Indian sub-continent. Therefore, in the case of the Ramnagar RamLila, 'the festival space (symbolic religious space and its logistic support) is intricately interwoven with the daily life of this north Indian town' (Bonnemaison and Macy, 1990, p.4).

One of the key issues in the interpretation of religious festivals in the contem-porary world is the degree of authenticity that the event represents. In the case of the Ramnagar RamLila the potential conflict between the desire to retain the sacredness of the event and accommodate larger audiences has led the Maharaja of Banares, who oversees the festival, to adopt a number of controls. The Maharaja has stated that he does not want the festival transformed into a living museum, therefore photography is generally forbidden 'because too many tourists were disrespectful to the holiness of the performing area'. In addition, gas lights rather than electric lights have been used to replace the traditional burning torches. The final point which deserves note is the nature of the audience the event is designed for and which determines the physical and social reconstruction of the RamLila. As Bonnemaison and Macy observed: 'The audience principally consists of people who have been there many times and the festival is experienced as a ritual, not as a way to acquire culture. Continuity is therefore very important' (1990, p.22).

Cultural Events

Cultural tourism may be defined as 'movements of persons for essentially cultural motivations such as study tours, performing arts and cultural tours, travel to festivals and other cultural events, visits to sites and monuments, travel to study nature, folklore or art, and pilgrimages' (World Tourism Organisation, 1985, p.6). While cultural events will share certain similarities with religious events, it should be noted that while religious events and festivals will provide a particular set of cultural expressions, cultural events will demonstrate characteristics of both the sacred and the profane. Zeppel and Hall (1992) identify two related but distinct forms of cultural tourism: arts tourism and heritage tourism, both of which identify events as significant components of the cultural tourist experience.

Heritage tourism is based on nostalgia for the past and the desire to experience diverse cultural forms. In a broad sense, the term heritage can be used 'simply to describe those things – cultural traditions as well as artefacts – that are inherited from the past' (Hardy, 1988, p.333). Therefore, heritage tourism also includes local cultural traditions, such as 'family patterns, religious practices and the subtleties of refined traditions that combine in various ways to make up what we describe as the heritage of a country' (Collins, 1983, p.58). According to Zeppel and Hall (1991, 1992), this community heritage embraces folkloric traditions, arts and crafts, ethnohistory (ways of life), social customs and cultural celebrations.

Folk festivals have become a focal point for the revitalisation of many cultural traditions within North America (see Table 2.3 on Folk Festival Themes) (Gutowski, 1978; Gillespie, 1987). In the case of folk festivals 'this self-conscious term comes into use when organizers are less involved with the material they present' (Wilson and Udall, 1982, p.4). In addition, the use of the term is relatively recent in origin (1894) and perhaps is indicative of the realisation of the diversity and richness of cultures within American society. The largest American folk festival, The Festival of American Folklife, has been held since 1967 on the Washington National Mall between the Smithsonian Institute and the National Park Service. In addition to demonstrating traditional music styles, the festival also stresses occupational skills, foodways, folk crafts and narrative sessions in order to present the participants in the festival within their cultural context.

Arts tourism is directed at the visitor experience of paintings, sculpture, theatre and all other creative forms of human expression and endeavour (Zeppel and Hall, 1992). Visiting art galleries and attending arts festivals are major forms of visitor activities in the events field. With the performing arts, well known companies or individual performers often become a significant visitor drawcard in their own right. Arts festivals are a regular feature on the tourist calendar of many cities, while the aesthetic, visual and theatrical appeal of the arts are increasingly being packaged and promoted as a special tourist experience (Isar, 1976; Carter, 1986; Dunstan, 1986; Noblet, 1986; Cameron, 1989; Zeppel and Hall, 1991, 1992). According to Hall and Zeppel (1990a, p.87) '[Arts] tourism is experiential tourism based on being involved in and stimulated by the performing arts, visual arts and festivals. Heritage tourism... is also experiential tourism in the sense of seeking an encounter with nature or feeling part of the history of a place'. Through participation in arts, culture and heritage individuals can seek to escape the routines of everyday life and improve their social status and self image. As Hughes (1987, p.212) commented, special cultural and artistic experiences 'are sources of arousal to compensate for the deficiencies of ordinary life'.

The growth in arts and heritage tourism, as with the growth of event tourism in general, can be attributed to an increasing awareness of cultural activities and attractions, greater affluence, more leisure time, greater mobility, increased access to the arts and higher levels of education (Eastaugh and Weiss, 1989), with tourism now providing the opportunities to acquire cultural knowledge and cultural experiences. 'Travel is no longer to *see* for the first time. It is to *experience*' (Collins, 1983, p.59). In arts and heritage tourism, consumer consumption has become increasingly oriented towards the purchase and consumption of cultural goods and

Table 2.3 Folk festival themes

Festival	Theme	Examples
Sacred festivals	Seasonal	Blessing of the Fleet, Blessing of the Fields
	Music	Harp Singing, Singing on the Mountain
	Annual rites	Midsummer observances, Mescalero Apache Maiden's Puberty Rites Ceremonial
	Miracles Recalled	Gift of Waters, Gift of Corn, Hill Cumorah Pageant
Harvest and food festivals	Vegetables	Watermelon, Sweet Corn, Pumpkin
	Animals	Blue Crab, Whale, Catfish, Shad
	Cooking	Chili, Gumbo, Boiled Cord, Johnny Cake
	Activity	Threshing, Sugaring Down, Sheep Shearing
Special activity festivals	Music	Bluegrass, Scottish fiddling, old-time music
	Local tradition	Mule Day, Trade Day, Dog Days Dance
	Contest	Fiddling, Piping, Hollering, Seed Spitting, Chicken Plucking
	Commemorative	Leif Ericson Day, Mud Springs Camp, Voyager Days
Festive subgroup gatherings	Ethnic	Dances of Rumania, Czech Days, Nordic Days
	Indian	Hopi Snake Dances, Rooster Pulls, Powwows
	Homecoming	Bethel Church Homecoming, Sutherland Family Reunion
	Occupational	Old Canalers Meeting
Regional and local folk arts festivals	Multistate	Mississippi Valley Folk Festival
	State	Tennessee Old-Time Fiddlers Convention
	Country	Wade County Crafts Festival
	Town	Benton Buck Dancing Contest

Source: Wilson and Udall, 1982

experiences (theatre, music, festivals, art galleries and museums) (Heinich, 1988). As MacCannell (1976, p.10) commented, 'All tourists desire this deeper involvement with society and culture to some degree; it is a basic component of their motivation to travel'.

Cultural events may be categorised in terms of their audience and the provider of the event. As Wilson and Udall (1982, p.3) commented, 'the motivations and aesthetics of the organizers are as important to the overall experience as what is being celebrated'. In the case of their typology of cultural festivals (Table 2.4), the classification illustrates

the movement of materials of folk culture away from the people who created them to people of the larger society. They also show how different organizers have applied their own concepts and aesthetics to problems of inclusion and exclusion. Much of the tension created by exclusion is relieved if the organizers have a clear idea of what they are celebrating, why they are celebrating it, and what presentations are appropriate to the celebration (1982, p.3).

Table 2.4   A typology of cultural festivals

Festival type	Characteristics
Indigenous	Celebrations which grow from, and are part of, particular cultures. The event is directed toward the culture at large and is controlled by members of that culture.
Evolving indigenous	Similar to indigenous festivals in that they grow from the culture depicted, are monocultural, are directed and controlled by members of that culture, and appeal primarily to an audience from within that culture. They differ because they consciously attempt to adapt cultural material to outsiders. This may involve adaptations of the cultural material to an aesthetic not wholly of that group, or some commercialisation of the event or both.
Commercialised	The commercial promotion of folk celebrations with the effect that the event moves primarily into popular culture even while retaining support from folk culture.
Non-community monocultural	Monocultural festivals organised by persons from outside the culture presented, having no support base in the cultural group presented, and making no attempt to involve persons of the culture as members of the audience.
Multicultural	Festivals representing the cultural materials of many cultures. With few exceptions, audiences tend to be people who are not of the cultures presented. Organisers tend to be academics or eclectic fans of the folk arts with control of the event likely to be in the hands of a non-profit institution.

Source: Adapted from Wilson and Udall, 1982, pp.4–6

Similarly, Dawson (1991) argues that three meaning systems can be attached to the analysis of ethno-cultural festivals. First, the 'cultural display' of living traditions. Second, a 'cultural text' of lived authenticity. Third, a 'cultural product' which meets the needs of commercial tourism.

Cultural display is the 'non-ordinary, framed, public events that require participation on the part of a substantial group' (Bendix, 1989, p.144). Through display cultural groups can hold events which demonstrate significant values and meanings to the wider public (Farber, 1983). Through such events, ethnic groups in multicultural nations such as Australia and Canada can highlight distinct cultural identities within the dominant culture. According to Dawson: 'This view of ethnic culture is completely in keeping with Canadian multicultural policy and ideology. The emphasis is on the rich diversity afforded by surviving, enduring social differences between ethnic groups, coupled with the avoidance of assimilation in the sense of the loss of one's ethnic identity' (1991, p.41).

The notion of cultural festivals as text is drawn from Lavenda *et al.* who perceived festivals as 'cultural texts that are performed anew each year, providing participants with one way in which they reflect upon experience and hence make sense out of their lives' (1984, p.34). From this perspective, cultural festivals and events allow a reading of the ongoing ethnic culture by allowing the participants to use common experiences as a cultural reference point which provides identity and an understanding of the nature of the tradition within the broader cultural context. For example, Low (1983, p.28) noted that the aboriginal themes of the Métis Heritage Days Festival helped to reaffirm the 'place for the Métis Nation within Canada', while the Powwow assists in the maintenance of North American Indian communities (Dyck, 1979, 1983).

The perspective of cultural events and festivals as tourism product emphasises the idea that cultural events may become commodified and festivals are transformed from community events to consumptive events which are marketed and promoted as products. According to Dawson

> ethnic and multicultural festivals may be seen as cultural products to be exploited for tourism ends. Individual ethnic cultures and multiculturalism itself are to be 'sold' using 'professional business practices', through the medium of festivals and other special events. Marketing initiatives and advertising campaigns are the means by which ethnic and multicultural festivals can promote themselves as 'sales packages' to tourists... When... an archaic revival of necrotic cultural practices takes place in order to satisfy the tastes of tourists, this deliberate, specialized revival renders ethnicity a commodity. It is valued for the profit it accrues through its exchange in the commercial tourism market and little more. (1991, pp.42–43)

As demonstrated above, the commodification of cultural events to provide 'inauthentic' and 'commercial' cultural products for tourists is generally seen in a negative light. However, while it may be easy for academics to criticise the selling of 'culture by the pound' (Greenwood, 1977), the key issue should probably be who is in control of the commercial process rather than the commercial process itself. For example, on the Indonesian island of Bali contrived performances of traditional Balinese theatre are specifically designed as commercial products for visitors. In addition to earning income from the performances, the Balinese have been able to continue performing their traditional plays (which often last for over ten hours) without their being undue disturbance from tourists. Therefore, at least in the case of Bali, commercialisation of certain aspects of cultural events has enabled the continuation rather than the desecration of traditional culture.

Moreover, there clearly needs to be a recognition that cultural display through events and festivals is not static. Cultural events are as dynamic as the host culture which responds to broader changes in society, technological innovation and contact with other cultures. Furthermore, there is a commercial element to almost any public festival. Even in the case of such culturally 'closed' societies as Saudi Arabia, the time of the Haj presents opportunities for Islamic merchants and hosts to benefit from the arrival of the Faithful in Mecca. Similarly, in the case of modern staged events, the nature of the festival may change over time in order to respond to broader economic and social needs. For example, in the case of the annual Kitchener-Waterloo Oktoberfest in Ontario, Canada, probably the largest Oktoberfest outside of Germany, the event has been transformed from a community-based celebration of German folk culture to a major tourist attraction which brings in substantial revenue for the Kitchener-Waterloo region (Wall and Hutchinson, 1978). Benefits still accrue from the event, although the benefits are now probably different from those intended when the initial objectives in hosting the event were established. Indeed, while Dawson may comment, 'Images of men dressed in lederhosen and toting kegs of brew on their shoulders are surely signs of archaic revival and the commercial exploitation of commodified culture, especially packaged for the benefit of tourism' (1991, p.46), it should be noted that the 'mother-event' in Munich has similarly been transformed in order to cater for both community and commercial needs.

Commercial Events: Markets and Fairs

> Popular gatherings and merrymakings seem, really, in this utilitarian generation, to be tolerated only as stimulants for provoking people to 'industry'… It is entirely reprehensible to celebrate with misplaced festivities what is in reality the greatest disgrace of all – viz, the necessity of securing the good conduct of the poor by artificial and secondary contrivances. (*The Times*, 24 September 1844, in Bailey, 1987, p.63)

The Great Exhibition at the Crystal Palace of 1851 was a concrete pivot of the change 'whereby leisure in its modern form became progressively more plentiful, more visible, more sought after and more controversial' (Bailey, 1987, p.68). The Great Exhibition saw the fusing of recreation with educational instruction and industry (Kusamitsu, 1980). Robert Baker, factory inspector, noted approvingly: 'The working class are moving about on the surface of their own country, visiting in turn exhibition after exhibition, spending the wealth they have acquired "in seeing the world" as the upper classes did in 1800, as the middle class did in 1850, and as they themselves are doing in 1875' (in Bailey, 1987, p.92). As Benedict (1983, p.2) reported: 'the fairs were not only selling goods, they were selling ideas: ideas about the relations between nations, the spread of education, the advancement of science, the form of cities, the nature of domestic life, the place of art in society'. Furthermore, they were an opportunity for nations to improve their image in an increasingly market conscious world. For example, according to Armstrong (1986, p.11), 'the first international exhibition, the Great Exposition of the Works of Industry of All Nations, held in Hyde Park London, in 1851 was held because, as Prince Albert stated, "It was the only way to out-do the French"'.

Commodity fairs and exhibitions have a long history dating back to ancient religious festivals. As Olds (1988, p.14) recognised, 'World Fairs are not merely overgrown amusement parks or simple trade fairs. They play a multitude of roles both explicit and implicit'. Such roles may include an elite statement concerning social and moral problems, demonstrations of confidence in technology, an educational institution, promotion of nationalistic sentiment, tools to effect labour

Table 2.5   The four periods of world fairs and expositions

Dates	Period	Fairs
1850–1889	Celebrations of the industrial revolution	London 1850, New York 1853, Munich 1854, Paris 1855, London 1862, Paris 1867, Vienna 1873, Philadelphia 1876, Paris 1878
1890–1930	The city beautiful	Chicago 1893, Omaha 1898, Buffalo 1901, St. Louis 1904, Portland 1905, Norfolk 1907, Seattle 1909, San Francisco 1915
1931–1961	The city efficient	Chicago 1933–4, New York 1939–40
1962–present	The city of renewal	Seattle 1962, New York 1964–5 (unofficial Fair), Montreal 1967, San Antonio 1968, Spokane 1974, Knoxville 1982, New Orleans 1984, Vancouver 1986, Brisbane 1988, Chicago 1992 (cancelled), Seville 1992

Sources: Zimmerman, 1974; Wachtel, 1986; Olds, 1988

relations, and the provision of spectacle by business and cultural elites (see, as a sample of some of the excellent literature available on World Fairs and international expositions: Allix, 1922; Curti, 1950; Hirschfield, 1957; Coates, 1964; Mandell, 1967; Cawelti, 1968; Doenecke, 1972; Lederer, 1973; Allwood, 1977; Rydell, 1978, 1981, 1983, 1984; Silverman, 1978; Badger, 1979; Harrison, 1980; Davidson, 1982/83, 1988; Benedict, 1983; Greenhalgh, 1988; Ley and Olds, 1988; Young, 1988).

Since the first international exposition in London in 1850 some four periods of World Fairs may be identified (Zimmerman, 1974; Wachtel, 1986; Olds, 1988), as shown in Table 2.5. However, regardless of the period, business and cultural elites have been critically important in promoting World Fairs (Rydell, 1984). For example, San Francisco's business elite attempted to use the 1915 Panama-Pacific International Exposition to attract investment to the city. According to Dobkin (1983, p.88) the main thrust of the city's campaign was:

> addressed to visiting businessmen. It was hoped that reconstruction of the city, and an exposition managed without labour disruptions would allay the fears of potential investors and drive home to the Atlantic states, where they conjure finance, and to New England, where they manufacture goods for export, the significance of San Francisco's geographical situation.

Anniversaries or 'marks of progress' (Olds, 1988, p.59) are also important in legitimising the hosting of World Fairs (French Revolution, 1889; 400th anniversary of the arrival of Columbus in America, 1893; tenth anniversary of the goldrush, 1909; Vancouver's 100th anniversary, 1986; Australia's bicentennary,

Table 2.6   Characteristics of major international exhibitions and fairs

Date	Place	Attendance (millions)	Profit (+) or loss (-)	Site acreage	Months open	National pavilions
1851	London	6.0	+	26	4.8	
1853	New York	1.3	-	13	15.5	
1855	Paris	5.2	-	34	6.7	
1862	London	6.2	-	25	5.7	
1867	Paris	6.8	+	215	7.2	20
1873	Vienna	7.3	-	42	6.2	7
1876	Philadelphia	9.9	-	285	5.3	8
1878	Paris	16.0	-	192	6.5	17
1889	Paris	32.4	+	237	5.7	31
1893	Chicago	27.5	+	685	6.1	17
1894	St. Louis	19.7				
1900	Paris	48.1	-	543	7.0	32
1901	Buffalo	8.1	-	350	6.1	
1904	St. Louis	19.7	-	1,272	6.1	19
1908	London	8.4		140	5.5	
1910	Brussels	13.0				
1915	San Francisco	18.9	+	635	9.8	
1924–5	London	27.1	-	216	12.0	
1931	Paris	33.5	+	500	6.0	
1933–4	Chicago	48.8	+	424	12.0	6
1935	Brussels	20.0				
1937	Paris	34.0	-	250	6.0	38
1939–40	New York	44.9	-	1,217	12.0	22
1939	San Francisco	19.05				
1958	Brussels	41.5	-	500	6.0	39
1964–5	New York	51.6	-	646	12.0	34
1967	Montreal	50.9	-	1,000	6.0	40
1970	Osaka	64.2	+	815	6.0	38
1992	Seville	est. 18		538	6.0	

Sources: Allwood, 1977; Benedict, 1983; Armstrong, 1986

1988). As Olds noted, 'this linkage is required in order to attract support from the community, all levels of government and the Bureau of International Expositions' (1988, p.67). However, World Fairs are not what they used to be. They have ceased to be the venue for important international meetings and congresses. Although while their amusement, educational and information function has diminished (Harrison, 1980; Benedict, 1983; Wachtel, 1986), their ability to attract tourists and investment and their value as a mechanism for urban redevelopment (Dungan, 1984), still makes them attractive to government and urban elites. Nevertheless, architect critic Ada Louise Huxtable has observed: 'The world's fair is a tired institution… It is a long time since it startled the world with its products or offered stimulating or controversial ideas. No longer an instrument of genuine

Table 2.7 Categories of international expositions sanctioned by the Bureau of International Expositions

Class	Theme	Minimum site acreage	Projected attendance	Participation	Examples
I (universal)	Broad, with universal appeal (e.g., peace, understanding, progress, discovery, harmony)	300	45–60 million	All 37 BIE signatory nations (host nation must provide space for pavilion rent-free to BIE members)	Montreal, Osaka, Seville
II (Special)	Specialised (e.g. energy, transport, fresh water)	70	10–12 million	Voluntary by BIE members (land or pavilion leases are negotiated)	Knoxville, Spokane, Vancouver, Brisbane

Source: After Dungan, 1984, p.84

intellectual exchange, it has been reduced to an expeditious shot in the arm and an instrument of national propaganda' (in Wachtel, 1986, p.40).

Table 2.6 illustrates some of the characteristics of major international exhibitions held between 1851 and 1970. Because of their lower cost and scale, specialised exhibitions have become more frequent in the 1980s (Knoxville, 1982; New Orleans, 1984; Tsukuba, 1985; Vancouver, 1986; Brisbane, 1988) (International Bureau of Exhibitions, 1989). Table 2.7 indicates the various categories of expositions sanctioned by the Bureau of International Expositions (BIE) based in Paris, an international organisation with some 37 signatory nations (Dungan, 1984). The BIE recognises two categories of expositions, Class I which are universal theme expositions and, Class II, which are special-category fairs.

The construction of purpose-built conference and exhibition centres is a major element in the development and promotion of urban areas, particularly because of the capacity of conferences to attract business interest in a region and the above-average expenditure profile of conference and exhibition goers (Law, 1987). The establishment of conference and exhibition facilities and associated infrastructure is also increasingly used as a mechanism to help revitalise core areas. For example, cities, such as Liverpool, Manchester and Birmingham in the United Kingdom, have utilised conference and exhibition centres as a means to transform their industrial image and develop tourism opportunities.

Despite the decline in the relative proportion of the population living in rural areas in the western world agricultural fairs remain as significant opportunities for both entertainment and business (Hughes, 1986; Kelly, 1986; Klassen, 1986). For example, agricultural shows are major visitor attractions in Saskatchewan with events such as the Canadian Western Agribition and the Western Farm Progress Show attracting over 150,000 and 30,000 people respectively (Derek Murray Consulting Associates, 1985, p.vi); while the 160,278 persons who visited the Wisconsin State Fair in 1988 spent a total of US$19,251,774 in the Milwaukee area (Gray, et al., 1988, p.1). The International Association of Fairs and Expositions founded in 1885 and with approximately 5,000 members worldwide, assists in the promotion, planning and management of fairs and events, often with an agricultural orientation (Goeldner and Long, 1987). Furthermore, the major provincial fairs of the nineteenth century have often been able to adapt to meet the changing external environment. For example, while the purposes of the Industrial Exhibition Association of Ontario formed in 1879 to promote agriculture, horticulture, arts and manufacturers, remain very similar to that of its successor, the Canadian National Exhibition (CNE), the present-day CNE is substantially different in its marketing, management and exhibition style (Oakes, 1986).

Sporting Events

Lines of cars and people start queuing up days before the race. When the gates open at 5.00 a.m. the lines stretch for miles. Every road leading to the speedway is clogged. In fact, if you are lucky enough to get a room at a downtown hotel, you will have to load up your car and get in line at 4.30 a.m. to drive just five miles to the track and make it comfortably in your seat before the race starts. By the time the orgy is over, thirty-three tons of trash will be deposited at and near the track, millions of hot dogs will be consumed, several children will be conceived, a dozen spectators will suffer heat attacks, an occasional motorist will be killed getting to and from the speedway, and a hundred or more persons will be treated for overdoses of both controlled and uncontrolled substances. Two hundred and twenty-five miles per hour on the track is an excuse for a one-day Middle American Babylon. (Edgely, 1987)

Sporting events probably constitute the most well-known form of hallmark event. 'Mega-sporting events are a powerful travel lure. The biggest draw large international audiences to the host site. Television provides free advertising and promotion to places which regularly stage mega-sports events. And this exposure attracts tourists to these places on a year-round basis' (Rooney, 1988, p.97). Mega-events such as the Olympic Games, the Commonwealth Games, the Indianapolis 500 (described above by Edgely) and major sporting events such as the World Cup (soccer) or the cricketing World Cup, have extremely high international and national profiles and are keenly sought after by nations and cities. Indeed, it is the profile which events can offer the hosts that provides the dominant rationale for the hosting of large-scale hallmark sporting events. As Okrant (1988, p.91) observed: 'The live audience and media coverage in attendance offer the likelihood of a substantial infusion of future visitors and dollars into the community. Further, well-timed, mega-sporting events may substantially increase the profitability of a destination's shoulder seasons'. The rationale for municipalities and/or organisations to host sporting events is indicated in the five goals and objectives which the Waterville Valley Ski Resort in the White Mountains of New Hampshire, United States, have in staging World Cup ski events at the resort (Corcoran, 1988):

1. Gain favourable media exposure and positioning for the resort.
2. Generate shoulder season revenues.
3. Stage event without out-of-pocket cost to the resort.
4. Create an event that instills pride in the resort by its employees.
5. Provide high quality ski competitions at 'home' to improve the US Ski Team's stature and world standings.

The rationales identified by Corcoran, the president of the Waterville Valley Ski Areas, are significant because the actual sports content of the event is the last objective which the hosting of the event is aimed at meeting. The primary rationale for the hosting of the event is the media coverage, marketing opportunities and extra income that World Cup skiing can bring to the resort and the region. 'Waterville Valley feels that the benefits of World Cup ski racing to its employees and its community are very substantial and that the exposure it has received through countless TV showings over time in major press stories has greatly enhanced Waterville Valley's name recognition and reputation' (Corcoran, 1988, p.102).

Rooney (1988) argues that there are a number of common factors in the hosting of mega-sport events. According to Rooney (1988, p.93) mega-sports events are surrounded by a great deal of tradition (some of which may be 'manufactured'); have 'developed a mystique' of their own; may benefit from media coverage, often at the international level; and are often accompanied by parades, festivals, and carnivals. In addition, some mega-events may be tied with specific places or hallowed grounds such as the holding of the Football Association Cup Final at Wembley Stadium in London or the Australian Football League Final at the Melbourne Cricket Ground.

Rooney (1988) also identifies three basic types of spatial organisation associated with mega-sport systems: 1.) events occurring periodically at different places over both regular and irregular time spans, for example, the Olympics are held every four years at a different site; 2.) events which occur periodically at a limited number of places over regular time spans, for example, the British and United States Golf Opens rotate among the premier golf courses of each nation; and 3.) events which occur periodically at regular intervals in a set place, for example, the United States Masters Golf Tournament is always held at the Augusta Golf Course. In addition, major league sports teams and franchises are located on a near-permanent basis in cities and stadia. However, while some major league teams and franchise may occupy an almost permanent position in their communities, for example, the Boston Celtic basketball team in Boston, the increasingly professional nature of sport may mean the relocation of franchises from one urban centre to another (Geddert and Semple, 1985). For example, the New Orleans Jazz basketball franchise was relocated from New Orleans to Utah in the late 1980s, resulting in the formation of the somewhat incongruously named Utah Jazz. Nevertheless, in general, a certain spatial stability can be associated with sporting franchises which brings with it significant economic and social dimensions for the host communities. As Rooney (1988, p.94) recognised:

Teams represent their places and become a part of a city's tradition, its social fabric, its culture. The Yankees, Cubs, Vikings, Lakers, Celtics, Canadians, Oilers, all connote strong city ties and attachments. Even college teams have come to represent their place, and as such are major attractions for alumni and a regional audience of sports enthusiasts. Certain forms of high school and youth sport have the power to unite a place and rally support for their efforts. As such high school tourneys and 'big games' can markedly influence travel behavior and tourism.

Table 2.8   Evaluation of candidate cities' bids for the 1996 Olympic Games by the Association of National Olympic Committees

A. Plus Points

Athens	Atlanta	Belgrade	Manchester	Melbourne	Toronto
Moral contribution to Olympic tradition and history in Greece. Centenary of modern Olympic Games	High concentration of very modern facilities. Convenient Olympic Village.	Many years quality experience in staging major international sports events.	Staging the Games will be of long-term benefit for the inhabitants in the area between Manchester, Liverpool, and Chester, considerably improving the environment.	85% of the venues within a radius of 6km from the Olympic Village.	Compact concept with the unique Skydrome and impressive lake front of Lake Ontario.
Olympic Sports Complex with Olympic Stadium, velodrome, sports hall, and other venues already completed.	Games will generate an enormous atmosphere with considerable financial profit to the benefit of the Olympic Movement.	Huge number of existing sports facilities, concentrated in the centre of the city.	Elegant concept at Barton Cross for Olympic Sports Centre and Olympic Village.	Financial subsidy for NOC delegations.	Good experience in staging major sports events including recent Olympic Games (Montreal '76, Calgary '88).
'Olympic Ring' concept – limited to three concentration points with maximum 29km from the Olympic Village.	Most of the venues are ready, situated in a green environment.	Moderate climate at the crossing point of two great rivers.	Solid experience in organising important international sports events, sport-enthusiastic crowd.	Long sporting tradition and excellence.	Special hospitality programme for athletes.

B. Minus Points

Athens	Atlanta	Belgrade	Manchester	Melbourne	Toronto
Probably traffic congestion and air pollution	Few major international sports events have been organised which could mean lack of experience (organisers, judges).	Most of the venues require considerable refurbishment.	Venues spread in the above-mentioned area.	Chosen date is the least convenient to the northern hemisphere, but might involve colder days.	Auxiliary Olympic Villages are not planned, but they would seem necessary bearing in mind distances to the shooting (105km) and canoe slalom (200km) sites.
Probably high temperature (up to 36°C) with low humidity and scarcely any precipitation.	Fairly high temperature (more than 30°C) with probably low precipitation.	Infrastructure of an old, naturally developed city may cause traffic problems (narrow streets, few parking places).	A request for additional accommodation for athletes competing in Liverpool and Chester is likely.	Long journey for most participating countries.	High hotel rates.
Olympic Games coincide with high tourist season.	Many high class hotels, but probably correspondingly high hotel rates.	Airport would need expansion.	Probably relatively low temperature and rain.	Probably high hotel rates.	The long lake front could cause strong winds.

Source: Association of National Olympic Committees, 1990.

Association of National Olympic Committees, 1990. Candidate Cities for the Games of the XXVI Olympiad, Appendix H in Sydney Olympic Games Review Committee, Appendix H in Sydney Olympic Games Review Committee

The Olympics

The impact of an Olympic Games on a host city is immense and profound, in terms of commitment by Governments, Business, Unions and the Community. The sporting program of the Games lasts only 16 days, yet their successful staging is the result of years of dedication and hard work by literally thousands of people.

If the commitment required to host the Olympic Games is immense, then so are the subsequent rewards for the host city and its citizens. An Olympic Games that is successfully staged and financially managed leaves a positive legacy for the host city in terms of new and upgraded sporting facilities and venues; new and improved infrastructure; enhanced international recognition; enhanced international reputation; increased tourism; new trade, investment and marketing opportunities; and increased participation in sport. (Sydney Olympic Games Review Committee, 1990, p.3)

The faces of entire cities have been permanently altered by the Games, and their impact on regional and national economies is considerable... The volume of symbolic exchange – interpersonal, national, and cross-cultural – defies quantitative description, but is even more prodigious and remarkable.

Not a few individuals have had their lives taken or saved, their pockets lined or emptied, their happiness ensured or stolen from them by the Olympics. For many, many more, the routines of daily life grind to a halt for two weeks every four years. Weddings are postponed, crops go untended, work is interrupted, and the Olympics crowd most other topics out of conversation. In short, the Games are an institution without parallel in nature and scope in the twentieth century. Insofar as there exists, in the hegelian-marxian phrase, a "world-historical process," the Olympics have emerged as its privileged expression and celebration. (MacAllon, 1984, pp.241–3)

The Olympics is probably the world's largest mega-event with substantial economic, social and political costs and benefits for the host nation, region, and city. Probably few events have the ability to focus the attention of the world as much as the Olympics. For example, two-and-a-half billion people viewed the 1984 Los Angeles Olympic Summer Games (Perelman, 1985). In addition, the Olympics provide an unprecedented opportunity for publicity, urban renewal, the construction of physical infrastructure and economic development. There are a number of goals and objectives in the hosting of an Olympics. According to Hiller (1989), the International Olympic Committee have two major objectives. First, the legacy of facilities that will stimulate athletic development which would not have been possible with inferior facilities. Second, to heighten the profile of the sports involved by providing better opportunities for training as well as sites for other national and international competitions. Therefore, 'to the Olympic organisation, the Olympic games are not merely an end in themselves but are meant to foster the broader goals of competitive sport. Impact is... measured in athletic terms' (Hiller, 1989, p.120). As an indication of the weighting that the Olympic Committee places on their objectives, Table 2.8 provides the evaluation of candidate cities' bids for the 1996 Olympic Games by the Association of National Olympic Committees.

Table 2.9   Olympic sponsorship and economic impact: 1984 Los Angeles
Summer Games and 1988 Calgary Winter Games

Item	Los Angeles	Calgary
Television income	$225 million	$309 million (ABC) $10 million (others)
Corporate sponsorship	$250 million	$187 million
Attendance	$17.5 million (season tickets)	$2 million
TV audiences	$1.5 billion	$1.5 billion
Volunteer workers	40,000	22,000
Construction	Minimal	$300 million Saddle dome ($98 million) Speed skating oval ($30 million) McMahon stadium expansion Olympic Plaza Ski complexes
Economic impact	$3.3 billion	$449 million – Calgary $650 million – Other Canada
Profits	$215 million	$29 million

Source: Rooney, 1988, p.99

For the host city and nation the goals of staging the Olympics are set in different terms. First, the sporting legacy provides a broad rationale for hosting the Games. Second, there is the honour and global recognition that comes from being chosen among international venues. Third, there is an infusion of external funding for capital projects which are justified by the event. Fourth, the economic stimulus that comes from the preparation for the event, the event itself and the tourism opportunities which follow the event. As McGeoch (1991, p.6) stated in respect of Sydney's bid for the 2000 Summer Olympics, 'the hosting of an Olympic Games results in a significant stimulus to the development industry in relation to direct requirements for the conduct of the games and improved opportunities for related investment'.

From a political perspective, 'the value of hosting the Olympics rests with the forum it offers for demonstrating the strengths and achievements of the host society and the value of participating is designed to do the same' (Richter, 1989, p.5) (see Chapter 5). For example, United States 'efforts to mobilize a boycott of the Moscow Olympic games as an international rebuke to the Soviets for the invasion of Afghanistan were intended to deny the USSR global respectability and prestige. Advocates of the boycott also saw the Olympic protest as a means of penetrating Soviet censorship and encouraging the domestic population to ques-

Table 2.10   The perceived significance of the Seoul Olympics to Korean tourism

Factor	Agree (%)	Neutral (%)	Disagree (%)	Mean Score
Increase in international awareness of Korea	100.00	0.0	0.0	4.9
Modification of Korea's image depicted by MASH	91.0	4.5	4.5	4.3
Opening up of new tourism markets	98.5	1.5	0.0	4.6
Decrease in the high dependency of Korean tourism industry on the Japanese market	67.1	20.9	12.0	3.9
Increase in Japanese visitor's length of stay	23.9	40.3	32.8	2.9
Potential growth in the female market	61.2	32.8	6.0	3.7

Scale ranges from 1 = strongly disagree to 5 = strongly agree

Source: Jeong, 1988, p.181

tion the legitimacy of the Soviet presence in Afghanistan' (Richter, 1989, p.6). Similarly, the Russians attempted the reverse in the Los Angeles Summer Games of 1984 and cited security fears as a reason for non-attendance. In retaliation, the Americans claimed that the Soviets were fearing defections.

Despite the undoubtedly political nature of such prominent events as the Olympics, the majority of research on the impacts of the Games on host regions has been on the economic, perceptual and tourism dimensions of hosting the Games. For example, the economic impacts of the 1984 Los Angeles Summer Olympics and the 1988 Calgary Winter Olympics are illustrated in Table 2.9. The significance of the Olympics for tourism was also indicated in Jeong's (1988) study of the perceptions of the impact of the 1988 Summer Olympics on Korea. In a survey of 67 high-level Korean tourism personnel, questions were asked about the preparation of the country for the Olympics and maximisation of the benefits of the Games for Korea. Jeong's survey revealed that the Seoul Olympics were a significant means to overcome the poor image of Korea in the international tourism market, particularly the United States, because of the devastation of the country following the Korean War, and the impression that Korea is a 'dangerous place to visit' (1988, p.176) (Table 2.10). In addition, the Korean tourism industry wished to reduce their dependence on the Japanese visitor market and stimulate further tourism traffic between Korea and the West. Furthermore, the Olympics were perceived as having significant economic, political and socio-cultural effect beyond the immediate impact of the Games on sport and tourism (Table 2.11). Jeong (1988, p.177) observed that 'the Olympics will fuel and foster the export-oriented growth process in Korea', although 'many respondents were concerned about the possible commercialization of the cultural values and traditions through the Olympics'.

Table 2.11 The perceived effects of the Seoul Olympics on the Korean economy, socio-culture, and politics

Factor	Agree (%)	Neutral (%)	Disagree (%)	Mean Score
Economic benefit				
Promotion of Korean-made products	85.1	10.4	4.5	4.2
Additional employment	71.6	20.9	7.5	3.9
Improvement of local infrastructure	64.2	23.9	10.4	3.7
Economic costs				
Inflation	23.9	37.3	38.8	2.8
Increase of imports	68.7	20.9	10.4	3.6
Real estate speculation	61.2	32.8	6.0	3.7
Socio-cultural benefits and costs				
Strengthening of cultural values	95.5	4.5	0.0	4.6
Increase in street crimes	11.9	28.3	59.7	2.3
Political benefits				
Popularity of the government	58.2	24.4	13.4	3.5
Fostering the spirit of national unity between North and South Korea	25.4	50.7	23.9	3.0
Improvement of diplomatic relations with the communist countries	80.6	17.9	1.5	4.1
Factors interfering with the successful hosting of the Olympics				
Unstable domestic political situation	55.2	19.4	23.9	3.4
Soviet boycott	64.2	23.8	12.0	3.6
Influence of terrorism	41.8	28.3	22.4	3.1
Factors reducing the number of foreign arrivals				
Unstable domestic political situation	53.7	23.9	22.4	3.1
Influence of terrorism	74.6	16.4	9.0	3.9

Scale ranges from 1 = strongly disagree to 5 = strongly agree

Source: After Jeong, 1988, p.182

Sport and Economic Development The relationship between sports events and economic development as seen in the Olympic Games which have been held over the past two decades is not new. The 1932 Los Angeles Summer Olympics were designed to promote tourism, while American College football games such as the Orange Bowl (Miami), Sugar Bowl (New Orleans), and the Cotton Bowl (Dallas), were established to help revive ailing cities during the great depression (Reiss, 1989). Similarly, the Superbowl is not only the pinnacle of the United States professional football season but also represents a massive injection of funds to the host city.

The hosting of major sporting events, such as the Superbowl, requires the construction of large sports facilities. Reiss (1981, 1989) has argued that the construction of stadia such as the Yankee Stadium in New York and the Los Angeles coliseum only went ahead because of the actions of elites within the municipal political structure. Indeed, the high costs of constructing sports facilities has often meant that the bidding for events and their associated economic impacts has become a major justification for establishing large sports facilities (Hiller, 1989; Thorne and Munro-Clark, 1989). Okner (1974) and Lipsitz (1984) provide several reasons for the role of government authorities in the development of major stadia

- prestige and 'big-town' image;
- the location of new industry and increased marketing power;
- the possible generation of additional employment, consumer sales, and tax collection which result from sporting events;
- additional recreational opportunities for community residents, especially if attendance at sporting events replaces other activities which are socially disruptive;
- beneficial effects on the morale of the citizens resulting from the presence of a successful sports team in the city; and
- encouragement of interest in sports among the young.

Most notably, Okner identifies the primary significance of the prestige factor with the construction of sports stadia. In North America, the supposed prestige associated with sports events and national league teams is witnessed in the desire of many cities to develop domed stadia, even though such stadia may only be used for a small proportion of the available time and require ongoing financial subsidies from municipal government. An example of the debt that municipalities are prepared to underwrite in order to construct sports stadia and host hallmark events is the 1976 Olympics in Montreal, Canada. Even though the 1976 Summer Olympics led to a Can.$600 million debt for the city, the Tourism Development Commissioner of the City of Montreal, Pierre Labrie, has justified the expenditure by arguing that 'one cannot look into the 1976 Olympics without examining the long-term spin-off effects, including the city's ability to host international activities such as world class amateur championships, professional and participation events'. He went on to note:

In order to fully assess the benefits reaped because of the Olympics, one must take into account intangible elements including the impact of the games on general participation in sports, increased use of public sports facilities, as well as the cultural impact of the event. One should look into the psychological impact on Montrealers, for example, pride in the city. One could argue that these cannot be measured accurately. (Labrie, 1988, p.103)

While sport event tourism is obviously a major factor in the hosting of hallmark events, the attention of researchers has primarily been on the economic impacts on the immediate region, rather than the relationship of the event to visitor motivations and the effects on participants and spectators. As Rooney (1988, p.94) commented 'We know very little about tourist motivation and behaviour relative to mega-sports. Nor do we know much about the precise role of mega-sports in attracting tourists to the location of the mega-event'. Furthermore, apart from a few isolated studies, the majority of research on sports events has neglected to examine the broader social and political effects of the hosting of events on the local community, a point which will be taken up in later chapters of this book. Unfortunately, there is an assumed view, often developed from inadequate re-search and studies of event impacts, that sports events are automatically 'good', this attitude is indicated in a study of the British Open at St. Andrews, Scotland:

> The question of spillovers – longer-term, dynamic and largely imponderable by-prod-ucts – is one to which we should draw attention but not one to which we can put numbers of any useful kind. On the beneficial side, the identification, through world-wide TV coverage, of St. Andrews with the world's premier golf championship must bring lasting advantages, affecting both local commerce and the Links Management Trusts. Against that, there may be some slight loss of goodwill among 'regular' holidaymakers... The benefits under the first heading *must* far outweigh the costs under the second. (Blake, 1979, in Rooney, 1988, pp.95-96; author's emphasis)

The focus on quantitative data by many researchers and the desire of govern-ment for such 'hard' data has meant that the social and political dimensions of events have often been neglected. Nevertheless, as the above discussion has illustrated, the impact of sports events, such as the Olympic Games, needs to be seen also in terms of the effect that events have on the image of the host city (Ritchie and Smith, 1991; Ritchie and Lyons, 1990), the event planning process, and the issue of who benefits from the hosting of such events.

Political Events

While mega-events such as the Olympic Games have undoubted political over-tones (see Chapter 5), political events such as visits by Royalty, the convention of a political party, or the hosting of a meeting of the World Bank/International Monetary Fund may also be seen as hallmark events. In the British Common-wealth and the United States, visits by the Queen and other notable members of the British royal family, such as the Prince and Princess of Wales, have the capacity to draw large numbers of people to host cities and/or to line the routes that they travel. In Australia, for example, on the occasion of tours by the Queen schoolchildren are requested by government and education departments to be present upon their arrival or departure from destinations. In the case of party conventions, the Republican and Democratic party congresses in the United States are much sought after events by cities, which perceive the media interest in the congresses, as well as the influx of delegates, to be of great benefit to the host city. In the United

Kingdom (Blackpool, Bournemouth, Brighton) and Australia (Hobart), several cities have come to be associated with annual party conferences which help to maintain the cities' presence in the valuable conference and exhibition market.

The political and economic significance of the International Monetary Fund and World Bank meeting also attracts significant numbers of visitors. In the case of the 1991 joint annual conference in Bangkok, the meeting was used to provide exposure for the new Queen Sirikit Convention Centre built at a cost of Baht 2.3 billion (US$90 million). The significance of such events require substantial security arrangements to be put in place. However, in the case of the Bangkok meeting other associated occurences included efforts to relocate 1,900 residents of the Khlong Pai Singtoh and Duang Phitak slums next to the Convention Centre, 'on the grounds that they could provide shelter for terrorists' although 'it is generally considered that the government is more worried about the image the slums would present to the world's bankers' (Handley, 1991, p.32). A national holiday was declared during the meeting in order to try and reduce the impacts of Bangkok's traffic jams on the delegates, while the police also attempted to restrain the city's 'hospitality girls' from being too open in their services. The police also announced 'a crackdown on streetwalking transvestites. Showing some sympathy, the police chief said only the most incorrigible transvestites will be disciplined, while the "nice ones" will be left alone' (Handley, 1991, p.32).

Summary

Bonnemaison (1990, p.25) has argued that there are two fundamentally different kinds of events that transform urban areas:

> official national or international events and community events. Military parades, for example, express patriotic attitudes, while ethnic festivals, carnivals or farmer's markets reflect a communal identity. The first category functions like a monument, supporting and reinforcing the image of established power, whether religious or secular.

Events of the second type, events which represent a community,

> serve a totemic function. They employ a collection of symbols that define the community and represent it to the outside world.

The above discussion has highlighted the part that both sets of functions play within the various categories of hallmark events.

Events are both inward and outward looking, while events can be a means of community celebration they can also be used to achieve economic and employment objectives. However, even when economic and visitor attraction goals are paramount, it can still be argued that such objectives will be a reflection of a certain set of socio-economic values that operate within that community. Furthermore, the focus of government, private industry, and certain sections of communities on the use of events to fulfil a variety of economic, social and promotional functions, means that the actual or potential tourist component of even the most 'traditional' event can no longer be ignored. The task then for researchers is to elucidate and articulate the mechanisms by which events can be of most value to host communities and ensure that such events retain their innate uniqueness which made the event attractive and valuable in the first place. Therefore, the following three chapters will examine the economic, social and political dimensions of events in order to highlight the basis from which the benefits of hosting events can be maximised and the costs minimised.

3 The Economic Impacts of Hallmark Events

Unfortunately, there can be no prior guarantee that benefits will entirely outweigh the costs accompanying mega-events. (Okrant, 1991, p.91)

By far the most detailed research on the impacts of hosting hallmark events has been conducted on the economic dimensions of event impact. Unfortunately, much of the research has been poorly conducted with inadequate consideration of significant methodological issues; thus, from a planning and decision-making perspective, it is relatively useless. This chapter will provide a discussion of the relevance of economic analysis for policy and decision-making, and methodological problems in impact assessment and forecasting. It will also suggest improvements in the manner in which research is conducted.

The Economic Dimensions of Events

Events are generally seen in a positive light by government and private industry because of the perceived economic, commercial and promotional benefits in the hosting of such events. Apart from the influx of visitors and the associated expenditure, events are also welcomed because they can generate economic activity through the construction of event-related facilities and infrastructure – such as stadia, accommodation, or improvements to transport networks – and attract broader commercial interest in the host city and region. Indeed, as Hall (1989b) observed, the location of an event or an event facility may be utilised to attempt to rejuvenate a run-down urban area, while the event itself is often used to arouse visitor interest in the host city and thereby attract further visitation. For example, as the Australian Department of Sport, Recreation and Tourism (1986, p.45) reported on the Aus\$5 million special grant provided by the Commonwealth for the initial Adelaide Grand Prix: 'The Commonwealth's support for the Grand Prix... acknowledged the unprecedented international exposure for Australia and the significant economic benefits in the areas of tourism, employment and business opportunities', while Bentick (1986), Van Der Lee (1987), and Van Der Lee and Williams (1986) reported that through the exposure of Adelaide on telecasts of the Grand Prix the city may hope to generate a greater level of tourism and attract entrepreneurs to South Australia. Similarly, according to CABR (1987, Part II, p.4), a significant longer-term benefit from the hosting of the 1987 America's Cup 'will be derived from the general exposure that the Cup achieved for the West Australian economy, and through the promotion of specific industries directly related to the Cup, such as the boat building and tourism industries'. However, as Cowie (1989, p.81) observed 'the influx of large numbers of visitors has a multitude of implications for the economy of the host community, especially if the community is unaccustomed to such an influx'.

Sports events have a substantial economic impact on their host communities (Lee, 1984). For example, the United States Golfing Masters Tournament at Augusta is estimated to have a US$25–30 million impact on the local economy during the Masters week. Similarly, the British Golf Open at St. Andrews has had a significant impact on the small, Scottish coastal town. Total visitor expenditure during the 1978 Open was estimated at £2,651,000 with total receipts of £3,231,000, adjusted for inflation, the 1988 benefit would be in excess of US$10 million (Rooney, 1988, p.95). However, sports events do not have to be as large as major golf tournaments to have significant economic impacts on small communities. For example, in a 1988 study of Scottsdale, the winter home of the San Francisco Giants, total expenditures in Scottsdale by fans attending Giants' home games in 1988 was estimated at US$7,137,499. The home attendance figure of 61,971 was generated by an estimated 29,662 spectators. 'Nearly 21,950 of these fans were out of state tourists... Scottsdale-resident fans spent $3,283,793 in the city. The other 18,220 tourists spent an estimated $22,582,898 while in Arizona, of which $3,226,128 went directly into the Scottsdale economy. Cactus League game-related expenditures in Scottsdale totalled $627,588' (Diffendererfer, 1989, pp.61–2).

A review of the impacts of a number of sports events in Australia indicated that sports events are able to contribute more than direct income and the generation of employment to local economies. Mazitelli (1989) argues that major sporting events have the potential to contribute substantially to tourism development because of the characteristics of event visitors as compared to other holiday-makers. According to Mazitelli (1989, pp.197–8) these fundamental sporting characteristics appear to be:

1. Visitors to major sporting events tend to equal or exceed the average length of stay of other holiday-makers.
2. Visitors to major sporting events tend to use accommodation options that equal or exceed the cost of those options used by average visitors – both domestic and international.
3. Visitors to major sporting events incur a level of per diem expenditure equalling or exceeding that of average visitors – both domestic and international.

For example, a study of the 1985 Fourth World Cup of Athletics staged in Canberra, Australia, indicated that the event attracted approximately 1,100 international visitors with an average length of stay of twenty-six days and average trip expenditure of Aus$1,846 (Department of Sport, Recreation and Tourism, 1986).

Table 3.1   Comparison of domestic tourist visitation and 1985 World Cup of
Athletics domestic visitation to Canberra, Australia

Number of nights away from home	Percentage of visitors stay in Canberra	
	Domestic	World Cup
1	28.4	14.5
2	25.4	26.4
3	14.6	26.1
4	6.5	14.6
5	4.0	7.1
6 – 7	6.9	5.2
8 or more	14.2	6.1
	100.0	100.0
Mean	3.1	3.4

Source: Mazitelli, 1989, p.198

In addition, approximately 9,000 residents from outside the Canberra region
visited the event with an average 3.4 nights spent in Canberra, 2.7 nights travelling
to, and 2.8 nights returning from Canberra, and expenditure of approximately
Aus$5 million (Department of Sport, Recreation and Tourism, 1986, Rey, 1987;
Mazitelli, 1989) (Table 3.1). At the national level Mazitelli (1989, p.199) argued
that the attraction of major sports events to Australia is compatible with the
broader tourism policies relating to the attraction of international visitors and is
comparable with attempts to attract international conventions, while at the regional level several other potentially significant advantages of hosting sports
events could be identified:

1. In regions with a scarcity of naturally occurring tourist attributes major sports events
   (or a program of sports events over the year) would provide an attraction for sports
   tourists who tend to spend more and stay longer than average visitors.
2. In regions with good tourist attributes and accommodation but with low utilisation
   levels the attraction of sports tourists is a better than average way of maximising the
   use of these resources.
3. In regions with good tourist attributes but with a shortfall in the stock of accommodation facilities the attraction of sports tourism is a mechanism to be considered for
   stimulating the development and upgrading of necessary infrastructure.

The above comments support the observation that rural communities may
perceive festivals and special events as a mechanism to attract non-resident and
tourist expenditure within their region (Reichert, 1978; Marsh, 1984; Thomason
and Perdue, 1987; Murphy and Carmichael, 1991). For example, in an examination of the economic impact of sport and recreation events on the Sunraysia district
in Victoria, Australia, it was reported that such events contributed an estimated
Aus$9.1 million to the regional economy, an amount equivalent to approximately
five per cent of the total income from the region's main industry, dried fruit
(Patterson, 1987). Undoubtedly, festivals and programmes of special events provide opportunities for communities to expand the markets of existing firms and
attract new businesses and commercial interests, and perhaps raise the overall

Table 3.2 Expenditures at three Ontario festivals (1985 Can$)

	Blyth	Niagara-on-the-Lake	Stratford
Total $	457,929	6,353,310	12,581,240
Total $ (less salaries)	186,411	3,376,668	4,017,339
Local $	95,987	3,376,833	281,213
% Local	51.4	5	7

Source: Wall and Mitchell, 1989, p.135

Table 3.3 Expenditures at three Ontario festivals per business (1985 Can$)

	Number of establishments	Local expenditure ($)	Expenditure/ business ($)
Blyth	28	95,987.3	3,428.1
Niagara-on-the-Lake	197	168,833.4	3,428.1
Stratford	606	281,213.0	464.0

Source: Wall and Mitchell, 1989, p.136

attractiveness of areas as places to settle. However, 'the nature of impacts varies with the age and status of the event and the size of the community in which it takes place' (Wall and Mitchell, 1989, p.132).

In a study of three Ontario festivals (Shakespearean Festival at Stratford, Blyth Festival at Blyth, and the Shaw Festival at Niagara-on-the-Lake), Wall and Mitchell (1989) reported substantial growth of accommodation and food and beverage sectors and other tourism-oriented establishments as a consequence of the festivals, and observed that the 'types of businesses in operation in the towns have changed over time, at least partially in response to the economic activity generated by the Festivals' (1989, p.134). According to their study 'smaller festivals in smaller towns may have larger impacts per local business' (Wall and Mitchell, 1989, p.135) (see Tables 3.2 and 3.3) although visitors tend to stay longer in larger communities primarily because there is more to do, a greater range and number of accommodation facilities, and therefore greater opportunity to spend money. In addition, they noted that 'as the festival becomes more established, its market area increases, and duration of stay and visitor expenditures expand' (Wall and Mitchell, 1989, p.136) with consequent flow-on effects for tourism oriented businesses and a perceived increased market potential to all firms within the local economy.

One of the most critical determinants in estimating the economic impacts of events on the host community is the balance of visitor versus local spending with the greater the amount of visitor spending the larger the potential positive flow-on to the host community. The potential for economic benefits from the hosting of events was demonstrated in Derek Murray Consulting Associates (1985) study of the impact of events on local economies in Saskatchewan, Canada. According to Derek Murray, in a survey of 24 events, an average of only 38.1 per cent of the attendance was drawn from the host community with the remainder travelling 50

Table 3.4 Actual and projected revenues for Olympic Summer Games (Aus$m)

Revenue item	Los Angeles 1984	Seoul 1988	Barcelona 1992	Atlanta 1996	Sydney 2000 bid
Media	372	444	587	731	636
Marketing	239	614	788	498	591
Ticket Sales	236	54	106	228	160
Operations	138	122	93	90	88
Government	0	0	159	0	180
Interest (holding costs)	–	–	–	–	37
Total	985	1234	1733	1547	1692

NOTES: All figures are presented in September 1990 Aus$ (Aus$1= US$1.27); marketing includes Olympic marketing, international marketing, suppliers and licensees, advertising, sponsorship and fundraising, lotteries, stamps and medals; operations includes accommodation, catering, publications and souvenirs, sales and property, and salvage of equipment; government includes federal, state, and local levels.

Source: Adapted from Sydney Olympic Games Review Committee, 1990, p.18

miles or more (the definitional criteria for tourist travel in Saskatchewan) to attend the event from within Saskatchewan or from out-of-Province destinations. The total visitor expenditure from event attendance was Can$68.2 million with the average per person expenditure being Can$175.87. However, from the perspective of gaining community support for the hosting of events it is important to note that it was estimated that for every Can$24.72 events received from tourists some Can$151.75 flowed on to the community (Derek Murray Consulting Associates, 1985, p.xiii). While these figures do not take into account the leakage of economic expenditures from the host community (see below) they do indicate how the economic potential of events may act to encourage government, municipalities and the private industry to become involved in event tourism.

Large-scale events or mega-events, such as the Olympic Games, are also keenly sought after by nations and cities because of their perceived economic benefits as well as the undoubted prestige and profile they bring to the host city (see Tables 3.4 and 3.5, for an account of Summer Olympic Games revenue and expenditure). However, while the Games themselves may be profitable the associated infrastructure development may be less economically beneficial, at least in the short term, to the host community. As the Sydney Olympic Games Review Committee (1990, p.39) reported, 'every post World War II Olympic Games has returned an operational profit, and only one has run at an overall loss. This was Montreal, which suffered from an ill-conceived, over ambitious and badly managed capital works program (including an underground rail system and new airport), compounded by major industrial difficulties' (see Table 3.6). In the case

Table 3.5 Actual and projected expenditures for Olympic Summer Games (Aus$m)

Expenditure item	Los Angeles 1984	Seoul 1988	Barcelona 1992	Atlanta 1996	Sydney 2000 bid
Operational					
• Venues operations	46	52	124	23	52
• Villages operations	60	61	–	42	70
• Cultural programme	13	64	47	19	40
• Ceremonies	13	–	32	33	20
• Signs and decorations	–	–	18	–	15
• Transport	17	9	17	16	25
• Airline subsidy	–	–	–	–	30
• Security	55	99	38	75	65
• Medical	–	5	18	10	10
• Insurance	–	–	–	27	20
• Public relations and marketing	–	132	38	76	35
• Protocol	–	11	20	17	25
• Technology	28	62	140	50	20
• Personnel	155	21	197	33	190
• Team costs paralympics	–	–	–	–	65
• Other/Operational contingency	86	138	196	193	25
Sub-total	473	654	885	614	707
Venues (including infrastructure)	138	470	430	478	692
Villages	8	0	248	79	60
Media (including telecommunications)	0	in technology	140	149	110
Contingency	0	0	0	0	50
Total	619	1124	1703	1320	1619

NOTES: All figures are presented in September 1990 Aus$. (Aus$1= US$1.27)

Source: Adapted from Sydney Olympic Games Review Committee, 1990, p.18

Table 3.6 Actual and projected operating profits for Olympic Summer Games (Aus$m)

	Los Angeles 1984	Seoul 1988	Barcelona 1992	Atlanta 1996	Sydney 2000 bid
Revenue	985	1800	1731	1548	1692
Expenditure	648	1124	1731	1339	1639
Profit	337	676	0	209	53

NOTES: All figures are presented in September, 1990, Aus$ (Aus$1= US$1.27)

Source: Adapted from Sydney Olympic Games Review Committee, 1990

of Montreal it should be noted that the associated infrastructure developments, such as improvements and changes to the transport network, were directly involved with Games expenditure. In the majority of Games developments, however, the Olympic operational costs are reported in separate financial statements to infrastructure costs. For example, the 1972 Munich Summer Olympics lost £178 million (at 1979 prices), with the loss being shared between the West German Government, the Bavarian Government and the City of Munich (Taylor and Gratton, 1988, p.33).

The above discussion illustrates the need for a careful consideration of the potential costs and benefits in the hosting of hallmark events and their potential to assist in regional and community development. The following section will examine in closer detail the potential of economic research to contribute to event planning and management and the techniques that can be utilised in economic impact assessment and forecasting.

The Relationship of Economic Research to Event Planning

The contribution of economic research to economic planning carries across the complete range of events and festivals. At the level of community events, economic research can help provide a clear assessment of the worth of the event to the local economy and help in the assessment of where resources and efforts should be focused. At the level of mega-events, economic research can determine the relative effectiveness of public funding and the distribution of costs and benefits as a result of both the event and the infrastructure development associated with it. However, 'research in this area has been biased towards exaggeration of the economic benefits in order to gain credibility and support for organizers, and has been flawed by theoretical and methodological problems' (Getz, 1991b, p.61). Similarly, Armstrong (1984, 1986) argues that it is a myth that international events are profitable and notes that grossly inflated multiplier effects are claimed by 'project boosters' in order to ensure that event proposals go ahead so that the prestige objectives in conducting an event can be met.

Given the large amount of public expenditure on many hallmark events there is a clear need for a more detailed appraisal of the success and impacts of these events, both pre- and post-event, than there has been in the past (Wall and Knapper, 1981; Travis and Croizé, 1987; Roche, 1988, Roche, 1991; Wang and Gitelson, 1988a, 1988b; Mazitelli, 1989; Hall, 1989a; Lawrence and Rosenthal, 1990; Foley, 1991a. As Zwolak (1987) reported, government is ever keen to pick winners before events are supported and staged. Therefore, the development of methodologies and an information base on the economic and employment benefits is of great benefit to government as well as to private industry (Fleming and Toepper, 1990).

From the perspective of the organiser the analysis of the economic impact of an event also has several substantial benefits. First, it helps provide a perspective on the potential benefit of the event on the local economy (often a criterion for the hosting of an event). Second, it helps provide an assessment of the event, including the level of attendance, which enables organisers to ensure that the event is meeting its objectives. Third, it assists in providing for an informed public debate on the merits of the event (Della Bitta, *et al*., 1977; Davidson and Schaffer, 1980; Kemp, 1984; McDonald, 1990a, b). The following section discusses some of the techniques that can be applied in the examination of economic impact.

Economic Impact Analysis

Economic impacts are the measured changes in specific economic variables (such as income, output and employment) in a defined economy arising from an impacting agent such as a hallmark event (Dryden, 1987). 'Economic impact can occur either as a result of attracting non-resident expenditures into the economy or by reducing the leakage of resident dollars from the economy' (Long and Perdue, 1990, p.10). The three most common forms of economic evaluation of an event are tourism multipliers, input-output analysis, and cost-benefit analysis.

Tourism Multipliers Tourism multipliers are concerned with 'the way in which expenditure on tourism filters throughout the economy, stimulating other sectors as it does so' (Pearce 1989, p.205), and are based on the Keynesian principles of the recirculation of a proportion of income by a region's recipients into consumption spending which then encourages further employment and income (Bull, 1991). Several different types of multiplier are used, each with its own economic emphasis (Archer, 1977, 1982; Della Bitta *et al*., 1977; Vaughan, 1977; Davidson and Schaffer, 1980; DPA Group, 1985; Roberts and McLeod, 1989). However, the multiplier may be regarded as 'a coefficient which expresses the amount of income generated in an area by an additional unit of tourist spending' (Archer 1982, p.236). It is the ratio of direct and secondary changes within an economic region to the direct initial change itself (Hall, 1991).

Primary and secondary impacts can be identified. Primary or direct impacts are those economic impacts which are a direct consequence of tourist spending. For instance, the purchase of food and beverage by a tourist at an event. Secondary impacts may be described as being either indirect or induced. Indirect impacts are those arising from the re-spending of money in the form of local business transactions, for example, new investment by event organisers in equipment and supplies. Induced impacts are those arising from the additional income generated by further consumer spending, for example the purchase of goods and services by event employees. However, it must be noted that for each round of spending per unit of initial tourist expenditure leakage will occur from the regional economy until little or no further re-spending is possible. In sum, 'the tourism multiplier is a measure of the total effects (direct plus secondary) which result, from the additional tourist expenditure' (Archer, 1982, p.237).

The size of the tourist multiplier will vary from region to region and will depend on various factors. These are the size of area of analysis, the proportion of goods and services imported into the region for consumption by event tourists, the rate of circulation, the nature of event tourist spending, the availability of suitable local products and services, and the patterns of economic behaviour for event tourists and locals alike. The size of the tourist multiplier is a significant measure of the economic benefit of event tourism because it will be a reflection of the circulation of tourist expenditure through an economic system. In general, the larger the size of the tourist multiplier the greater the self-sufficiency of that economy in the provision of tourist facilities and services. Therefore, a tourist multiplier will generally be larger at a national level than at a state or provincial level, because at a state or provincial level leakage will occur in the form of taxes to the national government and importation of goods and services from other states. Similarly, at the regional and local level, multipliers will reflect the high importation level of small communities, and tax payments to state/provincial and national governments (Hall, 1991).

As a measure of economic benefit from tourism, the multiplier technique has been increasingly subject to question, particularly as its use has often produced exaggerated results (Archer 1977, 1982; Hughes 1982; Frechtling 1987; Pearce 1989). As Hughes (1982, p.172) has argued in the British case, other forms of economic activity may produce similar regional multipliers, 'They are not consistently superior and do not warrant the special status accorded them'. Nevertheless, despite doubts about the accuracy of the multiplier technique, substantial attention is still paid to the results of hallmark event economic impact studies by government and private industry as a measure of the immediate success of the event and associated tourism development.

Input-Output Analysis 'Input-output analysis is a general equilibrium approach to examining the structure of an economy, its dependencies and the economic impact of exogenous changes in final demand' (Fletcher and Snee, 1989, p.223). Input-output analysis seeks to determine how the aggregate secondary effects of an economic activity, such as tourism spending, work their way through an economy, based on the specific supply and demand interactions between different economic agents such as industries or industry sectors (Bull, 1991, p.142). The technique is of use to policy-makers in determining changes in output, income, employment, government revenue, and inflow of foreign expenditure as a result of touristic activity, such as a hallmark event. The concept of interdependence between industries is central to input-output analysis as it is based upon the transactions between all producers and consumers within an economy. To establish a set of accounts or matrix of transactions it is necessary to (Bull, 1991, p.143):

- define industries and sectors [a difficult task in the case of tourism]
- identify the total output of each sector and the breakdown of where it goes, that is, whether it goes to other sectors or to consumption *per se* (final demand)
- identify the total outputs of each sector acquired from other sectors, and in particular, what marginal inputs are required to make a marginal increase in output

After allowing for leakages the derivation of disaggregated multipliers through input-output analysis allows for more precise measurement of economic changes in final demand (Dryden, 1987). However, the onerous data requirements of input-output analysis have tended to limit its use. Furthermore, there is a paucity of suitable economic data, particularly at the regional level at which many events occur, and there are substantial methodological difficulties in defining exactly what the tourism sector is (Socher, 1987; Bull, 1991).

Cost-benefit Analysis Cost-benefit analysis is a technique for assessing the externalities that result from tourism development decisions, and is a response to demands for a more complete examination of the social, environmental and economic effects of tourism. According to Bull (1991, p.164), cost-benefit analysis involves four main stages:

- identifying externalities
- valuing them where possible in money terms
- incorporating them as positive benefits, and negative costs, into some form of social account
- summing the resulting 'net' costs or benefits into a net present value which can be subtracted from, or added to, the commercial or private value of a development, to form a *social value*.

Despite the standard use of cost-benefit techniques as part of the environmental and social impact assessment procedures which governments often place on large projects such as hallmark events, substantial difficulties emerge in the assessment of non-market values such as environmental quality and aesthetics, and in the forecasting of outcomes (Socher, 1987; Socher and Tschurtschenthaler, 1987; Vanhove and Witt, 1987). Nevertheless, the technique will undoubtedly remain as an analytical tool in the assessment of the value of hosting large scale events for the host community. However, according to Burns and Mules (1986, p.8) much of the research in the application of cost-benefit analysis to event studies has been of poor quality and 'much of what has been done has been rather misleading' with excessively large cost-benefit ratios and multiplier effects being claimed. For example, in their study of the 12th Commonwealth Games in Brisbane, Lynch and Jensen (1984) claimed that a multiplier effect in the range of 1.9–2.3 existed.

Excessively large cost-benefit ratios in the study of hallmark events have emerged for several reasons (Burns and Mules, 1986, 1989; Burns, 1987; Hall, 1989b; McDonald, 1990b). First, there has been a failure to account for the economic impact that would have occurred anyway but has switched from one industry to another (see Lynch and Jensen, 1984, for an example of a study which has made this error). Second, the 'unfortunately common mistake' of attributing all the benefits received from the event to Government expenditure, instead of establishing the marginal impact of that contribution' (Burns and Mules, 1986, pp.8,10). Third, the counting of taxation benefits of expenditure generation as 'additional to the multiplier "flow-ons" when they have already been included'. Fourth, input-output rather than value-added multipliers, which can result in major over-estimates of the economic impact of events, are frequently uncritically used leading to double counting of gross output effects (Burns and Mules, 1986, 1989). Fifth, there has been a general failure to identify the size of the regional economy that is to be studied.

In their Adelaide Grand Prix study, Burns and Mules (1989, p.173) argued that the 'costs and benefits associated with the event should be measured from the viewpoint of South Australia as a whole, not just the viewpoint of the State Government'. The delineation of whose viewpoint costs and benefits are to be measured from is critical, as this will delimit the framework of analysis and the consequent set of results and conclusions. The delineation of the regional economy to be analysed is especially significant as this will determine 'who are visitors'. Since the benefits, in terms of expenditure, can only be included from participants and visitors from outside of the defined area (city, region, state or province, or nation), the expenditure of 'locals' (those within the boundaries of the defined area) should only be viewed as transfer expenditure (Gartner and Holecek, 1983; Redman, 1983). In addition, allowance has to be made for the phenomena of visitor 'time switching', where people bring forward intended visits that would have happened regardless of the event being conducted.

The viewpoint from which the study is conducted will also affect cost classifications. Staging and construction expenditure should also only be regarded as a benefit if it is from outside of the defined study region. In addition, attention needs to be paid to the significant opportunity costs associated with government funding for hallmark events which may have alternatively been spent on health, education, or public housing. Similarly, discounting of expenditure should also occur for the time switching that occurs in construction or investment expenditure, for example, when hotel projects that had been planned are brought forward in order to take advantage of the market opportunity that a hallmark event might provide.

In the case of the Adelaide Grand Prix, the approach of Burns and Mules (1986, 1989) in measuring the tangible benefits and costs of hosting the event was to identify the expenditure that occurred on account of the Grand Prix. They then estimated how much of this was an injection into the state economy, noting in particular how much was new as opposed to switched or transferred expenditure. The next step was to use input-output analysis to calculate the amount of income generated in South Australia by the injection of this new expenditure. The total of this income was the tangible economic benefit of the Grand Prix to South Australia. The tangible cost to the State was measured by the expenditure on the event that was funded within South Australia (Burns and Mules, 1986, 1989). The ratio between tangible benefit and tangible cost is illustrated in Table 3.7. According to Burns and Mules (1989, p.180):

> Even... adjusted figures show that the Grand Prix did better, on purely tangible costs and benefits, than just about any other use of the money. The South Australian input-output figures show that home building, for example, has a value added multiplier of 1.273, whilst farming is only 1.005. Only expenditure on communications, community services or public administration would have had a higher income generation impact than 1.36 and no expenditure would have had an impact of 1.57 or better.

The study of the 1985 Adelaide Grand Prix by the Centre for South Australian Economic Studies (Burns, Hatch and Mules, 1986) represented one of the first attempts to provide a thorough analysis of the impact of a major special event. The

Table 3.7 Benefit: cost ratio 1985 Adelaide Grand Prix (tangible economic benefits and costs only, Aus$m)

Benefits and costs	Upper bound	Lower bound
Benefits		
Visitor expenditure (including multiplier effects)	$9.865	$9.865
Event and construction costs (funded from outside the State and including multiplier effects)	$14.941	$13.765
Total benefits	$24.806	$23.630
Costs		
Event and capital costs (funded from State sources)	$6.571	$7.520
Total costs	$6.571	$7.520
Benefit-Cost Ratio	3.8:1	3.1:1

Source: Burns and Mules, 1989, p.179

study's authors argued that a framework of analysis was needed that:

a) established the nature of the benefits and costs involved;
b) indicated how they may be measured after the event, using multipliers where appropriate; and, knowing this
c) allowed reasonable estimates to be made before the event (Burns and Mules, 1986, p.9)

However, while the merits of the Adelaide study's approach may be lauded, the applicability of their methodology may not be transferable to the evaluation of smaller events where communities do not have the same financial resources to spend on evaluation. Indeed, Getz (1991b, p.74) does not recommend that 'such elaborate and expensive cost-benefit methods' as used in the Adelaide Grand Prix study be employed. Instead he argues that a relatively simple approach is needed in answering the key questions associated with the hosting of events including return-on-investment, number of tourist trips motivated by the event, and monetary impact. Details of how these economic factors can be assessed is provided in Table 3.8. The calculation of expenditure effects can be undertaken through several, relatively easily applied, techniques:

- direct surveys of participants, sponsors and visitors
- obtain information from recipients of expenditure including retail stores, accommodation, stall holders and petrol stations
- collection of attendance and participation statistics

It is of great significance to community groups and small municipalities running events that economic assessment and evaluation of events be cheap, easily

Table 3.8 Simple measures of economic impact

Economic activity	Measure
Return-on-investment	Traditional profit and loss statements Measures of direct job creation Numbers of tourists in attendance
Number of tourist trips motivated by event	Utilise random surveys to evaluate the relative importance of the event as a trip motivator to the community and determine the extent to which the event increased the length of stay and expenditure in the community (incremental measures). It is important in this study of economic activity to ensure that surveys are random and that visitors are defined in relation to a clearly defined area.
Monetary impact	Calculate incremental visitor expenditure, spending by residents should not be included as it is likely that this expenditure would have occurred within the community regardless of the hosting of the event.

Source: After Getz, 1991b

applied and replicable, so that comparisons can be made both over time and with other events (further detail of evaluation techniques is provided in Chapter 6 on the management of hallmark events). For example, Murphy and Carmichael (1991) have presented a data-gathering methodology designed for use with open-access hallmark events to detect tourist spending. This includes a triangulation estimate of spectator numbers (Stoddard, 1982), which when combined with participant numbers and the respective expenditure records provides an overall estimate of direct tourist spending. The level of tourist spending is arrived at through the following formula (Murphy and Carmichael, 1991, p.35):

Tourist spending = number of tourist spectators or participants x per cent reporting an expenditure x average daily expenditure per person x average number of days at Games.

The above discussion of the economic dimensions of event tourism indicates that there are a range of measures which can be used to evaluate economic impact, each with its own advantages and drawbacks. Therefore, it should be possible to identify both simple and complex measures of economic impact which meet the requirements of the organisers and the size of the events. The following section provides a closer analysis of the benefits and costs of events through an examination of two case studies of different size events; an exposition and a special athletics event.

Benefits and Costs of Events

Since the hosting of the 'free enterprise' Los Angeles Olympic Games in 1984 (Edwards, 1984), and increasing concern from political publics about the cost of holding large-scale events, governments at both the national and regional level have been seeking to minimise the overt financial costs of hallmark events (Taylor and Gratton, 1988). For example, the 1988 Seoul Olympics was promoted as an Olympics in which government outlays would be returned from promotion, advertising, increased visitor arrivals and television coverage. Similarly, the 1988 Brisbane Expo was also promoted as a free enterprise event which would receive no government subsidy. In fact, these principles were enshrined in Queensland State law. The Queensland Expo '88 Act stated, that it required the Brisbane Exposition and South Bank Redevelopment Authority (BESBRA) to 'secure the recovery of and an adequate return on moneys expended in or for the purpose of presenting Expo '88 or thereafter developing and improving those lands with a view to their disposal and to achieve a net financial result that will not impose a burden of cost on the government of Queensland' (Part II, section 19(c)).

In the case of the Expo no direct subsidies were received. However, substantial indirect subsidies did occur from national, state and municipal government in the form of the provision of infrastructure, facilities, and financial support for the event. According to Carrol and Donohue (1991, p.135), 'the historical accounting value of the indirect, public subsidies which have so far been identified amount to $129.7 million'. For example, indirect subsidies from the Queensland Government included the upgrading of railway facilities and services to the Exposition site; improvements to car parking, ferry, pedestrian access and road services; the provision of the Queensland Pavilion; and the provision of sub-market interest rates on loans raised by the Queensland Government on behalf of the Exposition Authority. The scale of the indirect subsidisation from government led Carrol and Donohue (1991, p.135) to conclude, 'thus it is debatable as to whether Expo '88 can be regarded as a success in terms of the criterion of no burden of cost to the taxpayer'. Indeed, the economic success of the Brisbane Exposition was even more debatable when it is noted that the final, audited, consolidated accounts for BESBRA as tabled in the Queensland Parliament revealed a total loss of Aus$11,148,000, 'which represented a negative rate of return on the total re-sources expended of -2.09 per cent, hardly a success in conventional accounting terms, and not including the indirect subsidies'.

> The financial performance of BESBRA is even gloomier when the value is adjusted to take into account inflation, and expressed in current accounting terms. The deficit of $11.1 million becomes an even larger deficit of approximately $31 million. If we apply the social discount measure, using a social discount rate of six and a half per cent, then the discounted real value of the project becomes a deficit of approximately $68 million. A questionable success. (Carrol and Donohue, 1991, p.135)

Furthermore, Carrol and Donohue went on to note that 'a preliminary study of the more tangible costs and benefits suggests that the net social costs of Expo '88 are in the order of Aus$700 million, with net social benefits of about $200 million', while in terms of the balance of payments, 'the impact of Expo '88 seems to be largely negative, with initial studies indicating a leakage overseas of over $230 million, a leakage that does not seem to have generated off-setting additional international tourists or business investment' (1991, p.137).

The case of the 1988 Brisbane exposition indicates support for Getz's observation that 'any claim of economic benefits to the host community should be matched by a statement of costs, including not only organizers' capital and operating costs, but also the grants and value of services invested in the event' (1991b, p.75). Nevertheless, despite both the overt and hidden costs of hosting events, substantial gains can be made through event tourism. The following case study of the Australian Masters Games in Tasmania highlights the potential benefits that appropriate planning and research can provide for the hosting of hallmark events.

The Australian Masters Games The first Australian Masters Games were staged in various communities throughout Tasmania, Australia, between 28 November and 12 December, 1987. The purpose of the Games was to encourage senior Australian sportsmen and women to maintain their participation in sporting activities while promoting a healthy lifestyle among the general population. The event was therefore designed to generate social as well as economic benefits. However, while the economic benefits and costs could be established relatively soon after the hosting of the event, any health and social benefits, such as an improved lifestyle, will have a far longer lead time before they can be accurately assessed. Nevertheless, as Patterson and Hagan (1988, p.2) observed: 'it is conceivable that the future staging of the Games may be uncertain unless it can be shown that net social and financial benefits are likely to accrue to the host State'.

The 1987 Games attracted over 3,695 participants and 582 accompanying persons. Of these, some 1,701 were from interstate or overseas. Of the non-Tasmanian participants total expenditure within the State amounted to Aus$1.34 million at an average expenditure of $791 dollars, or almost $99 per night. Of this, forty-three per cent was spent on personal items including registration ($577,500), forty per cent was spent on accommodation ($537,800), and seventeen per cent on transport ($229,500) (Patterson and Hagan, 1988, p.12). Therefore, the immediate short-term economic gains to Tasmania from hosting the Games may be regarded as quite significant. However, the Games may also have played a key role in encouraging the Games visitors to return to Tasmania. For example, of the respondents to a questionnaire concerning the Games, some 66.3 per cent stated that they intended returning to Tasmania for a vacation, while only 7.3 per cent indicated that they would not return. Of those who did intend to return, forty per cent stated that this decision had been 'very much' influenced by attending the Games, while only 24.8 per cent claimed that their decision to return had in no way been influenced by their Games trip (Patterson and Hagan, 1988, p.13).

The all-up costs of the Games to Tasmania was estimated at $1.41 million with benefits of almost $3 million. Therefore, the benefit-cost ratio was established at 1.92:1, while this is substantial and demonstrates the value in hosting such events it is noteworthy that 'prior to the commencement of the Games, and even the period when they were being held, predictions that the Games would be worth $12 million to Tasmanian Tourism were being made'. As Patterson and Hagan (1988, p.27) continue: 'Such a prognosis, well wide of the mark, underlines the necessity to treat claims made by organisers, or others close to the event, with a modicum of caution'. Nevertheless, it is apparent that hallmark events, such as the Masters Games, which take advantage of established facilities, off-season travel and accommodation, and substantial numbers of volunteers may provide positive economic benefits to host communities (Hall, 1991).

Spatial Distribution of Economic Effects Associated with Hallmark Events

In addition to examining the gross expenditure of event visitors, an important consideration in the analysis of the economic dimensions of events is the spatial distribution of economic impacts. The economic effects of hosting hallmark events are not distributed uniformly throughout the local economy because of the pattern of non-resident spending associated with the event, the potential displacement of non-event related tourist expenditure ('the displacement effect'), and the changed pattern of resident spending in the light of the hosting of the event. For example, in the case of the 1984 Los Angeles Summer Olympic Games, retail sales were down 15 per cent during the Games period (DPA Group, 1985, p.ix), contributing to a potential 'worst case' displacement value of US$168 million lost on regional resident expenditures at the Games and US$163 million of lost out-of-region visitor/tourist expenditures in southern California (Perelman, 1985). Similarly, during the 1987 America's Cup in Fremantle, Western Australia, major hotels experienced a downturn in food and beverage income despite increases in occupancy level while, in the case of restaurants, 60 per cent reported significant decreases in income and 20 per cent reported no change at all (Zwolak, 1987). Furthermore, other substantial changes to the normal pattern of expenditure occurred (Zwolak, 1987; Hall and Selwood, 1987, 1989; Hall, 1989e), including

- caravan parks outside Fremantle reported a downturn
- the clash of the Cup with the Chinese New Year meant a significant loss of regular visitors at this time
- the wildflower trail, a major tourist attraction within Western Australia, had extremely low patronage
- theme parks missed out on local patronage as well as visitor patronage
- other locations in the south-west of the state reported substantial increases in patronage, while others reported a lower patronage

The changes in expenditure patterns may be associated with what has been described as the 'Los Angeles' (Olympic Games) or 'London' (Royal Wedding) effect – where people stayed away because of a perception that the hallmark event would be marked by inflated prices, crowds and difficulties in finding accommodation (Hall and Selwood, 1989). In the case of Fremantle there were unfulfilled expectations which appeared to have been generated by the media hype that surrounded the Cup and which influenced business activities and decision-making. For example, a deputation of Fremantle businessmen approached the State

Table 3.9   Growth in visitor nights in commercial accommodation in
                  Queensland destination regions, 1983–88

Destination region	Percentage change 1987–88	Average annual percentage change 1983–87
Brisbane	+92.6	+9.5
Gold Coast	+7.2	+14.6
Sunshine Coast	+23.5	+12.8
Maryborough/Bundaberg	+19.7	+2.0
Rockhampton/Gladstone	-5.9	+10.6
Mackay/Whitsunday	+19.2	+13.8
Townsville/Bowen	+17.6	+9.0
Cairns/Tablelands	+3.3	+19.6
Other Queensland	+15.0	+5.0
Total Queensland	+17.1	+12.7

Source: Queensland Tourist and Travel Corporation, 1989, p.3

Government after the event demanding compensation for the lower than anticipated receipts (Hall and Selwood, 1989). In addition, there was what Hall (1989e)
described as a 'slop effect' where the hospitality industry in Perth lost trade to
Fremantle operators. Conversely, Fremantle's non-visitor oriented businesses
found their regular clientele abandoning them until after the Cup crowds had
receded. In other words, there was a great deal of turbulence within the business
sector without there necessarily being any significant increase in the overall
amount of trade (Howarth and Howarth, 1987).

The 1988 Brisbane Expo also had a significant impact on visitor activity in
Queensland (Queensland Tourist and Travel Corporation, 1989). However, the
effects were not equally distributed throughout the State (Table 3.9). Destination
regions on the main travel routes to Brisbane appeared to benefit substantially
from overnight stays from travellers to and from Expo. However, other destinations appeared to have lower visitor growth than normal because Expo provided an
alternative destination for potential tourists. Therefore, while the Queensland
economy appeared to benefit substantially in terms of increased visitation because
of Expo, certain regions did not.

A more detailed study of the spatial distribution of expenditures associated with
the hosting of an event is to be found in Long and Perdue's (1990) study of the
hosting of the 1986 Carbondale Mountain Fair in west-central Colorado, United
States. The 1986 Fair lasted for three days and had an official visitation of over
10,000 people with almost half (49.3 per cent) of the visitors spending more than
one day at the Fair (Goeldner and Long, 1987; Long, Perdue, and Behm, 1987). Of
the non-resident expenditures associated with the Festival, the mean percentage
spent in the community by the 235 survey respondents was 69.7 per cent. However, 77.9 per cent of this spending was to festival booths operated by non-local
operators. Indeed, of the US$43,689 spent by the survey respondents, US$32,719
(74.9 per cent) was to entities outside of the Carbondale economy (Long and
Perdue, 1990). As the authors reported:

at least in the instance of the 1986 Carbondale Mountain Fair, the results clearly show that a significant proportion of the expenditures associated with the rural arts and crafts festival may not accrue to the local community and, hence, would not contribute to the local economy. At a minimum, these results indicate that festival survey questions assessing visitor expenditures should ask 'how much money did you spend *in the community?*' as opposed to the generic 'how much money did you spend?' (Long and Perdue, 1990, p.13)

The results of the Carbondale Mountain Fair study illustrate that for the economic benefit of hosting events to be maximised for the host community then local stallholders (food, art and craft) should be encouraged to participate. In addition, they demonstrate the need for considerable methodological improvement in the analysis of the flow-on of event expenditure to local communities.

Ripple Effect As opposed to the above discussion of the local economic impact generated by the hosting of hallmark events, the term 'ripple effect' was used by Hall and Selwood (1989) in reference to the generation of activity immediately associated with participants in the hallmark event, but who are located externally to the focus of the activity. In the case of large-scale or mega-events, such as the Olympic Games, World Cup, World Fairs, or the America's Cup, which have a prolonged period of intense media coverage, they suggested that the ripple effect may reach substantial proportions as the events can stimulate international commercial interest. For example, an interesting aspect of the ripple effect in the case of the 1987 America's Cup was the way in which possible future sites for the event became subject to land speculation. Property prices on the Whangaporoa Peninsula, north of Auckland, soared in expectation of victory by the New Zealand entry as it reached the final of the challenge series. In addition, similar land speculation occurred at the same site during the 1989 and 1992 America's Cup events off San Diego, California, while the early success of the New Zealand yacht in 1992 led to a dramatic increase in the share price of Fay-Richwhite, the main New Zealand corporate supporter for the challenge.

Event Forecasting

One of the major problems in the hosting of a hallmark event is forecasting visitor demand. For instance, The Centre for Applied and Business Research (CABR) estimate of visitor numbers for the America's Cup in Western Australia was substantially overestimated. Although some 930,600 visitors were estimated to have come to Perth in the five months during which the America's Cup was held, this figure was 22 per cent (325,000) less than the 1.2 million forecast in March 1986 (CABR, 1985, 1987). In addition, less than half of the estimated interstate visitors came to the Cup (477,475 estimated compared with 225,000 actual). As Shaw (1989, p.45) noted 'The failure of interstate Australians to make the journey to Perth was largely responsible for the reduced economic impact of the defence series, down twenty to twenty-five per cent – depending on the calculation of the multipliers – on earlier estimates' (CABR, 1987).

Table 3.10   Alternative approaches to tourism demand forecasting

Qualitative	Quantitative
• Analysis of vacation surveys • Survey enquiries of potential visitors in tourism generating regions • Delphi Technique • Judgment-Aided Model	• Time Series Analysis • Gravity and Trip Generation Model • Multivariate Regression • Discrete Choice Models

Source: After Hall, 1989c, p.31

Forecasts of tourism demand are essential for tourism-related industries. The need for approximations on visitor numbers and travel patterns is crucial not only for the planning of tourism infrastructure and the minimisation of potentially negative impacts but also the marketing of the event to potential visitors, investors and, possibly, the host community. Tourism demand forecasting contributes data that helps answer at least four vital questions in the management and planning of hallmark events (Uysal and Crompton, 1985; Hall, 1989b):

1. How many tourists are likely to arrive at a destination in a given time period?
2. Which origin areas represent the best marketing opportunities for a destination? and
3. Which factors are most influential in determining future visitation to a destination?
4. What will be the likely economic, physical and social impacts of a given number of tourists in a given time period on a destination?

Table 3.10 identifies the various qualitative and quantitative approaches which have been used in forecasting tourism demand in general and which have also been applied to event forecasting. However, event forecasting often presents a range of additional problems to that encountered in 'normal' tourism forecasting, the most significant of which is the uniqueness of many events and therefore the lack of an established set of travel and demand patterns. Where events do occur in a regular fashion either at the same site, for example in the case of sporting events such as the FA Cup Final, or in the case of the same event in a different location, such as the Olympic or Commonwealth Games, World Cup, or World Fairs, a background of knowledge and experience may have been established (Pyo, Cook and Howell, 1988). Nevertheless, it is the fact that events are, by definition, exceptions to the norm, which will make their forecasting a challenging task.

One of the most cost-effective forms of analysis is the study of holiday surveys. Through the analysis of holiday surveys it may be possible to discern trends and patterns in visitor numbers to particular locations. This method may be refined by surveying potential visitors in tourism-generating regions in an attempt to approximate the number of visitors that may travel to the host community for an event. This method was utilised for the America's Cup in Fremantle but was relatively inaccurate (Centre for Applied and Business Research, 1987; McCloud and Syme, 1987). Other qualitative methods of forecasting demand include use of the Delphi Technique and a Judgement-Aided Model. The Delphi Technique is an attempt at reaching conclusion amongst experts through the application of a series of questionnaires, collating judgements and the provision of feedback to all participants (Runyan and Wu, 1979). 'Additions and comments from earlier rounds are taken into consideration so that ultimately the most desirable solution emerges from the collective knowledge of the experts' (Uysal and Crompton, 1985, p.8). Similarly, the Judgement-Aided Model assembles a panel of experts in an attempt to reach consensus on different tourism scenarios. Perhaps the most common quantitative approach, this method often takes the form of committee meetings or seminars (Hall, 1989b).

The most commonly employed method of quantitative analysis of event tourism demand are time series analysis, and econometric techniques including multivariate and linear regression models (Archer, 1980, 1987; Witt and Martin, 1987; Hall, 1989b; Witt, 1989a, b; Bull, 1991). Time series analysis consists of the collection of statistical data over time which may then be analysed in terms of the direction and magnitude of future patterns or trends (BarOn, 1975; Sheldon and Var, 1985; Witt, 1989b). Statistical methods usually employ either a Box-Jenkins model building technique or univariate analysis. The former is considerably more difficult than univariate analysis and requires considerable expertise on the part of the user. In addition, results of studies using these techniques indicate no clear advantage for either method. Gravity and trip generation models are similar to regression models except that their focus is on the effects of distance and journey time as a constraint to travel. Gravity models are widely used to predict flows of tourist travel. However, such models have been recorded as having a number of weaknesses (Uysal and Crompton, 1985; Hall, 1989b).

Multivariate regression is a means of identifying the relative influence of different variables upon tourism demand. Variables may include cost of travel, income of travellers, number of tourist attractions and per capita demand for travel. Slade, Picard and Blackorby (1986, pp.255–6) utilised linear regression analysis to determine the key factors which influenced attendance at international expositions. The technique of linear regression is used to determine a statistical relationship among variables. The technique approximates one variable by a mathematical relationship among the remaining variables. In their study they used the variables of total attendance, average price charged (1984 US$), size of the fair site in hectares, and number of foreign pavilions. Using data from previous World Fairs, they concluded that 93 per cent of the variation in attendance at the World Fairs they examined could be explained by three key factors: the admission price, the size of the site and the diversity of the fair, particularly as expressed by the number of foreign pavilions.

Louviere and Hensher (1983) developed an approach to forecasting event participation which utilised experimental observations of consumer choice derived for conjoint measurement type multiattribute alternatives that describe a preferred design for an exposition. A primary choice experiment based upon two interlocking fractional factorial designs examined items of interest to consumers such as:

• national and/or cultural exhibits and displays;

• industrial and/or technological exhibits and displays;
• merchandised foods and beverages of different national or ethnic origin;
• shows and spectacles; and
• rides, amusements and games.

A secondary choice experiment extended the inferences possible from the first study by concentrating upon more detailed aspects of exposition choice such as:

• type of exposition;
• size of crowds attending the exposition;
• what friends and media say about the exposition;
• cost per person to enter the grounds;
• city in which the exposition is located; and
• the time to get there by car or by public transport.

Following the surveys the choice data was analysed by means of discrete choice econometric models. A multinomial logic choice model was then applied to forecast the choice of attendance at various types of hypothetical international expositions. The value in using such an approach is that by varying any of the design variables within the data set (noted above), a planner could arrive at different forecasts for different 'models' of a particular event. However, it should be noted that the use of such a technique is relatively expensive, for example the Louviere and Hensher survey involved 680 individuals in 525 households, and will be too costly for many event organisers. According to Louviere and Hensher (1983, p.359) choice procedures 'are strong in providing insights to choice processes and in enabling analytical assumptions of choice models to be satisfied, but are weak in external validity and presently accommodate fewer attribute insights'. Nevertheless, despite such reservations they were able to optimistically state 'that considerable evidence now exists to indicate that experimentally de-signed simulation models can now predict the real choices of real individuals in real markets with a high degree of accuracy…, integration of econometric models and controlled simulation studies can now be undertaken' (1983, pp.359–60).

The need for information upon which to base planning decisions necessitates some form of estimation of the pattern of tourism demand for individual events. However, despite the sophistication of quantitative and econometric methods such as multivariate regression analysis and univariate time series methods , 'forecasts of tourism demand can produce only approximations' (Uysal and Crompton, 1985, p.13). Similarly, Witt (1989b, p.173) noted that 'in an industry as highly volatile as international tourism, and one that is influenced by so many factors, trend extrapolation is a technique which should be used with extreme care'. The characteristics of the hallmark events and festivals and the often incomplete nature of tourism and visitor statistics complicates the use of methods of forecasting for individual events (Hall, 1989b). 'The decision to attend a unique event depends on a variety of attributes of the event and characteristics of the individual(s)' (Louviere and Hensher, 1983, p.348). Therefore, the results of forecasts, even when expressed within a range rather than as absolute values, need to be regarded with the utmost caution when they are incorporated in to the planning process.

Summary

This chapter has indicated that although the economic effects of hallmark events can be extremely beneficial to host communities, substantial methodological problems remain in the evaluation of economic impacts. Zwolak's (1987) argument – that the methodology utilised in the analysis of the economic impacts of an event will differ according to the source of funding – does not hold true. According to this, events which are largely public funded require cost-benefit analyses and those in which most costs and benefits are privately borne require economic impact studies based solely on increased visitor and event staging expenditure. The choice of method of economic evaluation will be contingent upon cost, ease of assessment, scale and the original objectives for conducting the event. Regardless of the source of event funding, it is good, basic, management practice to gauge the costs and benefits of an investment decision. However, the assessment of the economic cost and benefits of an event is not value-free and is often tied up with the political significance of events. Getz comments that 'typical economic impact assessments... appear to serve only one purpose – that of exaggerating the economic effects of events to gain political advantage. The misuse of multipliers and econometric models is a symptom of this problem' (1991b, p.76). While this is perhaps somewhat exaggerated given the potential value of economic studies for planning and management, one can nevertheless support the observations of Roberts and McLeod (1989, p.246). They state that 'in economic impact studies it is probably better to err on the conservative side to minimise possible criticism and to reduce the likelihood of possible political over-emphasis... the results of an economic impact study should not be used as a promotional device'.

Although much event research has focused on the economic aspects of events, substantial consideration still needs to be paid to the less tangible costs and benefits of hosting events, such as social impacts, image and politics. For example, Wang and Gitelson (1988a, p.5) observed that the annual Spoleto Festival in Charleston, South Carolina, does not in itself appear to be economically justifiable, however the city continues to support the event in order to maintain a desirable image.

In the planning and development of hallmark events 'economic factors are mediated by less tangible psycho-social factors pertaining to civic boosterism, civic pride, and civic involvement to generate urban support before the event ever occurs' (Hiller, 1989, p.120). Hallmark events have an extremely important non-economic dimension which is rooted in the attitudes and social interaction of the host community. As Camacho commented 'Not only is it beneficial in economic and financial terms, it is right and proper that the people of a nation should be offered an opportunity to widen their horizons and to become aware of their history and their religious, cultural, industrial and political heritage' (1979, p.5). Therefore, the following two chapters will pay close attention to the analysis of the social and political dimension of hosting hallmark tourist events.

4 'Everybody Loves a Parade': The Social Dimension of Hallmark Events

Hallmark events leave more than visible traces. (Dovey, 1989, p.74)

Chapter 4 surveys the social implications of the hosting of events to the destination area. The chapter will also link the broader objectives in hosting events to the social planning process in order to emphasise the argument that to be successful, events must simultaneously address both social and economic planning issues. The chapter will provide examples of the social impact of events and highlight the need to improve social impact assessment procedures.

The Social Dimension of Hallmark Events

The social effects of hallmark events on host communities has, apart from several anthropological and sociological studies, received relatively little attention until recent years (Hall, 1988b, 1988c; Olds, 1988; Roche, 1990, 1991). Nevertheless, the development of negative reactions towards tourism development in some destination areas has meant that government and private industry are increasingly paying attention to community attitudes towards the hosting of hallmark events (Hall, 1991). For example, an expression of public concerns regarding the hosting of events is indicated in the responses to specific issues raised in the Olympic Games Social Impact Assessment Steering Committee (1989) a preliminary social impact assessment of the Melbourne 1996 Olympic Games bid (Table 4.1). Craik (1988a, p.26) has argued that, despite difficulties in quantifying the social impacts of tourism, 'it is perhaps the most important aspect of tourism development'. Therefore, an examination of the social dimensions of hosting hallmark tourist events is essential not only from the perspective of the affected community but also because without it, the successful hosting of hallmark events will be extremely difficult.

'The social impact of tourism refers to the manner in which tourism and travel effect changes in collective and individual value systems, behaviour patterns, community structures, lifestyle and the quality of life' (Hall, 1991, p.136). 'Broadly conceived, social impacts refer to all changes in the structure and functioning of patterned social ordering that occur in conjunction with an environmental, technological or social innovation or alteration' (Olsen and Merwin, 1977,

Table 4.1   Issues raised in submissions to the Melbourne 1996 Olympic
Games Social Impact Assessment Steering Committee regarding
social impact of the Games bid

Issues of concern	Number of Responses
Housing and accommodation	44
Employment and training	13
Goods and services	16
Transport	11
Social expenditure	15
Social and community infrastructure	9
Safety and security	5
The environment	14
Recreation and culture	1
The effect on disadvantaged groups	13
Other issues	11
Process issues	41
Number of Submissions	66

NOTE: As submissions often included comments on more than one issue, the total
number of comments was greater than the number of submissions
(15 from government bodies, 10 from members of the public, and
41 from community groups)

Source: Olympic Games Social Impact Assessment Steering Committee, 1989,
Appendix 5, p.2

p.44). Factors and associated social-indicators which contribute to social well-
being and the quality of life include economic security, employment, health,
personal safety, housing conditions, physical environment and recreational opportunities (Andressen, 1981). According to Matthews (1978) the scale of social
impact will be determined by the numbers of tourists in relation to the host
population and by the economic level of the host community as compared with that
of the tourists. However, to this should also be added other factors such as the
proximity to the development, cultural differences between host and guest, socio-
economic status, neighbourhood roles, political and social boundaries and the
visibility of the tourists and the tourism industry (Hall, 1991).

   The social impacts of event tourism are often cast in a negative light in terms of
such problems as increased crime, social dislocation and loss of community
identity. A longer-term effect may be a breakdown or loss of an individual's sense
of place as his surroundings are transformed to accommodate the hosting of an
event (Dovey, 1989). However, it should be noted that such problems tend to occur
in the case of large scale or mega events rather than in smaller scale and/or
community events. Indeed, event tourism can have substantial social benefits such
as increased cultural understanding, employment, the provision of social services
and improved community identity. For example, a number of benefits, including
recognition, increased tourism and economic benefits were reported for the 1988
Calgary Olympic Games (Ritchie and Lyons, 1990) (Table 4.2). Sporting events
may also assist in promoting regional identity:

Table 4.2   Calgary resident perceptions of benefits from the hosting of the 1988 Winter Olympics

Benefit	Per cent of cases (n=388)
Recognition for Calgary	50.0
Increased tourism	36.3
Economic benefits (more jobs, more business)	34.0
Olympic facilities	21.1
Enhanced Calgary's reputation/image	14.2
Citizen pride in city	8.8
Brought city/citizens together	4.9
Chance to meet other people	4.1
Excitement/atmosphere in city	2.8
Other[a]	1.5
Total[b]	177.8

[a] less than 1 per cent
[b] total adds up to more than 100 per cent because of multiple replies

Source: Ritchie and Lyons, 1990, p.16

> By providing a common area of interest, sport encourages communication and information exchange between geographically and/or socially differentiated groups. Contact with people from other country communities increases the social network of country residents. These networks have the ability to expand the quality, quantity and diversity of the community's information base. (Cowie, 1987, p.43)

Several studies have reported that in addition to economic and tourism benefits and the provision of new infrastructure such as sports facilities (Lipsitz, 1984), regional sporting events have made a positive contribution to community well-being and regional identity (Oakley, 1987; Pennington, 1987 [Glenelg Games]; Lloyd, 1987 [South West Games]; Saeniger, 1987 [North Queensland Regional Games]). McKinnon (1987) identified a number of positive social effects of events in the Warrnambool region of Victoria, Australia:

- personal skill development of committee members and club administrators
- the bringing together of diverse sporting individuals and groups – who otherwise rarely interact – towards a common goal
- increased social interaction
- involvement of all age groups
- family involvement
- involvement of non-regular participants in sport
- community group involvement
- increased prominence of minor sports
- civic pride and regional identity

One of the most difficult problems facing research on the social impacts of events is that the majority of research focuses on the effects of large-scale and mega-events. Therefore, the following discussion of the social dimensions of hallmark events should be recognised as only dealing with a relatively small, albeit extremely significant, proportion of the total number of tourist events. However, it should also be acknowledged that it is the larger-scale events, such as World Fairs, which consume the greatest amount of public funding and may also cause substantial dislocation in impacted communities.

The Social Implications of Hosting Mega-Events

The hosting of mega-events is often deliberately exploited in an attempt to 'rejuvenate' or develop urban areas through the construction and development of new infrastructure, including road and rail networks, airports, sewage, and housing. This has been used to revitalise inner-city locations that are regarded by government, municipalities and business interests as requiring renewal (Zimmerman, 1974; Peters, 1982; Armstrong, 1984; Olds, 1988). In Australia this approach was utilised in the 1987 America's Cup in Fremantle, Western Australia (Cowie, 1989; Hall and Selwood, 1989; Newman, 1989), the 1988 Brisbane Expo (Kingston, 1987), and the Darling Harbour Bicentennary project (Huxley and Kerkin, 1988; Thorne and Munro-Clark, 1989); and was a component of the Melbourne bid for the 1996 Summer Olympics. In North America, a similar strategy was employed in the False Creek area for the 1986 Vancouver World Expo (Olds, 1988, 1989) and the 1980 Winter Olympics at Lake Placid (Wall and Guzzi, 1987).

The Olympic Games has also been used to provide a boost to urban development projects. For example, in 1972 Munich gained not only new sports facilities but also new housing and transport improvements. 'The Olympics enabled the Bavarian capital to jump ten years ahead in its development programme and at less expense' as the federal government undertook 50 per cent of the investment, and the Bavarian government 25 per cent. Similarly, less than 5 per cent of the capital improvements for the 1964 Sapporo Winter Olympics were spent on sports facilities (Armstrong, 1984, p.60). Furthermore, although the reuse of earlier physical plant at the 1984 Los Angeles Games may have helped engender a renewed interest in hosting the Olympics (Travis and Croizé, 1987), the majority of bids for the 1996 and potential bids for the 2000 Summer Olympics still involve substantial investment in new capital and infrastructure. As Hiller commented in the case of the 1988 Calgary Winter Olympics, 'The overarching compelling rationale of preparation for the Olympics in general tended to minimise opposition and controversy thereby supporting capital cost expenditures' (1989, p.127)

The commonly-held perspective of many government authorities of the social benefits of using events as a component of city renewal programmes is presented by Hillman (1986, p.4): 'As center city revitalization continues to be viewed as a major ingredient of economic development, the questions of enlivening public spaces and extending usage of downtowns after 5 o'clock have become critical issues... Events are a proven animator capable of turning barren spaces into bustling places'. In contrast to the support Hillman shows for the role of events in animating the city and making them places of fun, Huxley (1991, p.141) argued in the case of Sydney's Darling Harbour redevelopment:

> The logo of Merlin International, developers and managers of Darling Harbour's Festival marketplace, displays a merlin falcon picked out in stars. It is a clever play on the name, invoking the freedom and beauty of a bird in flight and making reference to Merlin the magician. The accompanying motto is 'Making Cities Fun'. The whole concept of the city as 'fun' is redolent with the post-modernist approach to playful spectacle, display and ironical references to other eras. It is the essence of the 'yuppy' lifestyle and yet our cities contain increasing numbers of unemployed, homeless, disadvantaged people: urban infrastructure is inadequate or non-existent at the fringe and outdated and overloaded at the centre. What sort of 'fun' can Merlin bring to the city?

The post-industrial urban environment associated with contemporary hallmark events often has a major impact on the socio-economic groups that occupy the inner-city areas which are usually those designated for renewal. The creation of a 'desirable' middle-class environment invariably leads to increased rates and rents, and is accompanied by a corresponding breakdown in community structure, including ethnicity, as families and individuals are forced to relocate (Hall, 1991). Moreover, the people who are often most impacted by hallmark events are those who are least able to form community groups and protect their interests. This tends to lead to a situation in which residents are forced to relocate because of their economic circumstances. In the case of the Vancouver Expo, six hundred tenants were evicted (Olds, 1988) including long-term residents and low-income residents from hotels near the Expo site (O'Hara, 1986; White, 1986). Similarly, the 1987 America's Cup and the 1988 Brisbane Expo also led to resident dislocation (Day, 1988; Hall, 1989b, c; 1991).

Housing impacts can also be substantial in smaller centres. In the case of the 1980 Lake Placid Winter Olympics, tenant eviction increased dramatically for the two months of the Games (January, February). 'The amount of evictions is not recorded but the fact that a citizens rental coalition was formed gives some indication of the severity of the problem. Tenant turnover of rentals increased 20-30%, as many landlords rented to outside groups at high rental costs during the Games' (Wall and Guzzi, 1987, p.10). However, the eviction of tenants due to the hosting of hallmark events is not isolated to the West. For example, the Asian Coalition for Housing Rights (1989, p.92) noted that South Korea's preparations for the 1988 Olympic Games led to the 'rehabilitation' and 'beautification' of numerous areas of Seoul: 'Many communities were evicted from sites, simply because they were next to the path along which the Olympic torch was to be carried and the public authorities did not want these communities to be visible to the reporters and television cameras following the path of the torch'. In all the above situations, it appears that the political and economic benefits of the hallmark event to the local elite and the state appear to outweigh the costs to segments of the host community, usually the poor and the powerless.

The Post-Industrial City: The City of Renewal

A World Exposition, commonly referred to as an Expo or a World's fair is a unique gathering of nations brought together to review and exhibit man's achievements in a specific field of endeavour – the theme at a specific point in time. It offers an unsurpassable opportunity to participate in a technological and cultural exchange of world ideas. (Minnikin, 1987, p.1)

I'm not going to move unless they force me out. I'm not a piece of garbage. I've been here three years and don't mind if they raise the rent, but I won't move... Once you get used to a place, it's like a pair of shoes, they're comfortable. Even if they get worn out, you still put your old shoes on. This hotel to me is home. You go to the beer parlour, you know everybody. ...I like this place, but what they've done – it's inhuman. (Jon Muller, 59, evicted following the impacts of the Vancouver Exposition on Downtown Eastside, Vancouver, in Olds, 1989, p.49).

As noted in Chapter 2, World Fairs have long been used for reasons of urban development. Indeed, the period since the Seattle World Fair of 1962 has been described as 'the city of renewal'. The following section will outline the manner in which renewal has been sought at a number of expositions and relate the 'rejuvenation' theme to similar large-scale hallmark events.

The 1962 Seattle Fair heralded the beginning of a new period of the use of international fairs and expositions as a mechanism for urban and economic development. Although World Fairs have always been closely connected to the interests of local business elites it was not until 1962 that they were consistently used to redevelop run-down city areas. In the case of Seattle, the Fair was used to develop 50 acres of a publicly owned 'blighted area', while the unofficial 1964–65 New York Fair occupied the same site as that used for the 1939–1940 World Fair. However, while the Seattle experience was reasonably positive, the New York Fair was not so successful in meeting its objectives: 'A visitor to the site today will see an eerie wasteland, with a few aging relics, including the unisphere, the fair's symbol, scattered across hundreds of acres of largely unused parkland. "It's worse than the ash heap it was converted from", one critic said recently' (Peters, 1982, p.17).

The 1966 Montreal Expo has been generally recognised as one of the more successful fairs of the modern era. However, although the expo site was constructed on reclaimed land, the Fair still had substantial social impacts. According to Peters (1982, p.17), Expo 67 was used by the City of Montreal as 'an excuse to pyramid dozens of public projects including a new subway system (the metro), highway expansion (finished ten years ahead of schedule), and 745 acres of parkland in the middle of the St. Lawrence River'. The 1967 Exposition was the culmination of municipal attempts to encourage private investment and tourism. According to Melamed, Schaecter and Emo (1984) some 15,000 dwellings were demolished in 1966, but no formal social impact studies were conducted nor can direct links to the hosting of Expo be established.

The 1968 San Antonio World Fair was explicitly connected to a federal and locally funded inner-city renewal programme which acquired 147 acres of 'substandard housing' (Peters, 1982) for the Fair site. There were great expectations for the Fair as a mechanism for urban redevelopment:

> The two things fit beautifully: the urban renewal process provided the vehicle that made possible the land assembly and clearance necessary to get the fair up on time; at the same time the fair provided impetus that picked up the pace of public development action. Now, with the fair going and a slug of new public facilities up and operating, private investment on a massive scale has started in downtown San Antonio. (Montgomery, 1968, p.85)

Similar, hopes were expressed for the 1974 Expo in Spokane, where the Fair was used as a means 'to squeeze a revitalisation program that would have ordinarily taken 20 years into an intensive five-year effort' (Yake, 1974, p.55). The reasons for using Expo for redevelopment were explained by King Cole, President of the Spokane Expo:

> If it seems a complicated route to urban renewal, it was necessary. This city had a sort of resentment of its downtown area... Three times in the past, the city voters have turned out city councils that ran for office on a platform of downtown renewal... But when we started pushing the idea of a world fair, which would bring about downtown renewal incidentally, citizens bought the idea. (cited in Olds, 1988, p.40)

The San Antonio Fair was a failure as an urban renewal mechanism and did not attract business and capital to the city (Peters, 1982b). In contrast, the Spokane Fair did lead to a construction boom which in turn subjected some communities to development pressures and accelerated existing social changes (Olds, 1988). However, no account of the displacement effect of the Fair was produced.

The 1982 'International Energy Exposition' in Knoxville, Tennessee, and the 1984 New Orleans (Louisiana) Expo were both deliberate measures to alter existing patterns of development and encourage business and tourism to the cities (Evans, 1982; McDonald and Wheeler, 1983; Smith and Keller, 1983; Douglas, 1984). The Knoxville Fair had only moderate success as a method of urban renewal, although the conversion of rented accommodation for the Fair did see the displacement of a substantial number of tenants. Olds (1988) noted that up to 1,500 tenants were evicted although because of the smaller than anticipated crowds, the number of relocations was shortlived. Similarly, the New Orleans Fair was also a relative failure in terms of attendance and finance, although the fair did lead to major rehabilitation works in the inner city, including hotel, convention and riverfront construction which has improved the overall attractiveness of the city for tourism, especially its major claim to event fame, the Mardi Gras.

The 1986 Vancouver Expo Expo 86 in Vancouver, British Columbia, was constructed on seventy hectares (173 acres) of Vancouver's inner city waterfront land known as False Creek and a three hectare waterfront site on the north of the central business district. The main exposition site had been earmarked for redevelopment since the mid-1960s, and development of the south side of the former industrial area was well underway by the late 1970s. However, the 1986 Expo provided the mechanism to further redevelop the area in what Jimmy Pattison, Expo 86 Chairman described as 'the biggest urban development project in North America. It will change the face of Vancouver for ever' (21 October 1985, in Anderson and Wachtel, 1986, p.7). Similarly, Gutstein commented, 'Expo is really a gigantic urban redevelopment project, an expenditure of more than one billion dollars to spur public and private land development' (1986, p.65).

Olds (1988, 1989) study of Expo's effects on the residents of Vancouver's 'Downtown Eastside', which was situated next to the Expo site, was the first comprehensive account of the housing and social dislocation impacts of a hallmark event. The Eastside was characterised by a large number of lodging houses and apartment units which were rented by lower socio-economic groups. Indeed, 91 per cent of all Downtown Eastside tenants fell below the Canadian Government's poverty line as of March, 1984. As Gutstein (1986, p.89) recorded, the more than 2,000 lodging house and hotel residents are older (average age over 50), predominantly male (90 per cent), and surprisingly permanent (38 per cent of the residents have lived in the area for more than ten years). However, the presentation of facts and figures concerning the nature and composition of residential locations does not adequately convey the full picture of the life of an area (Hall, 1988a; Olds, 1988).

Inner-city locations, such as the Downtown Eastside, are typically communities with strongly developed social networks and sense of place. As Olds observed, 'Independence, combined with a history of struggle (in terms of work, personal life and community problems), links to community-based services and social networks has created for many a strong sense of community' (1988, p.92). The redevelopment of the area through the hosting of Expo may therefore have two substantial, interrelated effects. First, the alteration of physical space through the construction of new buildings and the refurbishment of old. Second, the displacement of short and perhaps more importantly, long-term residents through physical restructuring and rent increases, which may lead to the breakdown of a well-developed community structure (Hall, 1988a; Olds, 1988, 1989).

Although there was no direct on-site housing impact of the 1986 Expo there was substantial post-announcement speculative impact. Between 1,000 and 2,000 units were lost from the housing market between 1978 and 1984, while a further 600 lodging house units were permanently lost between 1984 and 1986. In addition, the rapid increase in value of downtown residential hotels further contributed to a destabilised housing market in the vicinity of Expo (Olds, 1988, pp.103–7; Olds, 1989). The promise of the tourist dollar to many hoteliers and the loss of low-cost had a substantial impact on the inner-city community. Olds (1988, p.109) estimated that 'between 500 and 850 evictions occurred in the Downtown Eastside lodging houses because of pre-Expo demand impact'. Furthermore, 'between 1,000 and 1,500 lodging house rooms were switched from monthly rental to tourist rental status during the spring of 1986'.

The post-event impacts of the Expo were mixed. Following the closure of Expo, many hotels failed to remain viable as tourist accommodation. In addition, it appears as if the rental and vacancy rates in lodging houses have returned to pre-Expo levels (Olds, 1988). Nevertheless, the Downtown Eastside housing market remains unstable and appears to show signs of further gentrification.

Walks through the community in 1987, 1988, and 1989 reveal considerable numbers of For Sale signs and several development permit applications. This signals that a potential exists for future post-Expo impacts. In all likelihood, current plans for the development of Expo '86 lands (now known as Pacific Place) will have a powerful effect on Downtown Eastside housing stock and, consequently, its residents. (Olds, 1989, p.52)

The Brisbane Expo and the America's Cup Considerable parallels can be drawn between the Vancouver Expo and two Australian events, the 1987 America's Cup and the 1988 Brisbane Expo. The 1988 Expo provided the Queensland and Brisbane city governments with an opportunity to redevelop a part of the city that was generally perceived as requiring redevelopment (Park and Feros, 1985; Craik, 1988a, 1988b). According to the general manager of the Brisbane Expo, 'the south Brisbane site won approval because of its central position, its suitability for an event such as World Expo 88, and its potential *for development from a run-down area to one of the most valuable, attractive precincts in Brisbane*' (Minnikin, 1987, p.3).

The Brisbane Expo had significant on-site impacts in the form of the displacement of small businesses through land resumption and payment of compensation. The Brisbane City Town Clerk, E.K. Campbell (30 July 1987, in Olds, 1988, p.53), noted that some 111 businesses had been displaced, while Minnikin (1987, p.6) stated that 73 properties (130 claims – 72 owners, 58 tenants) had been resumed. Off-site impacts were also substantial with significant increases in rental prices in the area of the Expo site and the conversion of low-budget hotels to backpackers and tourist accommodation. Since 1986 the Southside Urban Research Group recorded the following social impacts in the South Brisbane/West End area (Day, 1988, p.19):

• a substantial increase in rents;
• an increase in involuntary displacement and evictions;
• changes in the area's physical characteristics; and
• a breaking down of social networks.

SURG estimated that the increases in rents over the period June 1987 to June, 1988, were in the order of 62 per cent for a two-bedroom flat and 44 per cent for a three-bedroom house, compared with increases of 34 per cent and 29 per cent respectively for the Brisbane area as a whole. In terms of displacements, SURG documented 605 people as displaced since November 1987, in the Expo adjacent area, but they estimated that the total for the periods before and during Expo would be several times that figure (Day, 1988, p.20). However, the longer-term effects of the hosting of Expo are yet to be fully determined because of substantial delays in the redevelopment, in several stages, of the Expo site. The project is for mixed housing, open space and a convention centre, possibly associated with a casino. (Hall, 1988a, 1991; Queensland, 1990a, b). Nevertheless, as Craik (1988b, p.5) observed, 'It seems clear that whatever the shape of the redevelopment, it will favour large scale development of tourist and commercial facilities geared towards those who can afford it'.

Table 4.3 Fremantle Commonwealth Employment Service December Quarter employment figures 1985-88

	New vacancies notified	Persons registering for work
1985	1,284	3,344
1986	2,023	4,933
1987	950	2,553
1988	1,094	2,808

Source: Hall, 1989e

The America's Cup was part of an ongoing redevelopment of Fremantle and was described by one commentator as representing the new gold rush for the city (Newman, 1989). Undoubtedly, 'the Defence did promote the renovation and upgrading of a substantial part of the stock of low cost housing in and around Fremantle which is viewed by many as being a highly beneficial outcome' (Cowie, 1989, p.90). However, housing rental markets were distorted by expectations of heavy visitor demand for accommodation during the Cup races and some long-term tenants were forced to relocate through pressures of rent increases and renovation of low-cost rental properties (Lenngren, 1987; Hall, 1989e; Hall and Selwood, 1989). Although provision was made for their relocation (America's Cup Defence Tenancy Working Party, 1985; Cowie, 1986, 1989) the accommodation that was provided for this purpose neither met recommended targets nor did it satisfy the actual demand for low rent accommodation. For example, a hostel specifically designed to house people forced out of dwellings upgraded for the Cup was forced to turn applicants away on a daily basis throughout the latter part of 1986 and into the first months of 1987. Many of the applicants were people who had come to Fremantle in the hope of obtaining employment and who exacerbated pressures on the rental market (Hall, 1989e). In addition, rent increases prior to and during the period of the America's Cup defence were in many cases well over the consumer price index (Morrison, 1987; Quekkett and O'Connor, 1987). According to Mr. John Garland, President of the Real Estate Institute of Western Australia, 'The major impact of the America's Cup has been felt in parts of the rental market, with some movement in sale prices in Fremantle and surrounding suburbs' (*Fremantle Gazette*, 1986, p.23). Rental increases were justified by members of the real estate profession and others by their insistence that rises in Fremantle property values and rents were long overdue. However, while that might have been the case, the Cup races undoubtedly acted as a catalyst in bringing about such increases, although the relative impact of the event on rent increases was undoubtedly dependent on the location of rental properties in relation to such factors as transport routes, socially desirable suburbs, the Cup course, the coasts, and the Fremantle Boat Harbour.

The social dislocation which some lower income groups incurred in the unstable housing market was also matched by difficulties in meeting the expectations of disadvantaged groups, such as the unemployed, which had been raised in the 'boosting' of the event by government and private industry (Hall, 1989e). For

Table 4.4 Perceptions of living in Fremantle as a result of the America's Cup and related activities

Perception of Fremantle	per cent of respondents		
	July 1985 (n=430)	March 1986 (n = 462)	March 1987 (n = 534)
Much better	8	2	9
Better	30	34	59
About the same	22	17	23
Worse	26	33	6
Much worse	6	4	0
Don't know	8	10	3

Source: Soutar and McLeod, 1989, p.101

instance, although the number of vacancies filled during the Cup period in Fremantle was a substantial increase over the corresponding period for 1985–6 the number of applicants for positions increased by an even greater proportion (Table 4.3). According to the Fremantle Commonwealth Employment Service this was due, at least in part, to the labour market participation of a number of 'non-traditional labour sources', including married women, transients entering the area for the America's Cup period, and students on holidays (Walker, 1987, in Hall, 1989e). Several additional reasons were cited as to why, 'the expected increase in casual labour demand did not occur' (Walker, 1987, in Hall, 1989e):

1. The expected charter boom did not happen;
2. The expected tourist flow did not happen;
3. The finals races were over very rapidly;
4. A number of employers in the Fremantle district took on their optimum staff in September/October, rather than in December/January as originally anticipated; and
5. The retail concessions on souvenir sales, were not as busy as anticipated.

Regardless of the reasons as to why the expected level of Cup-related employment generation did not occur, the failure of employment growth combined with housing market instability does indicate that even if analysts are able to conclude that hallmark events do bring real net benefits to their hosts, there are clearly those whose quality of life is not improved and who lose out (Hall, 1989e; Hall and Selwood, 1989).

Impacts on Community Values

One of the outcomes of the hosting of hallmark events is their impacts on community values. As noted at the beginning of this chapter, regional sports events serve to reinforce regional identity and social cohesion, while in the case of community events 'perhaps the psychic benefits, the bonding of people to their place for a job well done, are the real and lasting justification for hosting such activities' (Rooney, 1988, p.97). Indeed, even in the case of the negative impacts

Table 4.5   Identified social costs and benefits of the 1985 Adelaide Grand Prix (Aus$)

Period	Social Costs	Social Benefits
Short term	Traffic congestion (time lost) ($6.2m.) Property damage ($0.26m.) Increased vehicle thefts and thefts from vehicles (n.a.) Noise (n.a.) Accidents ($3.2–5.8m.)	Psychic income ($28m.+) • general excitement • good opinions of oneself • extra shopping access • opportunity to have guests • home hosting opportunities • pleasure in 'experiencing' the event
Long term	Loss of amenity Increase in crime • vandalism • hooliganism • accidents	Increased tourism Expanded industry • exports • improved terms of trade Improved self image

Source: Burns and Mules, 1989, p.184

of the 1988 Brisbane Expo on the South Brisbane/West End community, Day (1988, p.iv) was able to report that 'one positive by-product... has been a re-affirmation of community spirit and militant activism transcending social and institutional boundaries'. This includes, perhaps somewhat ironically given the supposed celebratory function of Expo 88 as a festival of the people, 'a burgeoning of participatory cultural and social activities including the strikingly successful West End Street Festival in October, just before the closure of Expo, billed as "a celebration of our unity" and a demonstration that "we don't need large-scale high-technology" for a "participatory and affordable festival... on a human scale"' (Day, 1988, p.21). However, while it is generally accepted that events can influence individual and community values, both in the short- and long-term, relatively little research has been undertaken on the subject.

The conduct of three surveys by Soutar and McLeod (1989) of Fremantle residents gives some insights into the perceptions of a local community towards the hosting of hallmark events such as the America's Cup (Table 4.4). Surveys were conducted of residents in July 1985, July 1986, and March 1987, barely a month after the Cup defence was concluded. Data in the survey was collected from a random sample of residents at three points in time between July 1985, and March 1987. 'The representative sample frame of 740 households was selected by the Australian Bureau of Statistics (ABS) and ABS interviewers collected the data in all three surveys. In all cases, the response rate was over seventy per cent, although movement of residents between survey periods meant that only half the respondents answered all three surveys' (Soutar and McLeod, 1989, p.93). The survey results indicated that the sample of residents had generally perceived Fremantle as a better place to live because of the Cup, a result which indicated that 'in respect of both its positive and negative aspects the Cup turned out better than initial expectations of it suggested' (Soutar and McLeod, 1989, p.102). However, it is unfortunate that the last survey was taken only shortly after the Cup was completed as a survey taken further away from the euphoria of the Finals series may well produce a different perspective of longer-term perceptions (Hall, 1989e, Hall and Selwood, 1989).

A number of social benefits and costs were identified in a study of the Adelaide Grand Prix (Burns, Hatch and Mules, 1986). Short term social costs included the traffic congestion caused by using city roads for the race track, time lost to traffic detours, property damage incurred by residents, increased thefts of both vehicles and vehicle contents, noise and accidents. Short term social benefits were described as 'psychic income'. This category included: the general excitement created by the event, good self-opinions, extra access to shopping, the opportunity to have guests, home hosting opportunities, and the pleasure of experiencing the event (Burns and Mules, 1986, pp.24–30). The short-term costs and benefits were valued by Burns and Mules, producing an approximate pricing on social costs of Aus\$9.86–12.46 million and a psychic income of Aus\$28 million (lower bound) (1989, p.183) (Table 4.5). However, Getz (1991b, p.75) has argued that 'attempts to develop surrogate monetary measures of intangibles are subject to many questions of validity and should be used very cautiously, if at all'

Unlike the majority of research on event tourism the Grand Prix study also paid explicit attention to long term costs and benefits of hosting the event. Bentick (1986) indicated that the Grand Prix had the potential to attract the interest of entrepreneurs in South Australia, affect the attitude and confidence of local businessmen, workers and residents (an improved self image), promote investment and demonstrate the ability of the State to manage similar large-scale events. Longer term costs of hosting the event were identified as being a potential loss of amenity, an increase in crime, vandalism, hooliganism and accidents (Burns and Mules, 1986). The impact of the Grand Prix on the accident rate is examined below.

Hoon effect

One of the most fascinating by-products of the Adelaide Grand Prix study is what has been described as the 'hoon effect' (Stuart Innes, *The Advertiser*, 10 January 1986, in Fischer, Hatch and Paix 1986, p.152); a hoon being 'a reckless, irresponsible driver... which may or may not have been encouraged by the staging of the Grand Prix' (Fischer, Hatch and Paix 1986, p.152). In the five weeks around the time of the 1985 Adelaide Grand Prix, there was a 34 per cent increase in the number of casualties compared with the average of the equivalent weeks of the previous years 1980-84. Only a small fraction of this increase could be explained by reference to weather conditions, overall trends, or traffic volume. The Adelaide study inferred from this 'that the particular nature of the Grand Prix, its emphasis on speed and aggressive driving, contributed substantially to these accidents' (Fischer, Hatch and Paix 1986, p.160). Nevertheless, the researchers were 'castigated for even daring to suggest that Our Event might have an undesirable side effect' (Arnold, *et al.*, 1989, p.188).

The results of the study indicated that governments should be concerned with the possibility that negative spillover effects could, in the end, cancel the benefits of hosting a hallmark event. Furthermore, consideration of the long-term behaviour modification which may result from the connection between a major sponsor's product (in the case of the Grand Prix Fosters Beer) and the excitement and general well-being generated by the event, led the researchers to argue that 'governments should be prepared to make their subsidies conditional on events not being associated with drugs of addiction' (Arnold, *et al.*, 1989, p.187). Nevertheless, despite the undoubted significance of the hoon effect as a social consequence of tourist events, the Economic Centre's study was generally favourable to the social effects of the Adelaide Grand Prix. 'The effect of the Grand Prix making people feel good was considerably greater than the tangible economic effects' (Arnold, *et al.*, 1989, p.186).

The results of the South Australian research have had flow-on effects to studies of similar events. According to the New South Wales State Treasury, 'the hoon effect has not been evident in subsequent Grand Prix, possibly as a result of major media campaigns targeted at drivers that may have been influenced by the race' (1990, p.18). Therefore, in examining the potential impacts of the development of a raceway at Eastern Creek to the west of Sydney, the Treasury decided not to include costs due to increased traffic accidents in their cost-benefit study because of doubts of extrapolating from the Adelaide case to Sydney, and doubts as to the original findings in Adelaide.

Crime

The costs of policing hallmark events because of the threat of crime and/or terrorist activity may be quite substantial. For example, the Fourth World Cup in Athletics staged in Canberra in October 1985, necessitated the devotion of 12,565 police man hours (Australian Federal Police, 1986, p.25). In the case of the America's Cup, a special unit was established in order to deal with police duties. Undoubtedly, there must have been considerable costs associated with the 250 member police task force established for the duration of the Cup (Western Australian Police Department, 1987). However, no consideration was given to this in the official report on the economic impact of the Cup (Centre for Applied and Business Research, 1987). In spite of the potential increase of crime that events may bring to a destination, little published research is available on this topic or the associated problems of policing an event, perhaps partly because of the security risks inherent in the release of such studies (Economic Impact Resources Consulting, 1989).

Wall and Guzzi (1987) reported that there was an increase in crime rates at Lake Placid during the 1980 Olympic Winter Games with most incidents being perpetuated by, and against spectators. However, the impact of crime on residents was regarded as negligible. Hall and Selwood (1989) noted that there were significant increases in petty crime and vandalism associated with the hosting of the 1987 America's Cup in Fremantle. In addition, it appeared that in peak periods of visitor activity the police showed greater tolerance for rowdiness and street drinking associated with the America's Cup than would have been accepted under pre-Cup

conditions (Western Australian Police Department, 1986, 1987). According to the
West Australian Police Department (1987, p.5):

> During the period October 7, 1985 to February 16, 1986, prior to the America's Cup
> series, the Fremantle Police preferred a total of 5,502 charges. During the corresponding
> period while the America's Cup Defence Series was being conducted a total of 7,483
> charges were preferred by the America's Cup Division and Fremantle Police. This
> reflects a growth in the number of charges of 1,981 or 36%.

Over the same period the number of arrests in Fremantle increased by 62.19 per
cent. The number of charges processed by the courts also increased: the Fremantle
Traffic Court by 110.7 per cent, the Fremantle Petty Sessions by 23.5 per cent, and
the Children's Court by 44.7 per cent. Interestingly, the 'overwhelming majority'
of charges were preferred against permanent residents of the Fremantle area
(Western Australian Police Department, 1987, pp.5–6, appendices 'c' and 'd', in
Hall and Selwood, 1989, p.112). Police officers were instructed to avoid 'heavy-
handed and insensitive' action against visitors and this may have influenced the
statistics (Western Australian Police Department, 1986, p.19), but it should be
noted that the precise reason for these increases remains unclear. The evidence
does suggest, however, that there was a definite relationship between the hosting
of the event and an increase in petty crime (Selwood and Hall, 1988).

Prostitution and the America's Cup In addition to an increase in petty crime,
research by Selwood and Hall (1988) indicated that the increase in the number of
visitors to Western Australia for the America's Cup also attracted substantial
numbers of prostitutes to the State, and possibly also encouraged local females and
males to enter the sex industry. For example, an advertisement in the *Sunday Times*
personal column (15 December 1985, p.62) read, 'Now that the casino is here and
the America's Cup is close we need keen adventurous girls who enjoy meeting top
line business executives etc. Various levels of income depending on your ambitions. All nationalities welcome...'

Although prostitution in Western Australia is not against the law, 'many acts
ancillary to it are' (Edwards, 1986, p.4), for example, soliciting, keeping a brothel
and living off the earnings of prostitution. Under the West Australian police policy
of containment and conditional tolerance (Dixon, 1982), prostitution exists in
several forms: brothels and massage parlours, escort agencies, single private
operators and street prostitution, although an exact account of the number of
persons acting as prostitutes is exceedingly difficult to provide because of the
particular legal, social and economic characteristics of prostitution. The Commissioner of Police does not publicly provide statistics on the number of prostitutes
allowed to operate, but according to the 1986 *Annual Report* of the Commissioner
of Police, approximately 120 single operator prostitutes were registered with the
vice squad as of 30 June 1986. This figure represented an increase of 100 per cent
over the previous year (Commissioner of Police, 1986, p.26). The dramatic
increase may perhaps be attributed to the heavier demands expected to be placed
on the local prostitution industry through the large influx of Cup visitors. Although

media reports that 500 eastern states' prostitutes had arrived in Western Australia for the Cup period were denied, there seems little doubt that there was a significant increase in the level of prostitution (Selwood and Hall, 1988).

The West Australian Police Department (1986, Annexure E, p.1) did expect 'an influx of criminals and prostitutes to prey on [tourists]', and a newspaper article subsequently reported on the arrival of prostitutes from Asia and the eastern states of Australia for the Cup (*Fremantle Focus*, 25 August 1986). Mr. Kim Flatman, a director of Rochdale Nominees which owned the Fremantle Fitness Studio, claimed that 500 prostitutes had arrived from the eastern states. This figure was later forcefully denied by Mr. Flatman's wife, 'one of the city's leading brothel keepers', on the grounds that her husband was merely the accountant and knew nothing of the day-to-day running of the business. Furthermore, the enforcement of the income tax laws in Western Australia that required prostitutes to pay tax made it, 'virtually impossible to attract women from the eastern states' (*The West Australian*, 10 October 1986) and indeed, the precise number of arrivals did appear to have been inflated. Nevertheless, it was apparent from the research conducted by Selwood and Hall (1988) that a substantial increase in the level of prostitution did occur during the period of the America's Cup. However, the determination of the impact of prostitution on crime, community health and community perceptions of the social effects of the Cup was impossible without assistance from the respective government authorities.

That the event provided business opportunities for the sex industry is undeniable. The *Official America's Cup Directory* (Telecom Australia, *et al.*, 1986) contained four pages of advertisements for 14 escort agencies which promoted sexual services of one form or another. A fact which had an element of irony given West Australian Premier Burke's recommendation on the frontispiece to 'familiarise yourself with the contents of this complimentary guide and carry it with you at all times. It will help you achieve maximum enjoyment of your visit'. Premier Burke's 'endorsement' of the contents of the Directory were challenged by the Parliamentary Opposition and led to a heated exchange in the State Legislature. However, although the debate addressed the question of the Western Australian Tourist Commission's position on prostitution, strip shows and the like (Western Australia, Legislative Assembly, 1986, pp.4381–2), it failed to come to grips with the issue of tacit support of such activities by the Government as an element in the attractiveness of a destination to tourists (Selwood and Hall, 1988; Hall, 1989e).

The tacit acceptance of prostitution during the period of the America's Cup was indicative of the extent to which the State Government relaxed laws and regulations in order to cater for the perceived 'needs' of the international tourist (Selwood and Hall, 1988). Within the Perth metropolitan area, shopping hours were extended for the duration of the Cup so as to provide retailers with more opportunity to capture the tourist dollar (a similar relaxation also occurring in Brisbane for the 1988 Expo). However, the new trading hours were removed once the Cup period was over. Hotels, taverns and nightclubs were able to obtain special licenses to remain open over a greatly increased number of hours of the week. Nevertheless, after the Cup was lost a renewed concern for the public morality emerged, leading to a crackdown on hotel striptease and see-through barmaids and their removal from the less-pretentious hotel establishments (Selwood and Hall, 1988).

The social impacts of the America's Cup were varied and numerous. However, 'the complex interactions of tourist phenomena make total impact almost impossible to measure... primary impacts give rise to secondary and tertiary impacts and generate a myriad of successive repercussions which it is usually impossible to trace or monitor' (Mathieson and Wall, 1982, p.5). As Hall and Selwood (1989, p.113) observed, 'there is great difficulty in differentiating between changes attributable to pre-existing processes, such as gentrification in the case of Fremantle, and changes induced by the influx, or expected influx of tourists'.

Social Impacts: The Forgotten Dimension of Hallmark Events?

Fairs should be undertaken in the full knowledge of the history of their problems. Necessary optimism ought to be tempered by the reasonable expectation that the ratio of costs to benefits is steadily worsening. And more importantly, the social and economic context within which a fair occurs is crucial. A fair that happens by accident, that gets developed without any coherent vision, risks two major kinds of disaster. That it will find itself in the wrong place at the wrong time (a childish but useful definition of accident). And that it has nothing to say and nothing to leave behind. (Wachtel, 1986, p.41)

Events undoubtedly bring social benefits to host communities. Community celebrations and small-scale events, such as festivals and regional sports carnivals, undoubtedly have substantial benefits in terms of regional or cultural identity, civic pride and community development, while larger events, such as the Olympic Games, can also have substantial psychic benefits for certain members of the population (Ritchie and Aitken, 1984, 1985; Ritchie and Lyons, 1987, 1990). However, in the case of larger events it is apparent that some groups benefit more than others, while still other sections of a community do not benefit at all. Residents of a host community might feel themselves threatened by the advent of a major influx of visitors and accompanying changes to the local infrastructure if the event is of a large enough scale. Indeed, as witnessed in the case of several mega-events, such as the Brisbane and Vancouver Expos, perception of possible negative impacts on the social well-being of a community, (for example, resident displacement and area redevelopment) may give rise to interest group politics and a call for greater public participation to which the government faced with the need to construct infrastructure may be unable to respond (Day, 1988).

The social dimensions of hallmark events are unevenly distributed through a community in the same manner as the direct and indirect economic impacts of an event. Spectators clearly benefit, while many members of the host community will also receive significant psychic income (Burns and Mules, 1989). 'Even for people who do not actually attend a major event or those who benefit financially from the additional crowds generated, there are social or intangible benefits. These benefits are manifested in many ways, but they mainly originate in the excitement generated and the glamour of an event of worldwide interest' (New South Wales Treasury, 1990, p.9). However, although the majority of people may benefit from an event at a macro-level of evaluation and have their quality of life improved, at the micro-scale concerns clearly have to be raised as to those members of a community who suffer the psychic costs.

As this chapter has discussed, a number of significant negative social impacts such as social displacement, loss of community identity and crime have been associated with the hosting of large-scale events. Analysis of the social impacts of events have generally been afterthoughts, if they have been thought of at all, in the planning and management of hallmark events (Day, 1988; Hall, 1988c; Olds, 1988; Economic Impact Resources Consulting, 1989). In the general atmosphere of crisis which surrounds large-scale events, the development and construction of facilities and infrastructure is often 'fast-tracked' through planning procedures, and the evaluation of the social and economic dimensions of the event through a public consultation process remains incomplete (Hiller, 1990; Hall, 1991). However, social impact assessment will assist both government and the private sector in gaining community support for event projects.

Social impact analysis is a vital part of the event planning process that can lay the platform for community involvement and the minimisation of any negative impacts that may occur. Nevertheless, it should be recognised that social impact evaluation will ask the difficult question of who benefits? A question which goes to the very heart of why cities host hallmark events in order to improve or rejuvenate their image and attract tourism and investment. Indeed, one of the most significant social dimensions of tourism development is the extent to which non-local investment can reduce local control over tourist resources. As Krippendorf (1987, p.55) has questioned, 'Why has the loss of local autonomy – certainly the most negative long-term effect of tourism – been practically ignored? Why does the local population tolerate it?'. This question enters the political dimensions of the hosting of hallmark events and it is to this aspect that we will turn next.

5   The Politics of Hallmark Events

The speed with which the massive new stadia, the Olympic village, the numerous fly overs and new street lighting has been accomplished for the Asiad shows what the administration can achieve if the government is serious. The tragedy is that this urgency is exhibited for projects that bring no benefit to the common people...

As for the Asiad, its relevance can best be judged by the 'talisman' Gandhiji left to test measures claiming to be undertaken for the public good: 'Recall the face of the poorest and most helpless man you have seen and ask yourself if the step you contemplate is going to be of any use to him. Will he gain anything by it? Will it restore him to a control over his own life and destiny?'

The answer is obvious. (*Indian Express*, October 30, 1982, in Richter, 1989, pp.126, 127)

Politics is paramount in hallmark events, it is either naive or duplistic to pretend otherwise... events may change or legitimate political priorities in the short-term and socio-cultural reality in the longer term. Hallmark events represent the tournaments of old, fulfilling psychological and political needs through the winning of hosting over other locations and the winning of events themselves. Following a hallmark event some places will never be the same again, physically, economically, socially, and, perhaps most importantly of all, politically. (Hall, 1989c, p.236)

Hallmark tourist events are both explicit and implicit political occasions. The image building which accompanies such events creates a situation in which personal and institutional interests receive a high degree of visibility. This chapter will review a number of the political dimensions of hallmark events including industrial relations issues, legal rights, protest, and the relationship of events to election strategies and international relations. At a macro-political level, events may consciously or unconsciously advance particular political objectives or values, while at the micro-political level, hallmark events may be used for personal political ambitions or to realise institutional goals.

The Present State of Research: From Politics to Postmodernism

> the modernist penchant for monumentality... has been challenged by an 'official' post-modernist style that explores the architecture of festival and spectacle, with its sense of the emphemeral, of display, and of transitory but participatory pleasure. The display of the commodity became a central part of the spectacle, as crowds flock to gaze at them and at each other in intimate and secure places like Baltimore's Harbor Place, Boston's Faneuil Hall and a host of enclosed shopping malls that sprung up all over America. Even whole built environments became centrepieces of urban spectacle and display. (Harvey, 1987, pp.275–6)

Research into the political impacts of hallmark events has only received limited attention. Several factors can be recognised as accounting for this situation (Hall, 1989c). First, there has been an apparent unwillingness by researchers and individual and institutional actors in the political process to acknowledge the significance of hallmark events at both the macro- and micro-political level. Second, given the lack of official interest in conducting research into the political dimensions of events there has been little incentive to conduct such research. Indeed, as Ritchie (1984, p.10) observed, 'there are undoubtedly pressures in the opposite direction'. Third, there are substantial methodological difficulties in conducting political studies because of the ideological nature and political implications of such research.

The study of hallmark events, as with the majority of tourism research, has generally assumed a positivistic, non-critical approach to their subject matter (Hall 1989c; Britton, forthcoming b). In the tendency to focus on economic impacts, relatively little attention has been paid to the wider political implications of such work. Indeed, what few there are, have tended to focus on notions of efficiency and economy rather than ideas of equality or control of contested space. Important aspects of political economy have been virtually ignored and it is perhaps ironic that given the vital role of 'the image' in tourism, it is only recently that attention has been paid to the ideological nature of the tourist image (Hall, 1989c). The vast majority of researchers in tourism have either failed to detect Weber's (1968, p.1404) observation that 'the essence of politics is struggle', or have deliberately chosen to ignore it. However, research on the political dimensions of hallmark events may be of an extremely practical nature. The results of such research may indicate how the social impacts of events affect host communities and increase the understanding of related decision and policy-making processes (Humphreys and Walmsley, 1991). In addition, there is clearly a need for the development of oppositional perspectives on the broader implications of the hosting of hallmark events, particularly in a period when tourist experiences and urban spaces and places are becoming increasingly commodified (Berman, 1987; Haug, 1987; Zukin, 1987; Albertsen, 1988; Sack, 1988; Canan and Hennessy, 1989; Sawicki, 1989; Wolch and Law, 1989). As Matthews (1978, p.74) noted 'most ideological debate about tourism starts from the premise that the basic cluster of activities which we call tourism is likely to continue in the foreseeable future. The debate is not so much concerned with tourism versus no tourism as it is with what kind of tourism'.

Table 5.1 Specific variables measured in political impact studies and associated data collection and interpretation problems

Category of data	Nature of variables measured	Associated data collection and interpretation problems
Macro-political	Image enhancement	Degree to which event improves awareness and status of city/region for commercial and tourism purposes
	Ideology enhancement	Degree to which event promotes awareness and status of a particular political ideology
Micro-political	Career enhancement	Degree to which event provides key individuals with high visibility and improved career opportunities
	Athletic enhancement	Degree to which event permits greater opportunity for local athletes to participate in and/or learn from activities

Source: From Ritchie, 1984, p.10

In postmodern society the commercialisation of leisure has meant that tourism is often treated purely as a commodity to be sold through the established rules of marketing. 'Postmodernism... signals nothing more than a logical extension of the power of the market over the whole range of cultural production' (Harvey 1989, p.62). Events are transformed from totems of place and communal identity to monuments of symbolic capital. A city can be imaged through the organisation of spectacular urban space, as in the redevelopment of redundant dockland areas (Baltimore, Darling Harbour (Sydney), London) and through the staging of hall-mark events and spectacles, although the question remains of how a city can most effectively swallow large amounts of capital investment without indigestion? (Berry, 1988; Dovey, 1989). For example, in the case of the Baltimore inner harbour Harvey (1990, pp.421–2) commented:

The present carnival mask of the Inner Harbor redevelopment conceals the long history of struggle over this space. The urban renewal... effort was stymied by the unrest of the 1960s... The inner city was a space of disaffection and social disruption. But in the wake of the violence that rocked the city after Martin Luther King's assassination in 1968, a coalition sprang to life to try and restore a sense of unity and belonging to the city... One idea that emerged from that effort was to create a city fair in the inner city that would celebrate 'otherness'... but which would also celebrate the theme of civic unity within that diversity... By 1973, nearly two million came [to the Fair] and the inner harbor was reoccupied by the common populace in ways which it had been impossible to envisage in the 1960s... During the 1970s, in spite of considerable public opposition, the forces of commercialism and property development recaptured the space... The inner city space became a space of conspicuous consumption, celebrating commodities rather than civic values.

An event as a spectacle produces and consists of images, 'and the triangular relationship between the spectacle, its contents, and its contextual culture is "about" the relationship between image and reality, appearing and being' (MacAloon, 1984a, p.270; White, 1991). The imaging of a city through the creation of new urban spaces and events is a mechanism for attracting capital and people (of the 'right' sort) in a period of intense inter-urban competition and urban entrepreneurialism (Harvey, 1988; Canan and Hennessy, 1989; Mommaas and van der Poel, 1989). Hewison (1987, p.135) observed that the postmodernist stage of heritage tourism, incorporated into the hosting of many hallmark events, creates 'a shallow screen that intervenes between our present lives, our history. We have no understanding of history in depth, but instead are offered a contemporary creation, more costume drama and re-enactment than critical discourse'. Similarly, although the institutionalised commercialisation of leisure spaces and spectacles such as the Baltimore harbourplace, the Docklands of London, and the 1988 Korean Summer Olympics are often regarded as a success because they create a positive and high quality image of place, little consideration is given to the role that spectacles and events plays in the political process.

The Analysis of Political Impacts

'Tourism is particularly well-suited to assuaging elites and developing a clientele for authoritarian rule' (Richter, 1989, p.53). For instance, tourism was utilised by the Marcos Government as a means of creating a positive image of the regime in the eyes of tourists, particularly from North America, and foreign governments. The Marcos regime used such events as the 1984 Miss Universe contest and the 'Thriller in Manila' fight between Mohammed Ali and Joe Frazier to improve the international image of the country following the imposition of martial law. Richter (1989, p.56) noted that the Government 'promoted tourist events with a positively dazzling eclecticism that ranged from the "Miss Gay World Beauty Pageant" in Baguio to evangelist Rex Humbard's rally in Manila'. Similarly, the hosting of the 1976 International Monetary Fund – World Bank Conference led the regime to fast-track the construction of twelve luxury hotels, the Philippine International Convention Center, and the Philippine Center for International Trade and Exhibitions, all for the conference and all at enormous cost to the government. However, politically the Conference was a huge success for the Marcos Government:

> ...despite the fact that only 3,000 of the 5,000 anticipated participants came, few delegates seemed to note the incongruity of a New Society that was supposedly aimed at redressing inequities spending many times more for the construction of luxury hotels than for public housing and land reform. As was intended, most were impressed by the stability and attractiveness of the society, the tremendous growth in international investments, and the obvious improvement in law and order, at least in the tourist belt. Military and economic aid to the Marcos government increased, in both bi-lateral US–Philippines terms and in terms of IMF-World Bank aid. (Richter, 1989, p.58)

As noted above, substantial problems exist in undertaking research on the politics of hallmark events. Ritchie (1984) established a framework for the measurement of specific variables, and associated problems of data collection and interpretation (Table 5.1). The framework emphasises that political impact should be studied at both the macro- and micro-political level. However, severe problems exist in the conduct of political impact studies because of difficulties in obtaining appropriate data from government authorities and significant individuals who may be sensitive about the results of such research. At the macro-political level Ritchie (1984) recorded the importance of the hallmark event as a means to enhance images and ideology. A possible by-product of this may be the strengthening of the position of elites within local or regional power structures. At the micro-political level the event may enhance careers and athletic opportunities.

Ritchie's identification of ideology as a significant factor to be studied has been similarly noted by Mings (1978) within the overall context of tourism research. However, Mings also identified the loss of control to multinational investors as being a significant impact which requires further study. Indeed, the analysis of core-periphery relations (Keller, 1984) and the broader field of services (Britton, 1990, forthcoming a, b) within the international economic system should be of great assistance to the analysis of hallmark events and tourism in general (Hall, 1989c). Nevertheless, 'it is difficult to obtain short-term, quantitative measures related to such goals as increased status or ideology enhancement from a diverse and dispersed international or national population' (Ritchie, 1984, p.10). Indeed, this may well be a reason why Ritchie's study of the impacts of the 1988 Calgary Winter Olympic Games does not include the analysis of political impacts (Ritchie and Aitken, 1984, 1985; Ritchie and Lyons, 1987, 1990; Ritchie and Smith, 1991); though it may also be because of the general inapplicability of positivistic approaches to questions of ideology, power and social structure. Despite the potential for substantial methodological and philosophical dispute, however, it should still be possible to identify who benefits from the hosting of hallmark events and the manner in which interests are engaged in the decision and policy-making processes.

Who Benefits?

The impacts of a hallmark event will have both positive and negative effects depending on the scale of analysis and the perception and ideologies of those impacted and those studying the impacts (Hall, 1989c). Attention should be paid to the differential impact of tourism policies both within and between regions. As Greenwood (1976, p.141) observed, 'only the local people have learned about the "costs" of tourism. The outside investors and the government have been reaping huge profits and are well satisfied'. Similarly, in the case of the 1982 Asiad Games in India it was reported that

Hypocrisy and cynicism are even more evident than usual in New Delhi. The crores being spent on Asiad [The Asian Games of 1982] stand out in sharp relief against the real requirements of the people... The twisted values involved in advertising the luxuries and choice of expensive dishes available in five star hotels when millions are in search of food... descriptions of spacious air-conditioned suites each fitted with colour television sets... and other luxuries, appear side by side in the newspapers with grim reports of near famine conditions in large parts of the country. (*Indian Express*, 30 October 1982, in Richter, 1989, p.124)

The studies of Greenwood (1976) and Richter (1989) are something of an exception within the tourism literature as they purposely concentrate on the struggle for power within the context of tourism development. In addition, the politics of place is all but ignored in tourism research (Hall 1989a, c, d, 1991; Britton, forthcoming, b). Little attention is paid to consideration of the winners and losers of the political process or the forces that lead to the event being hosted. Although a useful starting point, the framework of Ritchie (1984), for example, failed to come to terms with the importance of conflict and power relations within the political dimensions of hallmark events and similar spectacles. As Thrift and Forbes (1983, p.247) declared: 'Any satisfactory account of politics and the political must contain the element of human conflict; of groups of human beings in constant struggle with each other over resources and ideas about the distribution of resources'. The vital questions of how, why, and even whether people struggle within the political arena of hallmark events and tourism are not only unanswered, but typically remain unset (Hall, 1989c), a point taken up in the next section on the politics of place creation.

Hallmark Event Impact at the Macro-Political Level: The Politics of Place Creation

The state appears ever keen to portray a favourable image of itself during hallmark events (Willens, 1978; Cribb, 1984). Indeed, 'City politicians see hallmark events as a growth industry. There is a trend throughout the world for more cities to bid for hallmark events on either a regular or a "one-off" basis in order to attract the notion of the economic boost for tourism and the social benefits of holding a "prestige" event' (Nancarrow, 1989, p.ix). The presentation of images that surround the hosting of an event is inextricably bound up with the presentation and promotion of ideology (Harvey, 1979, 1987; Thurot and Thurot, 1983; Uzzell, 1984).

The hallmark event 'functions like a monument, supporting and reinforcing the image of established power, whether religious or secular' (Bonnemaison, 1990, p.25). For example, in 1933 to commemorate the tenth anniversary of his rise to absolute power in Italy, Mussolini decreed the organisation of a cultural fair in Rome to glorify the Fascist revolution. The Fair featured works in a Futurist style providing an architectural expression of the totalitarianism of the time; a precursor to the architecture and spectacle of the 1936 Olympic Games and the Nuremberg Rallies (Hughes, 1980, pp.97–9). In a similar fashion, the Festival of Britain in 1951, while an attempt to restore some life to the post-war gloom, also served to reinforce orthodoxy in British cultural life

With the exception of Herbert Morrison, who was responsible to the Cabinet for the
Festival and who had very little to do with the actual form it took, there was almost no
one of working-class background concerned in planning the Festival, and nothing about
the result to suggest that the working classes were anything more than the lovable human
but essentially inert objects of benevolent administration. In fact Festival Britain was the
Britain of the radical middle classes – the do-gooders; the readers of the New Statesman,
the Guardian, and the Observer; the signers of petitions; the backbone of the BBC. In
short, the Herbivores, or gentle ruminants. (Michael Bryn, 1963, in Hewison, 1988,
p.65)

'All places have images – good, bad, and indifferent – that must be identified
and either changed or exploited' (Hunt, 1975, p.7). Hallmark events focus attention on a particular location for a short period of time and can provide a structured
set of socio-cultural experiences to both the visitor and the local. During such
events the host community is able to highlight certain images, themes and values.
For instance, the 'Olympic Games are concerned not only with athletics. They are
also about politics, ego, and the compulsion of cities to prove themselves' (Thomas, 1984, p.67). Indeed, it has been argued that spectacles, such as the Olympic
Games and World Fairs, have come to symbolise the power of commodity
relations and the dominance of hegemonic consciousness within modern western
society (Debord, 1973). The 1984 Los Angeles Olympics were as much a celebration of American capitalism and the processes of capitalist accumulation, as the
1980 Moscow Olympics attempted to show the success of state Marxism to the
western world. Similarly, at the micro-political level hallmark events may be used
to improve the international and domestic acceptance of unpopular and/or authoritarian regimes. For example, the 1990 Asian Games in Beijing were used by the
Chinese to help improve their image after the Tianenmen Square massacre of 4
June 1989. (Knipp, 1990). Indeed, it is a testimony to the power of political events
that the Square is now a tourist attraction in its own right.

Papson's (1981) study of the socio-cultural reality surrounding tourism marketing; routing and zoning; created community events and historical sites in the
Canadian provinces of Nova Scotia and Prince Edward Island, is of great relevance to research on hallmark events (Hall, 1989c). Papson concluded that the
tourism policies of the Provincial departments redefined social realities. This does
not mean that 'reality was falsified, but rather it was contrived, self-conscious and
alien to everyday reality. As such, reality becomes spurious' (1981, p.233). Hence,
a created community and hallmark event and the development of the space
associated with it, involves a redefinition of social realities through the transformation or definition of particular ideologies or myths. This may not only transform
the image of place but also the place itself (Phillips, 1984). For example, the
'Empire Village' set up for the 1962 Perth Commonwealth Games was an 'instant
ideal suburb of modern detached houses on quarter acre blocks', while with the
onset of the America's Cup in Fremantle in 1987 the ocean became a 'stadium'
and the city became a giant 'games village' (Dovey, 1989, pp.74–5). Both events
had consequent implications for social and symbolic meaning. Similarly, Fawcett
(1986, p.15) considered that the 1986 Vancouver Expo 'inadvertently resulted in

the creation of an unexpected but de facto new right wing force' in British Columbian politics. This is not to argue that the construction of particular realities by government or private industry is necessarily the result of a conscious attempt at exploitation. However, it must be recognised that the broader processes of capital accumulation and their relationship to power relationships, social and spatial structures, and the values which underly the conduct of a hallmark event, may well promote a particular picture of reality at the expense of others.

World fairs, in particular, have been the focus of dramatic expressions of urban spectacle and capitalist accumulation (Mills, 1990, 1991; Britton forthcoming b) which are concerned not only with goods and services but also notions of idealised social structures and relationships (Benedict, 1983). 'Spectacle... is full of events that make us notice and heed moral and social boundaries that have become blurred and banal in daily life' (MacAloon, 1984a, p.273). However, it has been argued that the range of social experience to be found at World Fairs may well broaden the potential scope of political hegemony (Susman, 1980; Ley and Olds, 1988). World Fairs, as with all large-scale hallmark events, are the product of urban elites. The fairs are built in the elite's image 'and thus present a dominant ideology' (Ley and Olds, 1988). Moreover, as evidenced in both the 1986 Vancouver and the 1988 Brisbane Expos, public consciousness becomes riveted on the 'bread and circuses' that the event has to offer (Craik, 1989), thereby providing both the elites and the state with an opportunity to expand patterns of social control. Similarly, MacAloon (1984a, p.275) observed that 'spectacle takes the "realities" of life and defuses them by converting them to be played with like toys, then cast away'.

In the 'party atmosphere' which hallmark events often create, elite hegemony and state interests may be enhanced through the promotion of politically dominant values. Moreover, the minority who represent the oppositional forces to the conduct of hallmark events are often held to be negative or downright 'evil'. As one Vancouver city priest noted: 'if one did resist Expo, boycott it, or tell the negative sides of this expensive party, you're a bad BC'er' (in Ley and Olds, 1988).

The Carnival as Contested Space

City governments have traditionally been in a double bind. On the one hand they are interested in events that make the city attractive to a large number of people, as money spent at events indirectly feeds the tax base. On the other hand they perceive events as a threat to the establishment because they are often spatially unstructured and involve large groups in playful activities. (Bonnemaison, 1990, p.25)

The notion of contested space may also be seen in the operation of carnivals and other ritualistic forms of celebration. For example, as discussed in Chapter 2, Turner's (1974) notion of social drama 'enables the observer to perceive the array of social structural principles and arrangements and their conflict and relative dominance over time' (MacAloon, 1984b, p.3); because social dramas allow latent conflicts of interest to become manifest through the social form of the celebration.

Carnival is a form of ritual travel in which the point of arrival is of little importance, instead what is of significance for both the participants and the viewers is the display of values contained in the nature of the procession. Furthermore, parades, processions and carnivals redefine the meaning that is attached to urban space.

> The commercial center of the city is closed to traffic so that people, whether or not they are associated with the typical corporations of carnival such as *blocos* and Samba Schools, can occupy it without difficulty. The street or avenue is thus domesticated. Most of the time, the streets of Rio and other Brazilian cities are deadly areas, with automobiles moving at high speeds. During Carnival, however, these tense, high-speed areas take on the aspect of a medieval plaza, where people walk in place of cars, watching or taking part in the festivities. The business district is transformed into a place for all the encounters and dramatizations typical of carnival. (Da Matta, 1984, p.221)

In contrast to the restructuring of inner-city and dockland areas to stage permanent leisure features, the redefinition of space and the accompanying transformation of place brought on by the carnival is often only temporary. The inversion of everyday social norms through carnival activity may be regarded as a form of opposition to the power structures within society (Gilmore, 1975; Cohen, 1982; Turner, 1983). However, opposition is channelled into a few days of 'playing carnival'. In the case of the famous carnival of Rio de Janeiro the channelling into time is also channelled into a space which is public not only in terms of the city but also for the tourists that have been encouraged to enjoy and 'share' in what has been marketed as a display of hedonism. For example, the Rio carnival has a specially constructed grandstand with seating for 60,000 people. In this atmosphere the original spirit behind carnival, the assertion of rights by Indians and Blacks in the face of existing, European-controlled, power structures, lies buried under the public ritual which is controlled by the city elite and which increasingly becomes a parody of its original self in order to satisfy demands so that the carnival is 'fun' but 'safe' for the local elite and the tourist (Edmondson, 1956; Pearse, 1956; Powrie, 1956; Gonzalez, 1970; Lavenda, 1980; O'Reilly, 1987). Nevertheless, the opportunity which carnival provides for self-expression among marginalised groups can still be seen in the Notting Hill carnival in London (Cohen, 1980, 1982; Manning, 1989) and the Gay Mardi Gras in Sydney (Waites, 1991/92), and may possibly be closely paralleled by the bike riots that occurred at the Bathurst Easter bike races in New South Wales, Australia, over a number of years (Cunneen and Lynch, 1988a, b; Cunneen, *et al.*, 1989).

The Australian bicentennary: the 'celebration of a nation' The 1988 Australian bicentennary provides a useful example of the manner in which hallmark events may construct particular definitions of contemporary and historical socio-cultural reality. The Australian Bicentennial Authority's (ABA) Aus$10.8 million national advertising campaign emphasised 'a celebration of a nation' that surely influenced both individual and collective images of nationhood. However, there was relatively little questioning of the political and ideological functions of the Australian bicentennary (Carroll, 1989; O'Brien, 1991). Indeed, at the ideological level the seemingly endless flow of royal visitors for the bicentennary may have reinforced Australia's colonial ties and strengthened aspects of conservative ideology through its appeal to the past, rather than the profession of cultural and political independence (Warhurst, 1987). The reinforcement of conservatism at the ideological level may be translated to conservatism at the operational level. As Warhurst (1988, p.6) argued: 'those who chose 1988 as the occasion for constitutional reform seriously underestimated the potential double-edged nature of that and similar occasions: reform has, under pressure, given way to reaction in such a way that traditional attachments to the status quo, including the monarchy, have been strengthened'.

Official sponsorship of historical celebrations can act to 'fortify the ideology of the existing power structure' (Chesneaux, 1978, p.18). In the case of the United States bicentennial, Lowenthal (1977) observed that history was perceived to have commenced with European colonization, while Manquis (1989) noted that celebrations of the bicentennial of the French revolution also served to reinforce particular national myths. Similarly, the Australian bicentennial was a celebration of the arrival of the first fleet of Europeans, not the forty thousand years of Aboriginal occupation. Hence, a particular picture of historical reality was painted by the Australian bicentennial which will have important ramifications for the manner in which Australians will come to understand their historical circumstances. Given that the centennial of Australian nationhood is 2001, the bicentennial may be best described as a celebration of colonialism rather than that of independence. In contrast to the Australian bicentennial, the Canadian preparations for their 125th Anniversary in 1992 have been geared towards a rededication of certain Canadian collective values. The delegates at the 'Toward 2000' Conference in Ottawa in 1989, which was drawn together to provide advice to the federal government, 'unanimously rejected the concept of an anniversary "celebration"... delegates insisted that the emphasis for the 1992 project should be on meeting and the exchange of ideas, rather than on entertainment and fireworks' (St-Onge, 1991, p.55).

Given the undoubted political ramifications of the bicentennial at the macro-political level it was therefore quite ironic that the ABA was expressing its apolitical character at the micro-political level. The ABA was evidently relieved that the Government called an early Commonwealth election in July 1987, so as not to appear to be taking advantage of the nationalistic fervour (Willis, 1987), otherwise described as 'manufactured whoopee', expected to be generated by the bicentennary (Richter and McGeough, 1987, p.6). Nevertheless, certain interest groups did see the bicentennary as a means to raise political issues in the Australian and international communities. Aboriginal activists threatened to use the high media profile of the bicentennial and associated events to highlight the plight of the Aboriginal people. For instance, twenty demonstrators were arrested over Aboriginal land rights during Australian bicentennial celebrations in Portsmouth at the launching of the reenactment of the departure of the first fleet. Protestors chanted '200 years of genocide', while one Aboriginal was dragged away from a First Fleet flag ceremony after she had questioned whether organisers had permission to fly the Aboriginal flag (*The West Australian*, 14 May, 1987, p.4). This example highlights the ability of hallmark events to provide a platform for political protest, a point taken up in the next section.

Protest

> For us who planned these Games of the 20th Olympiad with confidence in the good will of all men, today is a day of immense mourning. Even in the world of crime, there are still some taboos, a final limit of dehumanization beyond which one dares not go. The limit was crossed by those guilty of the attack on the Olympic Village. They brought murder into this great and fine celebration of the peoples of the world, this celebration that had been dedicated to peace. (Willi Duane, President of the Munich Olympic Organising Committee at the Olympic Memorial Service, 1972, in Groussard, 1975, p.438)

Given that one of the primary functions of the hallmark event is to focus national and international attention on the destination for a defined and usually short period of time (see Chapter 1), events may provide a ready mechanism for the display of political grievances. For example, South Africa's apartheid policy led to protest at sporting events at which South African individuals or teams participated for much of the last twenty-five years (Harris, 1972).

For a large part of its history the Olympic Games have been marred by, some-time violent, political controversy (Table 5.2 illustrates the relationships between political protest and the Olympics since 1968). Although the Olympics have never been without a political dimension, it is nevertheless important to recognise that the use of such large events to make political statements has gone hand-in-hand with the growth of media technology (Garnsey, 1984). Rather than just being a sporting event the Olympic spectacle has become a medium for the communica-tion of political discontent, diplomacy, and disagreement (Kanin, 1980; Shinnick, 1982; Edwards, 1984; Tomlinson and Whannel, 1984). As MacAloon (1984a, p.273–4) commented in relation to the Munich massacre of the Israeli Olympic team:

> Terrorism was nothing new in 1972. Who had not read about it or watched it on TV? One might even say that it had come to be taken for granted in the contemporary world as 'something we just have to live with.' But at Munich, terrorism was yanked out of the banal and burned into the hearts and minds of millions across the earth. The Games provided the ultimate stage for the terrorists, and the rest of the world an avenue by which terrorism was 're-bounded', returned from a 'fact of life' to a fact.

The Olympics is not the only major event to feel the effects of sporting diplomacy. The 1986 Commonwealth Games in Edinburgh were struck by the withdrawal of African, Asian and West Indian competitors over Mrs. Thatcher's policy on South Africa. The media attention given to the Games provided the boycotting countries an opportunity to attempt to pressure the British Government into altering its stand on relations with South Africa. Similarly, at the 1982

Table 5.2   Political protests and the Olympics

Summer Olympics	Form of Political Protest
1968 (Mexico City)	Black Power Salute. Substantial domestic unrest
1972 (Munich)	Israeli Team Massacre
1976 (Montreal)	Boycott by nations over South Africa
1980 (Moscow)	Boycott by western nations and individual competitors over Soviet invasion of Afganistan.
1984 (Los Angeles)	Boycott or partial boycott by several communist nations
1988 (Seoul)	Boycott by several communist nations over relations between North and South Korea. Substantial domestic unrest
1992 (Barcelona)	Substantial domestic unrest

Source: Hall, 1989c

Commonwealth Games in Brisbane, Aboriginal groups conducted demonstrations and protest marches in order to highlight issues of social inequality (McGregor, 1984; Ryan, 1984; Sutton, 1984; Watson, 1984). As McGregor (1984, p.11) reported: 'Over the ten days of the Games, land rights received such publicity that if all the reports and photographs of the subject published in *The Courier-Mail* during those ten days were collated, they would fill roughly the equivalent of the entire news columns of one edition of *The Courier-Mail*'.

The threat of violence at events is treated with great seriousness and is in itself an indication of the profile which hallmark events may have in domestic and international media. For example, the over 6,000 delegates to the 1980 American Society of Travel Agents (ASTA) Conference in Manila was seen by the Marcos Government as a means of creating a positive international image for the Regime. However, just minutes after President Ferdinand Marcos had given the opening address, a bomb exploded, missing the President but injuring several delegates. The Conference was cancelled despite pleas from the Government, and the number of visitors to the Philippines immediately began to decline following this audacious display of political opposition to the regime (Richter, 1989).

Such outbursts of violent protest are not isolated to authoritarian states. One of Australia's most publicised hallmark events in recent years, the 1986–87 America's Cup Defence, experienced a range of political protests. The Observation City hotel complex at Scarborough Beach then owned by the Cup defender, Alan Bond, and located just off the Cup course, was subject to a large bomb explosion during its construction phase. 'Permission to build the Observation City resort Hotel, against strong community opposition, was a gift for bringing the America's Cup to Perth' (Dovey, 1989, p.77). The complex dominated the beach and surrounding area and dramatically altered the nature of the area (Dovey, 1989). The violent protest appeared to have been directed at the multi-storey hotel by local residents who resented the physical and social changes to the area that the complex was likely to bring (Hall and Selwood, 1987, 1989). The explosion was the first in a series of incidents that continued throughout the lead-up to the Cup. Community environmental groups attempted to block the construction of a new marina at

Hillarys-Sorrento. Anonymous letters from people protesting rent and tax increases, perceived to be related to the hosting of the Cup, made threats to 'fix Australia III' and make the Aga Khan 'wish he stayed at home' (Hall and Selwood, 1989). Aborigines also threatened to 'disrupt' the event in order to focus attention on Aboriginal land rights in Western Australia. Yet somewhat surprisingly no Aboriginal protests came about (Hall and Selwood, 1988; Hall, 1989c).

Legal Rights and Industrial Relations

The importance and prestige attached to hallmark events by Governments often means a commitment to 'fast track' planning practices which ignore community opposition to the hosting of events (Thorne and Munro-Clarke, 1989). In the legal arena the significance of events for the image of government and political personalities may mean the suspension of the principles of natural justice and/or the enactment of legislation specific to the requirements of an event. For example, the construction of facilities for the 1982 Asiad Games in New Delhi was marked by extremely poor labour conditions which included industrial law violations, non-payment of the minimum wage, a lack of health and safety regulations and employment of young children (Lin and Patnaik, 1982).

However, the suspension of natural justice is not isolated to developing countries. In the case of the America's Cup, for instance, special legislation was passed by both the Western Australian State Government and the New Zealand Government in an attempt to ensure that the event would run without interference. Similarly, the Queensland Government passed legislation to control the affairs of the 1988 Brisbane Expo, while the effects of the Queensland *1982 Commonwealth Games Act* meant 'that the only protest allowed during the Games, and the only protest occurring during the Games, was that allowed by the authorities' (O'Gorman, 1984, p.43). Furthermore, legislation may be matched by the appointment of a minister with special responsibilities for the conduct of the hallmark event, as in the case of Western Australia and New Zealand for the America's Cup.

In the case of the 1986 Expo, the British Columbian Government proclaimed a law that stripped construction workers of negotiated contract rights at the Expo 86 site. Under the legislation, 'the area around False Creek in downtown Vancouver where the fair will be built is designated a special "economic development zone". The law prohibited work stoppages or lockouts on such sites' (Mulgrew, 1984a, p.8). The justification for the Act was supplied by Premier William Bennett (in Mulgrew, 1984b, p.1) earlier in the year:

> The Government will be introducing legislation to ensure that no one – whatever their motivation – has the power to stand in the way of Expo. And I know that British Columbians are not prepared to let any stumbling block stand in the way for Expo. Nor are they prepared to see the tentative economic recovery that is now under way tampered with.

The politics of 'lotusland', Warnock's (1987, p.10) description of the 'stupor-like dream world' of the British Columbian Government in which the 1986 Expo was created, are further evidenced by one of Premier Bennett's statements upon announcing the Expo project in 1980: 'It's more important to proceed than worry about how much it might cost' (Mulgrew, 1984c, p.1). A sentiment that appears to categorise many of the political statements that are attached to hallmark events by government and political leaders (Hall, 1989c).

The establishment of special acts and regulations to control hallmark events has important political dimensions. Acts and regulations may serve to reinforce the powerlessness of certain groups and individuals within the planning process. The law often acts to protect the integrity of the event not the impacts of the event on the host population. Greater attention therefore needs to be given to the ability of affected groups and individuals to participate in the decision-making process (Hall, 1989c).

The Promotion of Government and Individual Political Interests

The perceived political gain for government and certain actors within the policy-making process ensures that hallmark events will continue to be promoted as vital to the interests of the host state. By utilising the high media profiles attached to events, individuals can promote their own interests. Politicians, governments, administrators and significant individuals invariably want to portray themselves as winners and are therefore often associated with sporting events, particularly domestic finals or international competition of the highest quality (Auf der Maur, 1976; Ueberroth, 1985; Richter, 1989, pp.124–30). For example, the perceived success of the hosting of the 1988 Summer Olympics in Calgary appeared to reflect favourably on the various levels of government that were involved in the Games (Ritchie and Lyons, 1990).

The origins of large-scale hallmark or mega-events appears to lie in 'the efforts or influence of a powerful individual' with the instigator of a major event most often being a nation's president, a state or provincial premier, or a powerful mayor (Armstrong, 1986, p.16). However, the pursuit of personal profile may have substantial long-term impacts on tourist development and regional growth. As Richter observed in the case of the 1982 Asian Games:

> The decision to reverse an earlier administration and hold the Ninth Asian Games... in New Delhi was a political decision that went beyond tourism considerations, though it was defended in such terms... Prime Minister Indira Gandhi badly wanted the publicity and attention of such an event to focus world attention on her triumphal return to national power and domestic attention to focus on her ability to get things done and to attract massive world interest. By the time she was finished in November 1982, 22 months later, 12 five-star hotels with a total of over 3,284 rooms had been built or were under construction. Five giant stadia had been erected, seven highway overpasses built, an electrified ring railway completed, bus services expanded, an athletic village developed, and well over US$5 billion spent – all in New Delhi for a 15-day sports event. Additionally, an advanced hotel management institute was set up to begin a crash program to train personnel for the games. (1989, p.125)

Some ten years later, Delhi was still overbuilt, moreover, Indian tourism policy has been attempting to get tourists away from the 'golden triangle of Delhi-Agra-Jaipur' in order to develop tourism in other areas (Seth, 1990). The legacy of Asiad '82 for the development of international tourism in India has therefore been substantial delays and problems in the diversification of the country's tourism base.

In the case of the Sydney 2000 Olympics bid, Duffy (1991/92) attempted to explain why the State and Federal governments were so keen to support the Games when the economic prospects for the Games bid were comparatively marginal. His conclusion was that the bid helps to distract media attention, and hence public attention from more pressing matters such as the recession:

> Thus the front-page headline in Sydney's *Telegraph Mirror* in October: 'Games Boost' above a story about how Prince Albert of Monaco praised our bid as 'excellent'. Later in the story, inside the newspaper, it emerged that the prince hadn't actually been to any of the other bidding cities, and was confident that they too would be excellent. But by then bid supremo and transport minister Bruce Baird's name had been mentioned in a positive context four times. (1991/92, p.12)

Therefore, as the above examples illustrate, for the boosters of hallmark events, the event may be an opportunity to enhance and legitimise their own power. Conversely, the power of those who are excluded from the 'benefits' of hallmark events or who are excluded from the formal and legitimate decision-making process may be negatively reinforced. However, somewhat paradoxically, as noted above, hallmark events may provide a platform for the disenchanted and the excluded to air their grievances because of the profile that hallmark events are able to attain. Therefore, attention needs to be paid to the overall issue of the legitimation of activities, popular or not, through the use of hallmark events (Hall, 1989c).

Towards a Political Economy of Hallmark Events?

This chapter illustrates that hallmark events are undoubtedly political. Tourist developments 'create a political and economic context within which the hallmark event is used as an excuse to overrule planning legislation and participatory planning processes, and to sacrifice local places along the way' (Dovey, 1989, pp.79–80). Despite the potential for negative impact, events are almost invariably seen by urban elites, politicians and governments as beneficial at both collective and individual levels because of their ability to promote appropriate images of places and attract investment and tourism. Events may act to strengthen dominant ideologies or further individual interests. They may have a hidden agenda. Events may act to legitimise hegemonic relationships and change the meanings and structure of place. Furthermore, they can even be used to legitimise what would otherwise be unpopular decisions, particularly in the area of urban development. Events may promote outbursts of patriotism which can see a renewal of national pride at best, or racism and bigotism at worst. For example, O'Gorman (1984, p.43) noted 'the patriotism which sometimes bordered on jingoism and which took over during the lead up' to the 1982 Commonwealth Games in Brisbane, Australia.

Despite the political significance of events, the study of the political aspects of hallmark events at both the macro- and micro-level is poorly developed. Emphasis should be placed on the allocation of resources for events and the manner in which interests influence this process, particularly through the interaction of power, values, interests, place and the processes of capital accumulation (Hall, 1989c). Nevertheless, despite the clear importance of political analysis for planning, management and appropriate development practice, it is likely that political analysis will remain a 'blind-spot' for government. However, it is essential that groups and interests who are ignored by urban elites and government in their desire for spectacles and 'bread and circuses' utilise the potential of political analysis to regain community control of hallmark events and set objectives which maximise returns to the community.

6 The Management of Hallmark Events

Out of the hope for the benefits,... as well as out of fear, rational men yield to the will of others. (Kaufmann, 1964, p.6)

The management of organisations is 'generally complex, ambiguous, and paradoxical' (Morgan, 1986, p.17), the management of events more so. Events have two immediate implications for conventional approaches towards management. First, events, by their very definition, typically occur outside the normal routine of an organisation. 'Routine refers to regular schedules, programmes and operations which are repetitive. An event will be the opposite to the regular with extended times, different participants, and non-regular operations. Managing will be on the 'one-off' basis rather than the predictable and the regular' (Badmin, Coombs and Rayner, 1988, p.106). Second, organisational structures may be established solely to manage a particular event and will consequently have a finite lifespan.

Successful event management will depend on the ability of the organisers to define the objectives of hosting the event, understanding the audience, creating an organisational structure which meets the requirements of running the event, and evaluating the effectiveness of the event in meeting its initial set of objectives (United States Department of Housing and Urban Development, 1981; Robinson and Noël, 1991). Management sophistication may depend on the size of the community in which the event is being hosted, as this will affect the size of the pool of available volunteers and the level of management experience. Nevertheless, 'except for the magnitudes of scale and the intricate scheduling involved in their preparation, even the most modest local special event requires exactly the same kind of organization, planning, division of responsibility, and meticulous attention to detail' as large-scale or mega-events (Canadian Government Office of Tourism, 1982, p.3). However, the critical element in the success of hosting events is having a clearly defined management strategy which satisfies the motivations of both visitors and the hosts. As Frisby and Getz (1989, p.7) described in their study of community festivals in Ontario, 'Strategies for understanding and exploiting the external environment are often not in place, very few of the festivals were engaged in goal setting, marketing, strategic planning, and organized fund-raising ventures and accurate measures of attendance and economic impacts often were not available'.

The scale complexity, presentation, status and motivation of special events change but the underlying management principles remain the same (Canadian Government Office of Tourism, 1982; Tourism South Australia, 1990a). Event management should be integrated, flexible and dynamic. However, it must also establish clear management, operations, planning, and financial procedures, in order to maximise the benefits of holding an event, four key management problems, which are common to a range of events and festivals, need to be addressed:

1. Short-period in which events are held;
2. Dependence on volunteer support;
3. Dependence on community support; and
4. Motivations not only monetary.

'The general function of any sponsoring festival agency is to make available to its target audience satisfying, constructive leisure-time activities. To do so, the festival machinery must have available funds, leadership, organized programmes, services, areas and facilities. It must have management, planning and direction' (Zauhar and Kurtzman, 1991, p.364). Similarly, Frisby and Getz (1989, p.7) commented, 'undoubtedly, the ability of festivals to become successful tourist attractions depends in part on their goals and the way in which they are managed'.

Four major functions can be identified in the assessment of event management:

1. *Planning* – the determination of the development of events through the establishment of objectives and by designing and implementing the strategies required to achieve those objectives;
2. *Organising* – the determination of the specific activities that will be required to implement the event plan;
3. *Leading* – the motivation of staff (including volunteers), and the direction and communication of the responsibilities that must be fulfilled if the event is to succeed; and
4. *Controlling* – the adjustment and monitoring of activities in order to ensure that events develop in line with established objectives.

The following pages examine the management of hallmark events in the light of these four functions. Each section discusses the function in terms of the role of the event organiser and provides examples of successful management practice. The chapter concludes with a discussion of the importance of evaluation as a management and planning tool.

Planning

Planning is the most basic function in the management of hallmark events. 'To be effective, managers must know what they intend to accomplish' (Pearce and Robinson, 1989, p.163). Most fundamentally, the organisers and managers of events must set and use objectives to guide the development and planning of events. As Tourism South Australia (1990a, p.6) recognised, 'no festival or event can be successful unless the organisers identify at the outset what it is they are trying to achieve by staging the event'.

Table 6.1   Purposes of ten American cities in conducting urban fairs

City	Fair	Purpose
Baltimore, Maryland	City Fair	To celebrate the City of Baltimore, particularly the neighbourhoods; promote civic pride
Petersburg, Virginia	Nostalgiafest	Get citizens back downtown; attract tourists and new businesses
San Antonio, Texas	Fiesta	Celebrate history of Texas, especially heroes of the Alamo and highlight Anglo and Latin cultures
Ithaca, New York	Ithaca Festival (the arts)	Urban revitalization, arts and business working together
Austin, Texas	Aqua Festival	Increase business in August; entertain citizens; attract tourists; publicise Austin
Sioux City, Iowa	River-cade (Summer festival)	Civic pride; business; create goodwill; entertainment; tourism; focus on city as a port
Knoxville, Tennessee	The Dogwood Arts Festival	Civic pride; culture; education; business; social; recreation
Dayton, Ohio	Down by the Riverside	Generate interest in the development of the Miami River corridor
Minneapolis, Minnesota	Aquatennial/ Summer Break	Promote civic pride; commerce; entertainment; education; tourism; cultural exchange; sports celebration; economic
Gilroy, California	Garlic	Celebrate garlic; derive revenues to make chamber independent

Source: United States Department of Housing and Urban Development, 1981, pp.40–41

An objective is an intended end. In the case of event tourism a variety of measurable and non-measurable objectives can be identified. Objectives range from raising the profile of a destination, bringing income into a community or celebrating a festival or anniversary. Table 6.1 summarises the purposes of ten American cities in the hosting of urban fairs, while Table 6.2 lists the specific objectives of the Glenelg Games, a regional sporting competition in Victoria, Australia in 1986, which involved over 4,000 participants.

Objectives improve the management of events in a number of ways:

- provision guidance to appropriate organisational behaviour
- reduction of uncertainty and the lack of direction in the development of an event
- clearly defined objectives motivate people to work toward specific ends

Table 6.2   Objectives of the Glenelg Games

Objectives

- to promote growing community involvement in sport;
- to develop goodwill and cooperation amongst disparate sporting groups through competition;
- to generate revenue for clubs and associations hosting events;
- to generate revenue for local business in towns hosting the events;
- to generate revenue for the Glenelg Regional Sports Assembly;
- to bestow recognition for sporting achievement and participation;
- to assist sponsors to market and promote their goods and services;
- to share the benefits of hosting the Games amongst numerous district centres;
- to encourage family participation in sporting events.

Source: Oakley, 1987, p.90

Table 6.3   Objectives for the hosting of hallmark events

Objective

- to upgrade cultural activity in the community;
- to attract tourists;
- to involve the community in a civic celebration;
- to develop popular participation in the arts, crafts, sports or athletics;
- to advance and promote the community for the public benefit;
- to promote political and cultural exchanges;
- to create or strengthen a spirit of goodwill between the community's social or ethnic groups;
- to promote the utilisation of tourist facilities during the off-season;
- to call public attention to unique characteristics or attractions of the community;
- to earn revenue that can be used to provide a needed but otherwise unattainable social benefit for the community.

Source: Canadian Government Office of Tourism, 1982, p.7

- clearly defined objectives provide a measure with which to assess the success of events
- objectives provide a focal point for coordination of the event organisation

Objectives in the case of event tourism may include: overcoming the seasonal nature of tourism, spreading tourist demand by creating new attractions, developing new tourist markets and creating a favourable impression of the destination through appropriate imaging. For example, the United States Department of Housing and Urban Development (1981) promoted urban fairs as a means to overcome the problems of cities such as poor self image or reputation and urban blight, or to take advantage of a city's favourable assets. Table 6.3 lists a number of objectives for the hosting of events identified by the Canadian Government Office of Tourism (1982). However, it should be noted that not all of these objectives could be attributed to a single event, while several of the objectives may not be compatible with each other. In order to meet their objectives event organisers must identify a hierarchy of objectives which will prioritise the management and organisational demands of hosting an event. Furthermore, in the case of regularly occurring mega-events such as the World Cup or the Olympic Games the objectives of the sporting organisation may be somewhat different to that of the host city. For example, 'to the Olympic organisation, the Olympic Games are not merely an end in themselves but are meant to foster the broader goals of competitive sport. Impact is... measured in athletic terms' (Hiller, 1989, p.120). For the International Olympic Committee the goals and objectives in hosting an Olympics are to create a legacy of facilities that will stimulate athletic development which would not have been possible with inferior facilities, and to heighten the profile of the sports involved thereby providing better opportunities for training as well as sites for other national and international competitions (Hiller, 1989). For the host city the goals are (Hiller, 1989):

- a sporting legacy which provides a broad rationale for hosting the Games;
- honour and global recognition that comes from being chosen among international venues;
- the infusion of external funding for capital projects which are justified by the event; and
- the economic stimulus that comes from the preparation for the event, the event itself, and the opportunities which follow it, such as tourism.

A survey of community festivals in Ontario, indicated that some 73.5 per cent (36) festivals had formalised goals and objectives. The most frequently mentioned goals were to promote the community, provide a good programme, to make money, education and to increase market area (Getz and Frisby, 1987, p.15). In the case of event tourism in Saskatchewan, Derek Murray Consulting Associates (1985, p.xviii) reported that despite the substantial contribution that events made to the Provincial tourist economy, particularly the level of trip expenditure, there 'has been little development of linkages between events and attractions to improve Saskatchewan's destination image... Events have not been integrated with community tourism development and marketing'. The significance of the community-based planning component of the event management process for the development of successful events is further discussed in the following chapter.

A vital, yet often overlooked, aspect of the operating environment for which event managers must plan is understanding of competition which events may face. Competition may take the form of other tourist attractions or, more likely, other events. Therefore, event organisers need to ensure that their planned event is not only in keeping with the character of the local community but they also need to know the characteristics, potential markets, and location of other events and festivals in order to maximise visitation and returns to their own event. Market niches may be spatial (what other events occur in the region?), thematic (what themes do other events in the region focus on?), or seasonal (what other events would occur in the region at the same time?). One response to the potential limitations which are established by competing events may be to find a niche not in direct competition with other festivals (e.g. in a region with no festivals, none of an overlapping theme, or none at that time of year). An alternative response may be to seek out 'competition' and add a festival to an area with a reputation for festivals, or add another of the same theme or season to develop a concentration of similar festivals. (Butler and Smale, 1991, p.21)

Organising

Organising 'is the process of defining the essential relationships among people, tasks, and activities in such a way that all the organization's resources are integrated and coordinated to accomplish its objectives' (Pearce and Robinson, 1989, p.296). The organising function improves the efficiency and quality of the event management process, establishes accountability for decisions and resources and facilitates communication between the various personnel involved in event management and organisation, including salaried staff, committee members and volunteers.

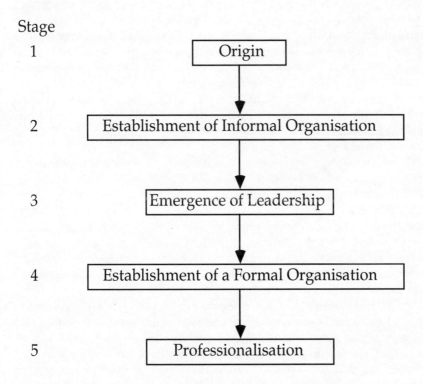

Figure 6.1 Stages in the growth of volunteer event organisations
Source: After Katz, 1981

Event organisation may take several forms. Katz (1981) suggested that volunteer-based organisations tend to go through five stages of development: (1) origin, (2) informal organisation, (3) emergence of a leadership, (4) the creation of a formal organisation, and (5) the professionalisation of the previously volunteer body (Figure 6.1). The five stages of development are akin to the stages by which organisational structures develop for community-based events (Getz and Frisby, 1988). However, the final two stages might not be reached because of a perceived belief that by professionalising the structure the community orientation of the organising body will be lost. As Frisby and Getz (1989, p.7) noted:

> Some organizers may see festivals as recreational pursuits that should be managed on a somewhat loose and informal basis. Others may resist the trend toward professionalism because they fear that community involvement and control may diminish if a 'business-like' approach develops. There may also be a concern that the event will become a 'tourist trap' in which authenticity diminishes or disappears and problems of overcrowding and commercialism take over.

The stages proposed by Katz (1981) in the development of volunteer organisations also apply equally well to a top-down model of event organisation. In the case of already established organisations, particularly municipal and government departments, the original idea will also pass through informal stages until leadership emerges to promote the virtues of the event concept through authority and/or persuasion. However, in a top-down model of event organisation the professionalised nature of event management will be a given, while the development of a formal structure will occur either within an existing institutional framework or will necessitate the creation of a new body structure specifically to deal with the new event.

The organisation of large scale, mega-events, such as international fairs and expositions, necessitates the establishment of a specific body in order to deal with the demands of such a complex organisational environment. For example, Carroll (1989) in his account of the origins of the Brisbane 1988 Exposition, noted that the idea to host the Expo during the Australian bicentennial year had been circulating through State and Federal Government circles for well over a decade prior to its hosting, and that it took decisive action from the Queensland Government under the personal authority of the Premier, Joh Bjelke Petersen, before the decision to apply to host the event was made.

In the development of events and festivals in Britain 'in nearly every case in which success is achieved, whether the idea springs from outside the area, arises spontaneously in a particular locality, or owes its origin to one man [sic], it has been essential to win the support of a sufficient number of people in the area, often including the local authorities' (Camacho, 1979, p.7). Similarly, at the level of community-based events in Canada, 'public discussion of the basic project is absolutely essential before a formal organization can be set up... In order to have a hope of success, a festival or special event must have the interest and support of the community' (Canadian Government Office of Tourism, 1982, p.8). Public discussion can be held either under the auspices of the local municipality or the

Table 6.4   Groups involved in community-run festivals in Ontario and their
                 tasks

Type of Group	No. of mentions	Main tasks	No. of mentions
Service Clubs	29	Running an Event	55
Government	10	Supplying Things	9
Sport Associations	10	Safety/Security	5
Children's Groups	9	Promotion	4
Volunteers	8	Overseeing	4
Police/Fire	7	Production	3
Business Associations	7	Other	3
Other	19		

Source: Getz and Frisby, 1987, p.24

originating group which has proposed the event. A public meeting may provide a
suitable opportunity to outline the project, gain public support and attract volunteers who may be willing to serve on the various committees associated with the
running of the event or who may assist while the event is being held. In addition,
events may be linked to specific community organisations such as service clubs.
However, each group will have its own agenda which has to be addressed by the
event organisation. As Frisby and Getz (1989, p. 8) observed: 'while involvement
of a wide range of community groups fosters community development, it greatly
increases the complexity of managing the festival'. Nevertheless, such public
support and involvement is necessary for the short- and long-term success of the
event. Table 6.4 outlines the groups involved in community-run festivals in
Ontario and the various tasks which they undertake.

In order to effectively organise events it is essential that an executive board,
group or committee is established which oversees the running of the event. The
executive board 'is responsible for the effective use of resources entrusted to them
in the presentation of a festival or special event which meets [its] original
objectives... it has full responsibility for directing the policies and finances,
establishing priorities and planning their execution' (Canadian Government Office
of Tourism, 1982, p.13). Sub-committees with specific responsibilities may be
established in order to handle areas such as accommodation, public relations and
promotion, fund-raising and finance, properties, transport, and security. Several of
the sub-committees, for example fundraising, may have a year-round lifespan,
while others may deal with specific concerns, such as parking, which only occur
while the event is being held. The number of committees will depend on the size of
the event. For example, Australia's premier wine event and one of South
Australia's largest tourist drawcards, the week-long Barossa Valley Vintage
Festival, has 25–30 fully operative major committees in addition to the board of
management (Wardlaw, 1990).

Executive boards should be small enough to be able to make effective decisions
and handle the ongoing management of an event. A chairperson or executive
director may also be appointed to deal with day-to-day issues that arise in event
organisation, for larger events this position will invariably be salaried. The

Table 6.5   Characteristics of members of executive boards and committees of
successful events.

Characteristics

- a capacity to visualise the potential for community development inherent in a
  local festival or special event;
- a recognition of the basic requirements of event management;
- a knowledge of community planning;
- leadership;
- business acumen and the ability to adapt sound business procedures to the
  event organisation;
- ability to command and administer the physical support system necessary for
  the functioning of the event;
- a willingness and ability to devote time and energy to the work during the
  months ahead; and
- no personal axes to grind with the management.

Source: After Canadian Government Office of Tourism, 1982, p.12

characteristics of committee members that have been found to contribute to the
success of events is illustrated in Table 6.5. In addition, the nature of the organising committee may change as the size of the event increases 'In large festivals it is
more likely that board members do not do as much committee work or help on the
operations, but concentrate on raising money and general support' (Getz and
Frisby, 1987, p.14). The problem of the appropriate size for an event executive board
or management committee has been well addressed by the Canadian Government
Office of Tourism (1982, p.12):

> The size of the board depends largely upon the size of the community and the size of the
> project itself. But where there are several projects running almost simultaneously or
> several separate events placed under the umbrella of the festival, it may require quite a
> large board to maintain effective control. Four out of five of experienced festival
> organizers asked for their opinions when this manual was planned voted for 'the
> smallest possible' executive board. Large boards, they report, are difficult to manage,
> have been known to create personality clashes, and may be manipulated by the develop-
> ment of power plays within the board room itself. A small, tightly knit group, on the
> other hand is able to keep its attention focused on the job at hand, because the
> communication problem is so much simpler. Every member of a small board simply has
> to pull his weight.

In order to maximise the level of community support for an event, an advisory
committee may be formed which has a broad representation from throughout the
host community and which includes members of government, service clubs,
educational institutions, churches, unions, cultural associations and youth groups.
Despite the emphasis that should be placed on involving as many stake-holders as
possible in the event management process, many events 'are "community-run"
only to the extent that many community groups take part – they are not truly
controlled by the public at large' (Getz and Frisby, 1987, p.13). Nevertheless, as
noted in a survey of Ontario events, 'while each festival has a small group of

volunteers that it can depend on, it must often struggle to get on-going commitments from a wide range of community groups to serve on boards and committees and to actually stage the event' (Frisby and Getz, 1989, p.10). Therefore, from the perspective of small, community-based events, the leadership function will be crucial in determining the life-span of any particular event.

Leading

Leadership 'is the process of influencing others to work toward the attainment of specific goals' (Pearce and Robinson, 1989, p.483). In the context of event management, a manager or member of a management committee is leading when he or she is able to influence members of the event organisation to direct their efforts toward the achievement of the events goals and objectives. The concept of leadership within event management is closely associated with motivating, group management, and communication functions.

Attracting tourists is only one motivation for the hosting of hallmark events. Events are also held in order to boost civic pride, involve community groups and promote community development. Meeting the human dimension of event management, the needs and motivations of participants, supporters, volunteers, and the interests of the wider community, requires substantial leadership and human resource management skills.

The brief period of time for which events are held is sometimes seen as a substantial challenge for event managers (Frisby and Getz, 1989). However, while it does undoubtedly pose organisational challenges, the brief burst of activity which marks the conducting of an event also provides a target towards which staff and volunteers can be motivated. In particular, events and festivals

> are organizations relying heavily on the 'synchrony' concept. Expectations of festival committees must interact not only with its committee members but also with its audiences. People working together towards one goal and seeking to involve people must determine a working climate leading to satisfaction, at least to some degree, for all concerned – participants as well as organizers; sponsors as well as grant giving institutions. (Zauhar and Kurtzman, 1991, p.365)

Managing Volunteers

Volunteers have a major role to play in the successful running of events (Kelly, 1986; Bratton, 1991). For example, in Edmonton a total of 19,684 volunteers were utilised for the 1983 World Student Games; almost 80,000 assisted in the running of the 1978 Commonwealth Games (Hamilton and Steadward, 1986) and over 28,700 volunteer staff were involved in the 1984 Olympics (Taylor and Gratton, 1988). However, the management of volunteers requires the development of a range of human resource management and leadership skills that will allow the maximisation of the human resource that is at the disposal of event organisers. Because volunteers are not paid, their reasons for becoming involved in events must be recognised by managers and the paid employees of the event organisation. More often than not volunteers become involved because they

- want to be part of the event, they want to 'belong' and 'be there';
- want to contribute to the community;
- wish to feel that they are productive members of the community;
- wish to develop their skills or feel that they have skills that can contribute to the success of the event.

In order to effectively use volunteer services it is essential that event managers have a clear idea of what their manpower requirements will be at various stages of the event. Potential volunteers should be screened so as to ensure that they are suitable for their positions and responsibilities. The roles and responsibilities must be clearly defined and managed but, most importantly of all, volunteers must be dealt with in a sensitive manner by the event organisation and their contribution should be appropriately recognised and rewarded (Hamilton and Steadward, 1986).

Controlling

Control is the means of making something happen the way it was planned to happen. Control is 'the process of monitoring and adjusting organizational activities in such a way as to facilitate accomplishment of organizational objectives' (Pearce and Robinson, 1989, p.580). Effective managerial controls go hand-in-hand with the planning process. Managerial control generally occurs at two levels. First, at the operational level, where event managers are concerned with utilising human, physical, financial and information resources in order to accomplish the event's objectives. Second, at the strategic level where managerial control is focused on the external environment within which the event occurs. For example, as noted in the planning section above, event organisers need to be aware of what competing events and tourist attractions are doing in order to ensure that their own event remains attractive to the visitor market. However, given the nature and structure of the majority of events organisations, it is likely that operational control will be of most concern to event managers.

Control over human resources will require selection of appropriate personnel, training, appraisal and meeting staff (including volunteer) needs. Control over physical resources will necessitate implementation of purchasing, inventory management and quality control techniques. Financial control involves the effective use of the capital available to event organisers through cost management. Information control requires the availability of timely and accurate information to support management activities, for example, the availability of information on attendee and visitor number forecasts, or advance booking details. The techniques most utilised by event managers to exercise control are budgets and audits. However, it should be emphasised that budgets not only detail financial advice but also generate information that allows decisions to be made concerning the overall

Table 6.6 Types of budget used in event management

Type	Characteristic
Attendance	A forecast of attendance, based on previous years' experience, market surveys, public opinion polls and economic information gives an indication of possible receipts from activities where admission is charged, or concessions of various kinds. This is useful for the cash and master budget, and also supplies an indication of whether additional capital and administrative expenses may be needed to meet increasing attendance.
Activity	Each committee produces budget estimates for the activity or activities assigned to it. In them, the expense items are of primary concern, but the budget should indicate potential revenues as well.
Receipts	This budget includes a consolidation of anticipated admission ticket sales, and receipts from the various activity budgets. The receipts budget is used as an input for the cash and master budgets.
Administrative expense	This budget includes all expenses not included in the activity budgets. These encompass management salaries, over-all publicity, licences, insurance, and taxes if it is not a non-profit organisation.
Capital expense	Required to cover all capitalised items, such as construction of facilities, purchase of major office equipment, or general improvement of festival buildings and grounds.
Cash budget	Derived from consolidating the activity budgets, receipt budgets, administrative expense, and capital expense budgets. It also helps management to programme its dispursements to ensure an orderly cash flow, to take advantage of cash discounts on purchases and/or the short-term investment of surplus funds, or else to warn of the necessity for short-term bank loans or more aggressive fundraising.
Master budget	This is the summary of the over-all operations of the event, enabling an executive board to make decisions concerning the number and type of short- and long-term activities which need to be considered in the running of an event. It also provides management with an operating summary so that comparison can be made with the results obtained by similar organisations in other parts of the region or country.

Source: After Canadian Government Office of Tourism, 1982, pp.18–19

management of resources. 'The budget is a formal statement of management plans to assist the organization in achieving its objectives. Without budgets, the operation would lack direction, problems would not be foreseen, leading to crisis management in which actions are taken to alleviate immediate problems without

Table 6.7   Revenue generators in Ontario community-run festivals

Sources	No. of Yes Responses	Per cent
Admission charges	33	64.7
Sales of goods	30	58.8
Lottery/raffle	25	49.0
Rent spaces to businesses	19	38.0
Donations	8	15.7
Other	18	35.3

Source: Getz and Frisby, 1987, p.24

regard to their future implications' (Canadian Government Office of Tourism, 1982, p.18). Seven different kinds of budget documents of use to event managers are explained in Table 6.6.

Of critical importance to the success of an event is the ability to generate enough revenue to cover costs, not only from the actual running of the event itself but also in the lead-up period during which preparation for the event occurs. As Frisby and Getz (1989, p.10) observed in their study of special events and festivals in Ontario, 'even the festivals which have been in existence for a long period of time and have full-time paid professionals have difficulty raising money and getting enough volunteers to run the event. Because the festivals do not rely on one predictable source of funding, they must work very hard to raise small amounts from numerous sources that often change year by year.'

Sponsorship is one mechanism by which costs can be lowered and/or income generated and this is dealt with in detail in Chapter 8. However, the sale of goods and services, and admission charges are the primary sources of revenue for any event organisation. The sources of revenue generation in Ontario festivals is shown in Table 6.7. In addition, substantial funds may be attracted to tourist attracting events from municipal, regional and national governments (Wallis-Smith, 1989). While mega-events of international and national status will almost certainly attract government funds, smaller events are increasingly drawing support from governments eager to promote tourism for its potential positive economic and employment effects.

Managing Risk

Risk is a significant factor in the management of events and is a critical component of the control function. In addition to the financial risks of event organisation 'relating to the costs and revenues of the event (a speculative risk – offering gain or loss), there is the risk of injury to persons and property due to accidents and terrorism (a pure risk-offering only the prospect of loss). If these risks are not well managed, they can impose both financial and social costs on the host' (Chang and Singh, 1990, p. 45). In their study of the 1988 Calgary Winter Olympics Chang and Singh (1990) noted that there were three major areas of exposure to the event organisers. First, risk exposure such as injury or death to employees, volunteers, visiting dignitaries, and participants. Given the large role that volunteers play in event organisation, the insurance liability component for volunteers would appear to be an important control item for the management of all sizes of events. Second, exposure to risks on property through the physical loss of, or damage to, all assets owned, leased, rented, and/or controlled by the event management body. Third, there is an exposure to risks in relation to the public that come to visit and spectate at events. For certain events, the size of the public may be enormous. For example, in the case of the Calgary Olympics the risk management committee estimated that 1,300,000 people would fall into the public risk category (Chang and Singh, 1990, p.47).

Risk management will clearly be a major contributor to the control function of event management and should have a clearly defined status within the organisation structure of an event. Risk management is not just applicable to mega-events such as the Olympic Games, although risks from terrorism and other acts of violence will undoubtedly be more substantial in relation to the size of the event. Therefore, all event organisers should consider a two-step process which aims to minimise the risks associated with the hosting of an event. The first step, is to 'identify and analyse risks through activities such as review of contracts, attendance at planning meetings, review of internal documents, physical inspection of venues, and review of documentation on previous events' (Chang and Singh, 1990, p.52). Risk exposures can be identified in terms of the three categories noted above. This step should occur from the earliest stages of the event management process. The second step is to manage the three categories of risk through financing and control programmes including insurance and self-insurance. Furthermore, risk management should be integrated with the other management functions through 'proper safety training, emergency response planning, and corrective actions after safety review' (Chang and Singh, 1990, p.52).

Learning From the Experience: Evaluation as a Strategic Tool

Evaluation is the often forgotten element in event management. Nevertheless, it is crucial that event organisers determine whether or not the event was a success in the light of the initial objectives for hosting an event; for example, through the use of a SWOT (Strengths, Weaknesses, Opportunities, Threats) analysis. Indeed, it may well be the case that some goals were met while others remained unfulfilled. The success or otherwise of an event will only remain hearsay and conjecture unless a formal evaluation occurs. Furthermore, evaluation is a continuation of the control function of management and helps develop management processes and procedures for the next hosting of the event. Evaluation is therefore a valuable means to learn from the mistakes and successes which have been realised throughout the management process, while also providing important information to use in further lobbying for government or private industry support in future years. Ongoing evaluation also allows the development of a body of knowledge and information as to the effectiveness that an event may have in meeting its objectives. Something that was successful five or ten years ago may not be appropriate now and therefore it becomes necessary for event organisers to adapt to the new

Table 6.8 General techniques for the evaluation and control of events

Technique
• Each committee records all the major problems encountered, the solutions reached, and a subsequent evaluation of the solution.
• Copies of all forms and form letters such as fund raising letters and registration forms should be filed.
• Copies of all publicity pieces produced such as tickets, booklets and flyers should be filed.
• The mailing list should be filed.
• Audited financial statements with a comparison to budgets should be reported and the reasons for being over or under the budget stated.
• Attendance figures need to be reported including where the audience came from, what they liked, and how they heard about the event.
• Figures on local commercial activity during the event such as traffic counts, gas station sales, hotel/motel occupancy rates, restaurant sales, and general merchants' sales, are most useful for giving the festival economic credibility in a particular locale.
• An overall evaluation of the event by the executive committee in terms of its financial success, acceptibility of individual events, and the success of individual publicity and promotion strategies is invaluable for the planning and management of any future event.

Source: After Canadian Government Office of Tourism, 1982, p.34

management environment. Table 6.8 outlines a number of general techniques for evaluating the success of an event. An example of the results of an evaluation of the management of events is detailed in the conclusions from an organisational review of festivals in the National Capital Region (Ottawa, Canada) presented in Table 6.9. In addition, the post-event evaluation should also include recognition of those individuals and organisations making a positive contribution to the running of the event.

Evaluation should not be regarded as an afterthought in event management. The costs of evaluation should be built into any event budget, as it should be regarded as a basic strategic management tool which assists event managers and organisations to find out where they have been, decide where they want to go, and identify how they are going to get there. Strategy is a means of achieving a desired end, for example the objectives identified for the hosting of the event (Chaffee, 1985). 'The strategy' as far as event managers should be concerned, is the event itself as a means of achieving two basic strategic objectives: sustaining its own existence; and enhancing the lives of the people who interact with it (Richardson and Richardson, 1989). Strategic analysis combines three different types of analysis:

1. *environmental analysis* which assists planners and managers to anticipate short and long term changes in the operational environment;
2. *resource analysis* which helps the event manager to understand the significance of the event's resource base to successful ongoing environmental adaptation; and
3. *aspirations analysis* which identifies the aspirations and interests of the major stakeholders in the event and assists management formulate their own strategic objectives in light of the desires, interests and power of others.

Table 6.9   Conclusions from an organisational review of festivals in the
National Capital Region (Ottawa, Canada)

- Mandates of most festivals are reviewed on a regular basis to ensure that activities and events continue to be relevant and are appropriately focused on the unique theme of the festival. This process should be continued.
- Members of the Board of Directors do not always participate actively and thereby make a valuable contribution to the success of the festival. Such members should be replaced.
- Some members have been on the Boards of festivals since inception. While this is commendable, limited tenures should be established, especially for the Executive, to ensure that there is an appropriate level of turnover.
- The Board members do not always contribute significantly to festival fund-raising activities. Active roles in this area are critical if the festivals are to increase the level of private sector support.
- Formal job descriptions are not always available and updated on a regular basis for full- and part-time festival staff. These are necessary to ensure that roles and responsibilities are clearly understood.
- Festivals vary in their ability to recruit volunteers and train and deploy them. Recruitment could be improved by ensuring that they have the necessary information and direction to work effectively and their skills are appropriately utilised for maximum benefit to both the festival and the volunteer.
- The planning and budgeting processes of the festivals are generally good, but the planning could be better documented for the majority of festivals. They need to improve so that they provide a critical path, with milestones and deadlines that will guide staff in their day-to-day efforts.
- All festivals could improve lines of communication between the Board, staff, volunteers and other participants. Roles, responsibilities and expectations for each group should be more clearly defined in order to avoid confusion, duplication of effort, or things not getting done at all.
- Most festivals should re-examine their approach to obtaining sponsorships, with a view to correcting identified shortcomings and strengthening their level of private sector support.

Source: Coopers and Lybrand Consulting Group, 1989, pp.28–9

As Richardson and Richardson (1989, p.58) observed: 'If performed effectively, strategic analysis can generate tremendous insight (particularly for first time users) into the factors which underpin present success/failure levels and into the organisational changes which make greatest sense in the context of the anticipated future'. Indeed, strategic analysis is part of the process by which events can be turned into 'learning organisations' that can constantly adapt to the demands of their stakeholders (Garratt, 1987; Tweed and Hall, 1991). Therefore, measures which event managers can take to evaluate the strategic basis for event management might include (Richardson and Richardson, 1989):

a) an aspirations analysis to determine who the important stakeholders are/will be and to ascertain their power positions, aspirations and propensities for or against alternative potential developments;

b) an environmental analysis for the insight this might stimulate on questions of organisational restructuring as well as potential product/market competitive developments;

c) pertinent market segmentation exercises;

d) analysis of the present and potential competitive market structure and identify the inherent attractiveness of the markets, and the openings which might exist for the event to exploit;

e) analysis of the wider and more futuristic environment in order to anticipate futures which the event might seek to exploit, change or avoid as necessary.

f) rank opportunities and threats in order of their perceived significance; and

g) conduct a resource analysis including an audit.

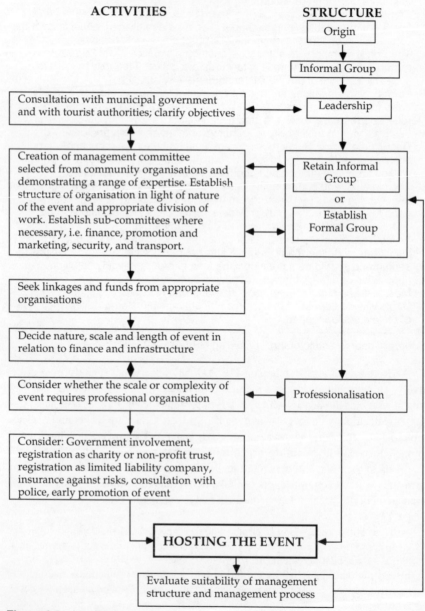

Figure 6.2   Idealised process of event management

Following this strategic analysis and evaluation of the organisation and management of the event, management can then proceed to generating the strategic developments that will make the event a success.

Summary

This chapter has illustrated that good management principles need to be applied to events regardless of their scale, complexity and objectives. The four major functions, planning, organising, leading and controlling, provide a basis not only for the assessment of event management but also as the guides by which events should be managed. Furthermore, evaluation and strategic analysis is shown to be a key element in not only achieving event objectives but also in realising essential strategic management objectives which will determine long- and short-term success.

The activities which events managers must undertake are explicitly connected to the organisational structure. Figure 6.2 provides an idealised diagram of the process by which an event is managed and how management principles can be put into operation. Management activities and organisational structure are part of a management process that will change over time in response to internal, (e.g. the human resource needs of volunteers) and external, (e.g. competition with other events) changes in the organisational environment of the event. Event management should, at all times, seek to evaluate and analyse its actions. However, it should be noted that 'even if the organization manipulates the environment well and secures desired inputs, the desired results cannot be guaranteed' (Frisby and Getz, 1989, p.10). Events, like all products, have a determinate lifespan, while the acquisition of human, physical and financial resources can pose major problems for event organisers. Nevertheless, it is anticipated that with application of good management practice, a clearly defined organisational structure, plus good planning and marketing techniques as described in the following two chapters, events can meet their defined objectives.

7 Planning Hallmark Events

Temporary urbanism is a concept that has not been a focus of Western architecture and planning. As a result, cyclical events in our cities have, for the most part, been tolerated rather than assisted by municipal, state and national authorities. In the United States there are some exceptions to this negative norm: daily food and flower markets in Boston, Los Angeles, and many other urban centres have permanent locations, but are cyclical in the sense that the vendors and their stalls come and go over time; gala events such as Macy's Thanksgiving Day Parade in New York City, Pasadena's Rose Parade on New Year's Day, New Orlean's Mardi Gras, and Minneapolis's summer Aquatennial Parades have defined routes and the support of necessary city services. (Friedmann, 1990)

This chapter will discuss the difficulties of planning for hallmark events given the short time-span in which the planning process will have to operate. Emphasis will be placed on the various factors which combine to ensure the success or otherwise of events. Items which will be discussed include intergovernmental relations, the establishment of planning structures, the role of public participation in the planning process and the need for careful event design.

Why Plan for Events?

The perceived potential of hallmark events to contribute to economic growth and attract investment and tourism has been almost universally sought by government and industry. However, in the rush to catch the tourist dollar 'relatively little thought is generally given to the nature of the planning process with which to maximise the benefits of tourism for the host community' (Hall, 1989b, p.20). Furthermore, 'while the short term impact of the architecture and planning is an important element in the effective staging of a hallmark event, it is usually the long term effect of the architecture and planning that is of major consequence to the host community. Many events are now remembered by their architectural and planning legacies rather than the event itself' (Kelly, 1989, pp.263–4).

Physical evidence of either the failure or lack of event planning is seen in the costly 'white elephants' that may be left once an event is over. For example, the long-term debt of the City of Montreal for the construction of the 1976 Olympic Games stadium; the ongoing financial support of the Brisbane City Council for the Queen Elizabeth II Stadium constructed for the 1982 Commonwealth Games; the long delay before the 1988 Brisbane Expo site was redeveloped; and the difficulties of Perth, Western Australia, and Christchurch, New Zealand, in finding events which can utilise their respective Commonwealth Games stadia. Social evidence of the failure of event planning is witnessed in the social dislocation and community impacts which marred the 1986 Vancouver Expo, the 1987 America's Cup, and the 1988 Brisbane Expo (See Chapter 4). Hence, effective planning measures are essential not only for the short-term success of the hallmark event itself but also in realising the longer-term benefits that can accrue to a community in the holding of such events (Hall, 1989b, p.20; Palmer, 1989).

Planning is 'an ordered sequence of operations designed to lead to the achievement of either a single goal or to a balance between several goals' (Hall, 1970, p.4). Tourism planning occurs in a number of forms (development, infrastructure, labour force, promotion and marketing), a number of structures (different government and industry organisations), and a number of scales (international, national, regional, local, sectoral) (Hall, 1991, p.98). The emergence of public concern over social, economic and environmental impacts resulting from tourism development have led to demands for government regulation and planning of touristic activity. As Smith (1977, p.6) noted: 'the economist and the planner, frequently cite the gross profits to be derived from tourism but gloss over the real human costs of tourism residual in the disruption of locally-functioning economic systems without providing sustained, proven alternatives'. Therefore, from this perspective, event planning 'should be concerned with the anticipation and regulation of the effects of the event on the host community, and the promotion of associated development in a manner which maximises short- and long-term economic, environmental and social benefits (Hall, 1989b, p.21). However, according to Armstrong (1986), from an examination of thirty international mega-events and projects, one of the great myths concerning such events is that they are planned according to a rational planning process:

> the planners who worked on the projects had one main role and that was to provide support for decisions already made. The planning process for prestige projects excludes the following traditional stages: recognition and definition of the problem, definition of the planning task, data collection, analysis and forecasting, determination of constraints, testing of alternatives, plan evaluation and project evaluation (1986, p.18).

Instead, the typical planning process of mega-events is outlined in Table 7.1. Furthermore, Armstrong went on to argue that the greater the level of government involvement the higher will be the cost overruns and concluded, 'that the less government involvement in the design, construction, and operation of an event, ... the more cost effective it will be' (1986, p.18).

Tourism planning, and hence planning for hallmark events, has generally followed a top-down style of planning and promotion that has left tourism 'destination communities with little input or control over their own destinies'

Table 7.1   The typical planning process for international events

Stage	Characteristics
1	Preliminary, vague or subjective identification of a need for a specific project.
2	Development of a cursory report.
3	Decision taking
4	Development of a plan to justify the project
5	Building programme
6	Implementation

Source: Armstrong, J., 1986, p.20

(Murphy, 1985, p.153). This centralist style of planning has had mixed outcomes. Tourism has contributed, in some circumstances, to rapid economic growth and regional development, but its accompanying impacts and spillover effects have often been ignored (Mathieson and Wall, 1982; Getz, 1986; Hall, 1991). One result of the failure of government, industry and planners to meet community needs and concerns has been the development of negative resident attitudes towards tourists and the tourist industry, and a level of tourist dissatisfaction with the destination (Pearce, 1980; Hall, 1991). However, if government and private industry seek to use hallmark events as a mechanism to attract tourism and investment, then they simply cannot afford such negative attitudes. This is because, 'Tourism, like no other industry, relies on the goodwill and cooperation of local people because they are part of the product. Where development and planning does fit in with local aspirations and capacities, resistance and hostility can raise the cost of business or destroy the industry's potential altogether' (Murphy, 1985, p.153). Therefore, a careful consideration of the dynamics of event planning is a necessary condition for the successful hosting of hallmark events in terms of the event's objectives. Consequently, successful event planning will need to 'manage the precarious balance between success and spirit' (Bonnemaison, 1990, p.29) which characterises hallmark events, festivals and community celebrations.

The Planning Challenge

One of the major problems in planning events is that 'more often than not, a successful event acquires its own momentum and it becomes difficult to maintain community identity when the number of participants grows every year' (Bonnemaison, 1990, p.27). Therefore, event organisers have to find ways to guide growth while still maintaining the features of the event which made it popular in the first place. For example, in planning for events as large as a World Fair or the Olympic Games, substantial problems emerge in the provision of facilities, infrastructure, accommodation, security and transport.

Table 7.2   Estimated impact on net international arrivals in Sydney through hosting of the 2000 Summer Olympic Games

Year	Pre Games preparation (000's)	Direct Games (000's)	Induced Volume (range) (000's)	Totals (000's)
1994	1.0	–	30	30–31
1995	1.0	–	33–65	34–66
1996	1.5	–	71–141	72–142
1997	1.5	–	113–151	114–153
1998	7.0	–	160–240	167–247
1999	14.0	–	213–340	227–354
2000	–	100–124	224–448	324–572
2001	–	–	241–335	241–385
2002	–	–	207–311	207–311
2003	–	–	167–223	167–223
2004	–	–	120	120
Totals	26.0	100–124	1578–2455	1703–2604

Source: McGeoch, 1991, p.5

The Summer Olympics are undoubtedly the world's largest regular sporting mega-event the scale of which is enormous. For example, the estimated impact on net international arrivals of Sydney's hosting of the Games in 2000 is indicated in Table 7.2. Furthermore, in the case of Sydney's bid for the 2000 Summer Olympics planning is underway for an international competition of 16 days consisting of:

- approximately 10,000 athletes in one location;
- around 4.8 million ticket sales;
- 550,000–800,000 individual spectators; with a likely 35 per cent of those from interstate or overseas;
- 9,000 representatives of television, radio and press media; and
- television audiences in excess of 2.4 billion people (McGeoch, 1991, p.2).

In order to meet the demands of the Olympics the planning of the venues, facilities and operational arrangements necessary for the Games will require the provision of

- venues for 29 Olympic sports, plus one or two demonstration sports, and appropriate training facilities; everything from athletics, football and weight-lifting to synchronised swimming and canoeing;
- an Olympic Village for 15,000 athletes and team personnel (in essence a new suburb);
- a media village for 6,000 media representatives and other village accommodation for judges and events officials (1,500 people);
- a media centre comprising international broadcasting and press centres (60-70,000m^2);
- services plans for transport/medical/security/quarantine/catering and others;

• appropriate capacity in infrastructure and telecommunications; and
• financial planning and budgeting for games hosting. (McGeoch, 1991, p.2)

On the other hand, smaller events can also have a dramatic demand on host communities. As noted in the opening chapter, a hallmark event can be described as such in relation to the size of the community which is hosting the event. Therefore, all cities and communities hosting an event need to take careful consideration of the demands that an event will make on their infrastructure and human resources.

The Planning Response

Considered event planning has the potential to minimise negative impacts, and maximise economic and social returns to the host community. Nevertheless, event planning may appear as a contradiction because tourism implies non-directed, voluntary and personal goal-oriented travel and 'free-enterprise' development (Gunn, 1977, 1988). However, unregulated tourism development would 'lead to the degradation of the physical and social resource base upon which tourism depends. Therefore, what is being planned is not the travel experience itself but the opportunity to achieve that experience within an appropriate economic, environmental and social setting for the hosts' (Hall, 1991, p.102).

While the desirability for event planning is now generally recognised, the form and method of the most effective method of planning remains a contested concept (Hall, 1991). Gunn (1988) has identified a number of key elements in the development of an overall approach towards tourism planning:

a) only planning can avert negative impacts, although for planning to be effective, all 'actors' must be involved – not just professional planners, government, and the private sector;
b) tourism is often symbiotic with conservation values, not a conflicting use with irreconcilably incompatible objectives or effects;
c) planning should be pluralistic, and integrate social, economic and physical dimensions and concerns;
d) planning is political, and as such there is a vital need to take into account societal objectives and balance these in the context of other (often conflicting) aspirations;
e) tourism planning must be strategic and integrative; and
f) tourism planning must have a regional planning perspective – because many problems arise at the interface of smaller areas and/or impacts may spill over from one locale to another, a broader planning horizon is essential.

The elements identified by Gunn (1988) provide a valuable basis for realising the benefits of event tourism. However, 'the consequences of tourism development are wide ranging and often unpredictable. As a result, planning can often only articulate concerns or uncertainties, society must guide planners in assessing their acceptability' (Hall, 1991, p.102). Nevertheless, given the economic, social and political dimensions of hallmark events (see Chapters 3, 4 and 5), it is apparent that a 'self-conscious approach' to event planning and policy-making

> is necessary at all levels of government. Presently most decisions are made on a case-by-case basis, and are dictated by common sense. Policy planning needs to occur at all three levels of government (municipal, regional, and national), since extensive research is needed before adequate policy can be formulated and guidelines developed for both cyclical and temporary urbanism. (Bonnemaison, 1990, p.31)

As the following sections indicate, therefore, planning offers numerous possibilities to assist in the hosting of events through the establishment of appropriate management structures, encouraging public participation in event planning, the development of appropriate facilities and land use, and ensuring that events fit in to the communities in which they are held.

The Establishment of Management Structures

The establishment of appropriate management structures is a basic task of event organisers. As Chapter 6 indicated, the manner in which event management is structured will affect how management activities are organised and operationalised. Event organisations can serve several purposes: they can manage and coordinate events, they can bid for events and they can act as a link between government and the host community.

Given the 'organizational axiom that every required function must be clearly vested in some specific role' (Katz and Kahn, 1966, p.210), responsibilities for large-scale events are often placed within specifically established agencies or coordinating committees (Hall, 1989b). For example, New Zealand has a Special Events Unit operating within the tourism ministry which assists in the development and marketing of event tourism opportunities. In the case of the 1987 America's Cup in Western Australia, an intergovernmental committee was established consisting of members of Commonwealth and State Cabinet and the Mayor of Fremantle in order 'to ensure the fullest co-operation and co-ordination between Commonwealth, State and local government' in the handling of the America's Cup Defence Series (America's Cup Support Group, 1984, p.2). In addition, both the State and Federal Governments established special groups to coordinate America's Cup activities, although it was only after substantial pressuring and lobbying that the State and Commonwealth (Federal) Governments agreed to use existing agency and local government structures for managing the development of Cup-related facilities and infrastructure (Hipkins, 1989).

In order to secure the cooperation of all levels of government and especially municipalities in the Perth metropolitan region, perhaps the most effective means of gaining the assistance of the relevant government agencies was the Aus.$82 million of State and Federal funds that was made available for America's Cup-related projects, a technique of constituent policy-making described by Lowi (1972) as 'log-rolling'. However, perhaps significantly in terms of the coordination of the various Cup related activities no allowance was made for wider public participation in the policy-making process beyond the involvement of municipal authorities (America's Cup Information Centre 1985, 1987; Hall, 1989b). Nevertheless, there were still significant benefits to be gained from the Cup for some of the local residents as funds were spent on renewing and expanding infrastructure, foreshore improvements, developing community facilities, and the construction of new public housing for low income residents expected to be displaced by Cup activities. While many of the projects had been planned for some time, the Cup provided the opportunity to tap State and Commonwealth Government funding that may have otherwise been unavailable (Hipkins, 1989).

Specialised event bodies or corporations may also be established at the national or provincial/state level in order to secure national and international events so as to attract tourists and promote investment opportunities. For example, the International Sporting Events Council (ISEC) was established in New South Wales, Australia, in April 1989, in order to examine the feasibility of international events and the bidding for international events. Since that time ISEC has successfully bid for a number of events including:

• 25th Congress and General Assembly of the General Association of International Sports Federations (GAISF), 16–19 October 1991
• World Amateur Boxing Championships, 13–25 November 1991
• Womens World Basketball Championships, July 1994
• Mens World Hockey Cup, September/October 1994

In addition, it should be noted that by establishing a track record of successful events at one level, government and private industry may be able to bid for larger, supposedly more lucrative events. For example, the hosting of the GAISF Congress was a component of Sydney's bid for the 2000 Summer Olympics and the hosting of other major sporting events. Indeed, it was not coincidental that during the Congress, held in facilities at Darling Harbour earmarked for Olympic activities should Sydney's bid be successful, every effort was made to welcome GAISF delegates and demonstrate that Sydney was a sporting centre capable of hosting international sporting events. Similarly, in April 1991, the New South Wales Government gave the race promoter of the Australian 500cc Motorcycle Grand Prix Aus$400,000 in '"sponsorship" in exchange for trackside signs "advertising" Sydney's Olympic 2000 bid: thus one potential financial disaster was used as an excuse to pour yet more money into another... These same people now propose a similar project expected to cost more than $1,600 million' (Duffy, 1991/92, p.12). (In September, 1991, the State Government took over the circuit and more than Aus$30 million of bad loans and loan guarantees from the private consortium involved with the race track. The total cost for the government, when items such as roads and land purchases are included, appears to be more than $90 million [Duffy, 1991/92, p.12]).

Local governments can encourage and manage events in a variety of ways. Cities and towns will often create support structures within the local government administration in order to encourage community initiatives in the development and hosting of events. For example, San Francisco, 'one of the first cities to recognize the positive aspects of cyclical event and... create policies to support their growth' (Bonnemaison, 1990, p.26), provided a support structure for events by institutionalising a Hotel Tax Fund of one per cent a year on hotel revenues which was then distributed to the arts organisations that attracted tourists to the city. This meant that event providers as diverse as the San Francisco Ballet, the San Francisco Opera, and event organisers such as City Celebration were able to utilise the funds to maintain and promote cultural events. In addition, San Francisco maintains a common pool of equipment which is then rented to community event organisers at relatively low prices. However, the City also has costs to cover from the hosting of events. In the summer of 1988 San Francisco passed a law which required event organisers to cover part of the costs of policing events such as Chinese New Year (US$60,000) and the Gay and Lesbian Freedom Day (US$32,000). Similarly, street food vendors were required to pay a $50 fee for a health department check at the time of establishment. As Bonnemaison (1990, p.26) observed: 'These new measures were badly received by small event organisers who raised the flag of free speech and refused to pay extra for public services such as police supervision. As San Francisco had encouraged outdoor cyclical events, this sudden change of attitude, due to financial stress, came as a great surprise to its citizens'.

The support structure provided by San Francisco can be contrasted with a city which encourages the establishment of events but does not provide a detailed support structure. For example, in the case of Vancouver, British Columbia, the Provincial Government has contracted a local insurance company to insure event organisations for a small fee (about Can$100 for a one day event). Thereby assisting in the hosting of events in which organisers have other substantial costs to bear such as barricades and road closures (Bonnemaison, 1990).

Public Participation in the Planning Process

Perception of the possibility of negative impacts on the physical and social well-being of a community, such as resident displacement and architectural pollution, may give rise to interest group politics and a call for greater public participation to which the government, faced with the need to quickly construct infrastructure, may be unable to respond. The importance and prestige attached to hallmark events by government often means a commitment to 'fast track' planning practices which ignore community resistance to either the hosting of the event or the construction of associated infrastructure (Hall, 1989c, 1991; Roche, 1991). As Thorne, Munro-Clarke and Boers, (1987) commented in the case of Sydney's Darling Harbour bicentennial project:

> National 'hallmark' events... are prone to generate (at least in prospect) a heady atmosphere. In some government quarters in particular, time comes to be experienced as a count-down interval, in which everything must be made ready for the day the show begins, and any call for deliberation amounts to sabotage. In the excitement of putting a good face on things, more sober, long-term commitments are apt to be lost sight of or denied, and normal legal safeguards are set aside, in the spirit of a state-of-emergency.

The exigencies created by the demands of events led, in the case of the Darling Harbour Redevelopment Project, 'the focal point of the bicentenary celebrations for New South Wales' (Unsworth, 1984, p.1485), to the denial of consultation and community participation in the decision-making process. All this taking 'place under a government whose own recent legislation explicitly enshrined community participation and provided for the dissemination of information through the publication of environmental impact statements' (Thorne and Munro-Clark, 1989, p.156). As Premier Unsworth commented 'It means we are determined to have this done – to see it finished – and we're not going to be frustrated by legal technicalities... This is a national project, it's something for Australia, and we cannot have government aldermen or anyone else frustrating our intentions to achieve one of the great features of 1988' (*The Australian*, 2 May, 1984, p.13).

In the case of public participation in the case of the Sydney 2000 Summer Olympics bid consultations took place with significant individuals and leaders of interest groups including labour, key public sector agencies, and the Director of the NSW Office of Aboriginal Affairs. In addition, a telephone poll was conducted to gauge reaction to a potential Sydney bid for the 2000 Summer Olympics. According to the Sydney Olympic Games Review Committee (1990, p.47), 'The poll showed widespread community support for a bid by Sydney... with 82% of respondents either strongly or mildly in favour'. Furthermore, 'While the Committee felt the poll results were more favourable than members had anticipated, the results were nevertheless highly encouraging', and concluded 'As a result of these meetings and consultations, the Committee is confident that a Sydney bid would have bi-partisan political support and the support of leading media executives and news editors, the aboriginal community, the NSW Labor Council and key trade unions, along with critical public sector agencies' (1990, p.47). The Sydney Olympic bid exercise supports the notion that Olympic bids are increasingly becoming tests of public relations strength (Hiller, 1989, 1990; Thorne and Munro-Clark, 1989) in which public participation in the decision-making process and community consultation occurs through media opinion polls rather than any independent social analysis or formal, ongoing, process of community participation.

> Moreover, assessment of 'public opinion' in a contrived climate of ignorance is no more than a propaganda exercise. If any weight at all is to be placed upon the corrective value of the judgement of ordinary citizens in such practical issues, it needs to be informed by an adequate knowledge of real contexts and consequences, and some basis for comparing and weighing alternatives. (Thorne and Munro-Clark, 1989, p.168)

The failure of public participatory measures in event planning is not restricted to Australia. For example, the proponents of the city of London's (Ontario, Canada) bid for the 1991 Pan American Games or the 1994 Commonwealth Games did not seek public opinion and comment. 'At no stage during the bid preparation process was any real attempt made to determine the reaction of the local population to the proposal to host the Games. This is not surprising perhaps, as residents' viewpoints are rarely part of the decision making process for such an event' (Butler and Grigg, 1989, p.144). As Heenan (1978, p.30) recognised, 'the process of tourism development only occurs when the permanent residents of the community are convinced that attracting visitors is essential for the area's future survival and growth'. Similarly, Butler and Grigg, (1989, p.151) reported, 'if citizens are uninformed about the details of... impacts before the event is being staged, or have not been involved in the decision making process, they may not be prepared to take the consequences willingly'

'The call for participatory planning is a criticism of the business and physical orientation of past tourism planning and its failure to keep abreast with developments in urban and environmental planning' (Murphy, 1985, p.171). However, there are a number of other reasons for encouraging community participation in event planning. According to Hall (1989b, pp.33–4), community involvement encourages greater variation and local flavour in the nature of the event and the tourist destination, assists in the protection of the tourist resource, and reduces opposition to tourist development. Events are 'tourism products, but they cannot simply be built like a hotel, nor forced to become tourist attractions if their organizers or host communities are opposed or uninterested. The promotion of [events] as tourist attractions without regard for the wishes of the community is not only questionable ethics, but also likely to be unproductive' (Getz, 1991a, p.164). Indeed, by using consultative measures to encourage residents to assist in the planning of and for the event, residents may come to feel that they 'own' the event, so it becomes a source of community pride which may actually encourage further appropriate tourism development (Cooke, 1982). Public participation is therefore an essential part of impact monitoring and event evaluation, for who is the event for if not the public?

> The inclusion of complex impact considerations in a tourism planning process strongly implies relatively wide community involvement in impact assessment. Increased involvement in estimating complex impacts contributes to the reliability of the estimates. Such involvement also serves as a constructive vehicle for appraisal of impacts by individuals and groups other than those which are 'expert', a body of interests most planners believe should be included in a planning process. (Runyan and Wu, 1979, p.451)

Site Considerations

Event planners have to consider a number of site and management considerations in the event planning process, including facility design and land use, site planning, accessibility, security, and environmental constraints. The following sections discuss these factors and provide several examples of strategies by which planners can successfully manage site attributes.

Facilities and Land Use

The issue of facilities and land use is critical for festivals and events. A pleasant, attractive, site is integral to an event's success, of course a motivation for the hosting of an event may be the development of such an attractive space. Parks provide one such opportunity for the hosting of events. Indeed, in many small towns the park becomes the focal point for anniversaries, national celebrations and picnic days. Nevertheless, park space may become overused and the hosting of events may prevent recreationists from utilising the open space of the park. Therefore, municipalities should strive not only to develop more open space in cities but also to make such open space usable. For example, in the Australian city of Brisbane, the city government has encouraged the holding of Sunday markets in the central business district in spaces between riverside office blocks and along the walk path beside the river.

Another strategy designed to facilitate the hosting of events is to allocate permanent space to event buildings or structures. For example, in Australia, New Zealand, and many parts of rural North America and Europe, nearly every town and city has a showground designed to accommodate the annual agricultural show, which is utilised for sports events the remainder of the year. However, such facilities tend to have a relatively low rate of utilisation and their upkeep and maintenance may provide a major drain on agricultural society and municipal funds.

Bandshells or music bowls are another means of creating spaces within parks and other open areas which may be utilised for certain types of events. However, yet again, they require significant funds (often municipal) for their upkeep. Moreover, as Bonnemaison (1990, p.31) argued, 'They are... unsuccessful, not only because their acoustic qualities are limited to a certain kind of performance, but more important, because they are permanent. It is better to have the space open and free when nothing is happening, as unused facilities create a vacant feeling while a simple open space does not'. Instead, municipalities should seek to develop multi-use facilities which are flexible enough in design to be able to meet the demands of a variety of events and community needs.

One of the greatest problems in event facility design and management is the issue of long-term use, particularly if the event for which the facility was constructed is 'lost' or ceases to run. For example, the Asian Games Centre in Beijing, China, built to accommodate the Eleventh Asian Games held in September 1990, converted to use as an international convention and exhibition complex known as the Beijing International Convention Centre once the Games were over (China Travel Press, 1989). Furthermore, if a facility is constructed for a specific type of event then it has to ensure that it can continue to host that event for a period which makes the facility economical. For example, in examining the development of a raceway facility on the western suburbs of Sydney, to host major race meetings, such as the Australian Motorbike Grand Prix, the State Treasury reported:

Over the 20 year project period, the raceway generates substantial benefits, which at a 7% real discount rate are estimated to have a present value of $478 million and are more than twice the costs of $230 million (all figures in 1990 dollars). However, the analysis has shown that, from a community view, the success of the raceway hinges on the ability to attract major international motor sports events. The above levels of benefit and cost are based on the assumption that one major event will be held at the raceway each year. (New South Wales Treasury, 1990, p.i)

Table 7.3   Factors in site planning and preparation

Factor	Consideration
Space	The site should have enough space to accommodate participants, visitors and any displays.
Transport	The site should be accessible by both public and private transport. Clear guidance should be given to visitors as to the best means to reach the event site. Adequate parking should be available for private vehicles. If on-site parking is in short supply then satellite parking may need to be considered.
Visitor flow	Access to the site should be controlled not only for visitor safety but also to ensure that admission fees are collected. Temporary fencing may be required if an outdoor venue is utilised.
	Displays and exhibits should have a logical flow with themes and focal points being established for display areas. Depending on the management strategy and the nature of the event, food and drink stalls can be either bunched together or spread out so as to encourage even flow.
	Information booths, clear signage, and other interpretive facilities will greatly improve the flow of visitors and lead to increased visitor satisfaction.
Infrastructure	Power and water must be available on site. Adequate toilet facilities for participants and visitors must be provided. Portable toilets may need to be provided.
	The event site and associated areas such as car parks must have adequate lighting.
	Garbage plans must be available throughout the site and visitors should be persuaded to utilise them. Nothing will make an event look more unattractive to visitors than an unclean site. Garbage will also need to be regularly cleaned from the site. Volunteer groups may be able to assist in site clean up duties.
	First aid and emergency support must have access to the event.
	Participants in the event must have clear on-site access.
Site problems	On-site areas such as unpaved spaces which may become muddy or worn with overuse should be avoided or, if that is not possible, modified so as to minimise damage and visitor inconvenience.
	Inconvenience to residents in the vicinity of the event, through such things as noise and unavailability of parking, should be minimised.

Source: After United States Department of Housing and Urban Development, 1981; Canadian Government Office of Tourism, 1982; Tourism South Australia, 1990a

Site Planning

A number of criteria can be identified as being significant in on-site planning. Table 7.3 presents a checklist of site planning and preparation factors which event organisers need to manage. Visitor flow is a primary consideration in site planning and managers will need to examine how walkways will assist or hinder visitor traffic. Enclaves, such as open squares, may be created in the site design to provide a point for visitors to mingle. In addition, focal or reference points can be established which can serve to attract visitors to specific items of interest and may also help orient the visitor to the overall site design.

Accessibility

Accessibility is a major problem in event planning. Increased traffic can place stress on existing public transport networks and road infrastructure (O'Connell, 1985). Strategies which can increase the accessibility of events to patrons include

- increased advertising of available public transport;
- placement of change and ticket booths if this is not already provided by transport authorities;
- advertising available commercial parking lots in the areas surrounding the event site;
- provision of discounted tickets which link public transport use and event admission;
- provision of shuttle services from parking lots and public transport points, such as railway stations, to the event; and
- provision of more on-ground parking through removal of exhibitor and part-time staff parking.

In the case of the Klondike Days Exposition in Edmonton the latter two strategies have been used with some success. The operation of a free shuttle system between the commercial parking lots to the Exposition cost Can$12,000 with a per capita cost use of 97 cents, while although the removal of parking privileges proved unpopular it did lead to an 18 per cent increase in parking revenue to the Exposition (Hughes, 1986, p.229).

Security Security is an important element of event planning. While the vast majority of events do not experience the political protests outlined in Chapter 5, event managers nevertheless have to ensure that sites are secure. Good security not only serves to ensure the protection of personnel and property but also assists in creating a feeling of visitor confidence in the event. Mechanisms to encourage participant and visitor safety include good lighting, uniformed police officers and/ or security guards.

Environmental Constraints Appropriate site planning should also include consideration of the environmental impacts of the event and associated facilities, not only on the immediate site but also on the associated areas (Hall and Selwood, 1989). As the majority of events are hosted in urban areas, the majority of environmental impacts are concentrated on urban resource management concerns such as sewage and effluent disposal, littering, water quality, air quality, and aesthetic effects, all of which have significant flow-on effects on social quality-of-life indicators (Andressen, 1981; Maher, 1986). For example, submissions to the Social Impact Steering Committee regarding the implications of Melbourne hosting the 1996 Summer Olympics, identified the following areas of environmental concern:

- there may be problems of air pollution, particularly if the volume of traffic is increased;
- the storage and transport of dangerous chemicals near the Olympic Village and other venues will pose a problem;
- the process for approving new projects should not circumvent existing planning guidelines;
- the impact of the large number of visitors on waste disposal facilities should be assessed;
- the opportunity should be taken in construction for the Olympics to implement and demonstrate energy-efficient design principles; and
- any new developments should not affect existing natural habitats (Economic Impact Resources Consulting, 1989, p.67)

The development of event facilities in rural regions, such as the construction of ski runs for the Winter Olympic Games at Lake Placid, Calgary and Albertville, may have considerable physical and aesthetic impacts on a natural or semi-natural area (Wall and Guzzi, 1987). Similarly, outdoor sporting events, such as whitewater rafting or endurance competitions, which attract significant amounts of spectators and competitors may have to be closely monitored in order to ensure that environmentally sensitive areas are not damaged through littering or trampling.

The emergence of a greater degree of environmental awareness among many communities about the negative impacts of tourism on natural and cultural heritage and the corresponding growth in conservation organisations has meant that government, tourism developers and event organisers can no longer ignore the environmental impacts of event tourism. In addition, many countries now have environmental impact legislation in place which requires the proponents of large-scale projects, such as those associated with mega-events, to provide environmental impact information to legislatures or environmental protection agencies prior to final approval for the project being given. However, a major concern in the environmental impact assessment process is that the size of investment in both the impact report and the project itself is so substantial that only marginal changes, if any, will be made to projects by overseeing bodies (Hall and Selwood, 1989).

Making Events Unique

Every year across Canada scores of ethnic and multicultural festivals are held. Some are small, one-day neighbourhood gatherings which invoke a few hundred local participants from a particular ethnic community, while others offer a week-long showcase of dozens of ethnic groups and attract hundreds of thousands of tourists from far and wide. Many of these ethno-cultural festivals feature ethnic food and drink, song and dance, parades, and even beauty contests. One is reminded of ancient Rome where garish spectacles were staged for the denizens of the Forum who sought no more than bread and circus-like entertainment. Are ethnic and multicultural festivals merely showy spectacles orchestrated merely for the pleasure of voyeuristic onlookers, or do they represent an authentic celebration of a group's cultural heritage? (Dawson, 1991, p.35)

Authenticity is one of the key motivational forces for visitors to many cultural and religious events and festivals. For example, Pyo, Uysal and Howell (1988) reported that authenticity was a sought after experience for visitors to the Seoul Olympic Games. However, some tourism commentators, such as Boorstin (1973), have argued that much modern tourism trivialises culture and has led to the creation of superficial and contrived tourist experiences which he described as 'pseudo-events', 'In order to satisfy the exaggerated expectations of tour agents and tourists, people everywhere obligingly became dishonest mimics of themselves. To provide a full schedule of events at the best seasons and at convenient hours, they travesty their solemn rituals, holidays, and folk celebrations – all for the benefit of tourists' (Boorstin 1973, p.103). Similarly, according to Getz (1989, p.127), many of the tangible products of events, such as competitions, entertainment, exhibitions, merchandising (food and beverage, souvenirs, speciality sales), parades and shows, 'are really a "facade" presented to the public. They are the mechanisms by which visitor experiences are partially created, although there must be a synergistic process involving these products and many intangibles to create atmosphere or "ambience" that makes events special'.

MacCannell (1973, 1976) argued that tourists are often caught in an all-embracing 'tourist space', constructed by the tourism industry, in which authenticity is staged. However, as Cohen (1979) noted, such 'staged authenticity' may not be an inevitable consequence of tourism. Cohen (1979) identified a dual interpretation of 'authenticity' which distinguished between the perceptions of the tourist and the nature of the scene provided by the hosts (Table 7.4). The 'ideal' situation is one in which both the hosts and the tourist accept that an event is authentic (i.e. authenticity). Alternatively, events may be deliberately staged for tourists but the tourist may accept the contrived scene as real (i.e. staged authenticity). The reverse of staged authenticity occurs where although the event is real for the host, the visitor may suspect that the scene is inauthentic and that the tourist is being manipulated (i.e. denial of authenticity). The final situation is that of an 'overt tourism space', in which an event is openly contrived by the tourist industry and is seen as such by the tourist (i.e. contrived).

Cohen's typology is a useful conceptual device for analysing the nature of the tourist experience at particular events and the satisfaction of visitors, hosts and participants (Hall, 1991). On this basis, while encouraging communities throughout the state to become involved in event and festival tourism, Tourism South Australia has cautioned that 'it is only in exceptional circumstances that an event will succeed outside its legitimate location (1990a, p.4). The legitimate location for both host and guest is one where the event will be authentic.

Notions of authenticity are particularly important in arts and cultural festivals

Table 7.4   Types of touristic situations

		Tourist's impression of scene		
Nature of scene		Real		Staged
Real	(1)	Authentic	(3)	Denial of authenticity (staging suspicion)
Staged	(2)	Staged authenticity (covert tourist space)	(4)	Contrived (Overt space)

Source: Cohen, 1979, p.26

where authenticity is one of the major motivational forces behind the special interest tourism market (Hall and Weiler, 1992; Zeppel and Hall, 1992) and in religious and sacred events. As noted in Chapter 2, in the case of many cultural and folk festivals the motivations of the organisers are crucial to the experience of what is being celebrated (Wilson and Udall, 1982; Dawson, 1991). For example, in the case of the Festival of Pacific Arts, a major international cultural festival which brings together participants from throughout the Pacific, Zeppel (1992) reported that the special interest by international visitors in experiencing 'authentic' Pacific culture has contributed to the Festival becoming a major tourist event.

> The participating cultural groups at the Festival varied in the amount of western influence, the degree of authenticity in costumes and dance styles and the extent to which performances were oriented towards a tourist audience. While dance styles were largely based on traditional forms, the attire worn by performers ranged from traditional costumes to modified traditional items (commercial face paints, artificial leis) and also contemporary clothing (sarongs, thongs, watches). The overall colour, drama and spectacle of the Festival, however, more than fulfilled most visitor expectations of experiencing 'traditional' Pacific culture. (Zeppel, 1992, p.73)

The growing success of the Festival of the Pacific as a tourist attraction (Zeppel, 1992) is indicative of the problem in keeping events meaningful and authentic to both participant and visitor. As Friedmann (1990) noted, although many large-scale urban festivities 'are successful and appear to grow in size every year, they also tend to become increasingly commercialized and... the problem is not how to popularize such events, but how to maintain the precarious balance between success and the spirit that must be at the core of such activities'. Therefore, cities should not only be planned to ensure that communities are consulted and can participate in event decision-making processes but they should also be planned with events in mind (see Corporation of the City of Melbourne, 1989). As Bonnemaison (1990, p.31) observed 'planning has traditionally been involved with the permanent urban fabric, with little thought for a cyclical layer'.

Planning of the physical environment for hallmark events requires the creation of pre-industrialised urban spaces such as squares and piazzas which allow the holding of fairs and markets. The design of permanent event space is akin to

Jackson's (1984) conception of a 'third landscape'. In the third landscape, 'place means the people in it, not simply the natural environment', and mobility is accommodated within the design and planning process. According to Bonnemaison (1990, p.32), the notion of the third landscape helps explain why 'community events are so successful: they satisfy a tremendous need to feel part of something'. Indeed, she goes on to argue that 'rediscovering the value of cyclical events, whether a small farmers' market or a large festival, is the first step toward realizing a balance between permanent and temporary urbanism'.

Towards Appropriate Planning Strategies for Hallmark Events

> Part of what makes an event special is its infrequency, its uniqueness, even its spontaneity – all of which are antithetical to total programming and control. (Getz, 1991a, p.13).

Tourism planning does not just refer specifically to tourism development and promotion, although these are certainly important. Appropriate tourism planning may well need no tourism at all. Community-oriented tourism planning means development within, rather than of, the community. Therefore, tourism must be integrated within the wider planning process in order to promote certain goals of economic, social and environmental enhancement that may be achieved through appropriate tourism development (Hall, 1989b). For example, in the case of the Melbourne bid for the 1996 Summer Olympics, special attention was paid to the development of a preliminary social impact statement (Economic Impact Resources Consulting, 1989) that met the objectives of the Victorian Government's (1984) economic strategy:

- to facilitate economic growth through improving the economic environment; and,
- to enhance Victoria's 'competitive strengths' through identifying and encouraging particular strengths or potential strengths of the Victorian economy;

and the principles of the social justice strategy (1987):

- *equity* – to reduce disadvantage caused by unequal access to economic resources and power;
- *access* – to increase access to essential goods and services according to need;
- *participation* – to expand opportunities for genuine participation by all Victorians in decisions which affect their lives; and
- *rights* – to protect, extend and ensure the effective exercise of equal legal, industrial and political rights.

An example of the way in which the influence of the principles and objectives could have been operationalised is to be found in the area of the likely effect an Olympics might have on housing (for a discussion of studies of the impact of mega-events on housing refer to Chapter 4 on the social dimension of hallmark events). Although the Games would accelerate 'the continuing process of inner urban gentrification, with consequent increases in land values and private rents and pressure for land use changes' (Economic Impact Resources Consulting, 1989, p.43), it was also acknowledged that the Games would also provide opportunities to supply significant additions to the public housing stock which have aimed to compensate for any negative effects of the Games on prices, rents and tenure (Olympic Games Social Impact Assessment Steering Committee, 1989). In addition, the impacted communities would have been consulted through a series of public meetings, local government initiatives, and the activities of a social impact assessment panel which had 'the two-fold task of conducting consultations with community and special interest groups and assessing and developing strategies to minimize possible adverse effects of staging the Games' (Melbourne Olympic Candidature 1996, 1990, p.2).

This chapter supports the notion that event planning can meet the demands of both the physical and social fabric of a community. The establishment of appropriate planning and management structures, maximisation of the role of public participation in the planning process, and the development of the appropriate event and facility design, management and planning will all assist communities in meeting their objectives in hosting hallmark events. A community-oriented strategy is applicable in both large and small scale events and is essential for the maximisation of desired benefits to the host community, a point returned to in the final chapter. However, different types of hallmark events will offer themselves to different segments of the tourist market thereby setting new planning and management challenges. Therefore, event organisers must ensure that their event is marketed to ensure that there is an appropriate match between the event, visitors, and the host community, a point which is central to the event marketing process described in the next chapter.

8 Marketing, Sponsorship and Image

The underlying purposes and motivations of… celebrations are varied, but all of them to a greater or lesser extent are dependent upon the degree to which they can awaken interest and attract visitors from the locality, from the country as a whole and, more importantly from a national point of view, from abroad. Without those visitors and tourists the event is a failure and the cost out of all proportion, whatever the merits of the events. (Camacho, 1979, p.2)

Chapter 8 will examine the manner in which events are marketed and the images that they help create. The event marketing process will be outlined and attention given to the role of sponsorships in event management and promotion. The contribution that events can make to the development of positive destination images will also be discussed, while examples will be provided of the marketing strategies that are employed in promoting both the event and the destination area. The chapter will conclude with a discussion of the means by which the benefits of marketing hallmark events can be maximised.

The Event Marketing Process

Marketing is a critical element in the hosting and management of a successful event. To modify Kotler and Levy's (1969) definition of marketing in event terms: marketing is that function of event management that can keep in touch with the event's participants and visitors (consumers), read their needs and motivations, develop products that meet these needs, and build a communication programme which expresses the event's purpose and objectives. Certainly selling and influencing will be large components of event marketing; but, properly seen, selling follows rather than precedes the event management's desire to create experiences (products) which satisfy its consumers. Market research should be an integral part of event management and planning. For example, in 1983 the Canadian National Exhibition in Toronto established its own research department:

Through the results of our research surveys, we have the information which is used to tailor and design programs, events, and exhibits. Research results are employed in all aspects of our advertising, publicity, and promotion; from creative concepts through to media placement. Research also provides us with sales incentives and presentation material which are effective in attracting desirable sponsors and exhibitors. Finally, through our research we have the best means to check and review our across the board operations and make any necessary adjustments. (Oakes, 1986, p.208)

A successful marketing plan will focus on the development of a marketing process which revolves around activities and decisions in three main areas:

1. market segmentation and targeting;
2. market entry strategy, including time and location of event; and
3. marketing mix variables.

Unfortunately, many events are conducted without the benefit of a marketing plan or strategy. For example, in their survey of events and festivals in Ontario, Getz and Frisby (1987, p. 17) found that, 'Twenty-one organizations (43%) had a marketing plan, compared to 28 without. In 24 cases (46%), a visitor survey had been completed'. Although empirical evidence is scarce, it is highly likely that the Ontario situation is not unusual in international terms. While high profile mega-events such as international sporting events or national cultural festivals do tend to have clear marketing plans (Brissenden, 1987; Smith, 1987; Pyo, Cook and Howell, 1988; Coopers and Lybrand, 1989; Wells and Dunn, 1991), many mid-level and smaller size events do not (Shire of Bright, 1988). However, even at this scale, event managers can benefit from developing a marketing plan which is appropriate to the objectives of hosting an event. As noted in the quotation from Camacho (1979) at the beginning of this chapter, an event will not succeed unless it can meet the motivations, expectations and needs of the participants, which will often be the local community, and the visitors. Marketing is the key which will help make this possible. The following sections will examine the major elements of the event marketing process.

The Market: Market Segmentation and Targeting

Visitors to events may appear to organisers to be a diverse market. However, no event can be all things to all people. Therefore, it is essential that any community, destination or organisation that is planning an event should incorporate an under-standing of the behaviour of event visitors into their marketing and promotional strategies. Event managers should identify market segments which are in tune with the nature and character of an event or, alternatively, the event should be staged in such a way as to meet the needs of the market. A market segment is identifiable by grouping together all those potential participants and visitors with similar motivations and/or propensities towards particular types of events or features of events and/or particular ways of promoting and supplying them. Segments may be identified along three main lines:

Table 8.1   Demographic profile of American travellers participating in festival and special event travel

Attribute	Frequency	Per cent[1]
Age		
Under 30	177	33.8
30 to 50	229	43.8
51 to 64	68	13.0
65 or over	43	8.2
Sex		
Male	271	51.8
Female	243	46.5
Marital Status		
Single	166	31.7
Married	243	67.5
Family Size		
One or two	170	32.5
Three or four	242	46.3
Five or over	111	21.2
Education		
High School or less	237	45.3
Some college	138	26.4
Graduated from college	94	18.0
Graduate work	49	9.4
Income		
Under $25,000	165	31.5
25,000 to 39,000	150	28.7
40,000 to 59,000	99	18.9
60,000 or over	33	6.3

[1] Percentages do not total 100 due to non response

Source: Uysal, *et al.*, 1991, p.205

1 *Geographical segmentation*: Event organisers should know how many people there are in the 'catchment region' of both existing and planned events and what distances people are away from the event site in terms of different public and private modes of transport.

2. *Demographic segmentation*: Event markets may be segmented along the lines of such variables as age, sex, occupation, level of income, ethnic association, religion, level of education and class. For example, an ethnic festival which celebrates the culture of a particular ethnic group will obviously be an attraction to the members of that ethnic group.

3. *Psychographic segmentation*: Markets may be identified in terms of people's motivations and self-images. For example, some cultural events such as art exhibitions may be deliberately structured so as to appeal to 'up-scale' markets which seek exclusiveness, prestige, and status.

Nevertheless, whatever way the market is segmented, it should be emphasised that an attractive market for an event will be one in which:

- the market segment is of sufficient size to make the event viable;
- the market segment has the potential for growth;
- the market segment is not 'taken' or 'owned' by existing events; and
- the market segment has a relatively unsatisfied interest or motivation that the event can satisfy.

Size

While size is not everything in ensuring whether or not an event is successful, event organisers must be able to ensure that there are enough people to make the event financially viable. Again, the initial objectives and reasons for holding an event will be an important determinant in estimating the desired number of attendees. Event organisers must recognise that the larger the amount of purpose-built or utilised infrastructure and facilities needed for hosting an event, the larger will be the required audience to make such an event financially viable.

Growth

Although it is not essential that events must grow in size each year, event organisers may want, for example, to be able to ensure that the market can be expanded in order to repay investment on purpose-built infrastructure or to use the event as a means of encouraging increased visitation; and corresponding levels of employment and economic development. Nevertheless, in the case of many community-based events and festivals it is highly desirable that they do not grow in order to keep their local flavour and ensure community control of the event. However, in both the grow and non-grow options it is essential to recognise that events, like any product, will be part of a product/market life cycle and will have a definite life-span, a point that will be returned to at the end of the chapter.

Existing Events

Event organisers must be aware of how their event compares with other events and attractions that may be competing for the same or similar market segments. Therefore, event organisers must be aware of competition from other events and attractions in terms of their region, timing and markets. However, it should also be noted that existing events and attractions may also represent substantial opportunities for joint promotions and the 'piggy-backing' of one event onto another event or tourist attraction.

Motivations

Events, as with many tourist attractions, fulfil particular participant and visitor motivations (physical, cultural and social). Successful event organisation requires the satisfaction of those motivations. Therefore, it is essential that event managers become aware of the motivations and expectations of their participants and visitors through such techniques, for example, as visitor surveys (Mashiach, 1977; Groves, 1985a, b; Pyo, Uysal and Howell, 1988).

In a study of a sub-sample drawn from the 1985 national survey of American travel behaviour conducted for Tourism Canada, Uysal *et al.* (1991) examined the motivations and activities associated with a festival/special event/exhibition trip. For the purposes of the study, 'a festival/special event/exhibition trip was defined as a vacation taken primarily for the purposes of visiting a major theme park or exhibition or special event such as a Super Bowl, World's Fair, or Olympic Games' (1991, p.204). While the inclusion of theme park visitation may distort the overall profile of event travel, the study may still provide some insights into the motivations of event tourists. According to Uysal *et al.* (1991, p.205), in terms of demographic profile (Table 8.1):

> Descriptive analysis of the study revealed that US festival goers are more likely to be married, some college or less educated, and under fifty years of age (33.8% under 30; and 43.8% 30 to 50). They tend to visit or go on a festival/special event/exhibition trip with one or two (32.5%) or more family members (three to four people 46.3%; and five or over 21.2%). Almost 60 per cent of this group had an income of less than $40,000.

In terms of the motivations and desired event activities the findings of the Uysal *et al.* study suggested that, as may be expected, 'event attendees may not be homogeneous and may require a combination of segmentation strategies' (1991, p. 216). Family, excitement, socializing and relaxation were identified as significant motivations, an observation which supports a number of studies of hallmark events, for example Ley and Olds (1988) and Getz (1990). However, the importance attached to excitement as a motivation appeared to decline as age increases. If this is the case, the nature of the marketing process for particular events should be adapted to suit the needs of the target market. 'If the target market is made of older citizens, marketing should not emphasise excitement related elements of the event to these individuals. On the other hand if the target market is comprised of single young adults the element of excitement should be emphasized' (Uysal *et al.*, 1991, p. 217).

The Festival State: The South Australian Festival and Special Event Market Position South Australia has deliberately adopted festivals and special events as an integral component of its tourism marketing strategy and is known as 'The Festival State'. Using such premier events as the Adelaide Festival of the Arts and the Adelaide Grand Prix as the starting point, the state government has encouraged communities to develop their own festivals and events in order to enhance South Australia's attractions and image, broaden the travel experience for visitors, generate longer stay visitation, and encourage the state's residents to travel more within the state (Roeper, 1986; Hand, 1990; Hall, 1991).

Tourism South Australia has identified a number of benefits that a festival or special event can provide which may increase tourist visitation (Table 8.2).

Table 8.2   Consumer benefits of event visitation

Benefit	
Change	Experiencing something different to that at home
Escapism	Getting away from the humdrum of day to day existence
Indulgence	Being waited on and pampered
Understanding	A quest for learning about new, different or exciting cultures, places or lifestyles
Adventure	Doing things that are exciting, daring and challenging
Companionship	Making new contacts and friends

Source: Tourism South Australia, 1990a, p.4

However, depending on the nature of the event only some of these benefits will be provided. Furthermore, 'Organisers must offer and provide what the visitors want to see, do or experience otherwise they will not support the event. An important factor in presenting the right combination of experiences to visitors is to have the full support of the local community' (Tourism South Australia, 1990a, p.4). Nevertheless, event organisers in South Australia have been encouraged to focus on a market segment which allows for a specific set of experiences available at events to be matched with a particular set of consumer needs. According to Tourism South Australia (1990a, p.5) the priority target segment describes travellers that:

- are discerning and confident
- are experiential but fairly passive
- have a preference for creature comforts
- are food and wine oriented
- have a strong sense of authenticity and heritage
- are interested in ideas and creativity
- are environmentally conscious
- have indulgent spending habits but are nevertheless practical

From the identification of a target market segment, Tourism South Australia has been able to develop a target market position that will assist in the identification of a market entry strategy and the development of an appropriate marketing mix for the event product. Therefore, 'South Australia's tourism market position is to set itself apart as the pre-eminent destination [in Australia] for discerning travellers to enjoy accessible and surprising nature, heritage, food, wine and festive experiences – with the emphasis on friendly, personalised hospitality, authenticity, quality and value for money' (Tourism South Australia, 1990a, p.5).

Market Entry Strategy

Each new event needs to develop a market entry strategy. Although many events are constrained in terms of their location, especially community events that must, by definition, be based within the community, the timing of when an event is held will be crucial to its success in attracting visitors. The objectives which underlie an event are again crucial to decisions regarding the timing of holding an event. Anniversaries are clearly limited to specific dates, unless they are of such significance, such as the anniversary of the landing of Columbus in the Americas, that the 'celebrations' can be drawn out well over a 12 month period. However, where there is some flexibility in hosting an event, organisers should consider a) what other events and attractions the event will be competing with; and b) given the seasonality of visitation to the destination, can the event be utilised to boost visitor arrivals in shoulder-season and off-peak periods? Indeed, as Ritchie and Beliveau (1974) noted in their seminal work on event tourism, in many cases the hallmark event is a strategic response to the problems that seasonal variations in demand pose for the tourist industry.

The Marketing Mix

The design of an appropriate marketing strategy for an event consists of analysing market opportunities, identifying and targeting market segments, and developing an appropriate market mix for each segment. The traditional 'four Ps' of the marketing mix are:

- Product/service characteristics;
- Promotional decisions concerning channels and messages;
- Prices to be charged for products/services; and
- Places and methods of distribution of products/services.

In addition to the traditional four Ps of marketing, tourism analysts such as Morrison (1989, pp. 37–8) suggest another four Ps that may be held as especially important in tourism and travel marketing: people, packaging, programming, and partnership, while the Economic Planning Group of Canada (n.d., in Getz, 1991a, p.197) also suggest a further 'P' in the marketing mix: positioning. However, while positioning is undoubtedly important in the event marketing process, the present work sees positioning as being a component of the market entry strategy and of the other eight Ps.

Product/Service Characteristics

Event management must understand the difference between the generic needs the event is serving and the specific products or services it is offering. Similarly, Getz (1991b, p.75) observed, 'the marketing challenge, especially within an event tourism context, is to add specialist interests to the generic, broad appeal of festivals and events'. Given the growth and recognition of events as visitor attractions it is readily apparent that events have an appeal to a wide range of audiences. However, in order to meet the demands of the marketplace, it is essential that event managers focus the event product/s in light of the needs of specific market segments. For example, while museums and art galleries have long held special exhibitions, the art world now recognises that specific events or a range of events can be used to appeal to a variety of market segments, including audiences who would at one time never have been considered an 'art audience'. Museum and art gallery exhibitions have been transformed from a flock of

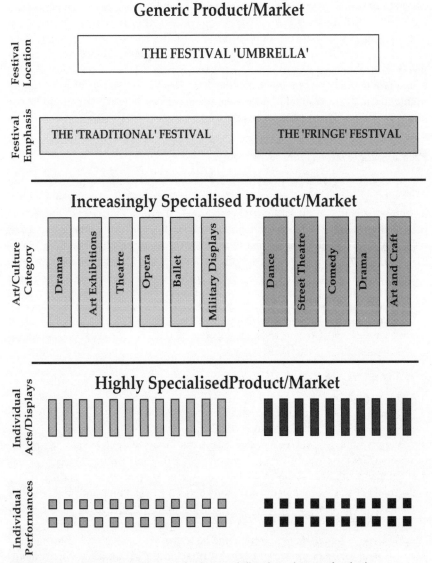

Figure 8.1   The layer of increasingly specialised markets at festivals

related objects to multimedia spectaculars or blockbusters. Furthermore, art galleries and museums no longer just show art or artefacts but they also sell a range of exhibition merchandise, including T-shirts, posters, napkins, books, diaries, replicas, and tableware, which also represents a broadening of the traditional exhibition product in order to meet new market needs.

Another indication of the use of specific products to maximise the market attraction of a generic product is the holding of events within events. For example, many international cultural festivals, such as the Edinburgh, Adelaide, or Wellington festivals, operate a fringe festival in association with the main festival. The fringe festivals, which provide an opportunity for newer or more *avant garde* artists to perform, appeal to a different range of audiences/market segments than the 'traditional' festival fare. In addition, each performance or event which operates under the festival umbrella has a far more specific market than at the 'generic' festival level. Therefore, in the case of many cultural festivals there is a layering of increasingly specialised markets (Figure 8.1), with the nature of the event product/market ranging from the generic at the festival level to highly segmented at the individual performance level, with each level/cultural product in turn requiring different marketing strategies.

Promotional Channels and Messages

'Promotional programs for even the most modest local event require exactly the same kind of organisation, planning, division of responsibility and the meticulous attention to detail that the larger events require' (Tourism South Australia, 1990a, p.3). In promoting events to the market various promotional methods are used, including advertising, personal selling, sales promotion and publicity. The Coopers and Lybrand study of festivals in the Ottawa region, Canada, reported:

> the most frequently mentioned sources of information about the festivals are newspapers and word-of-mouth. Non-local participants generally learn about most festivals only after arriving in the Region. This demonstrates the need to improve marketing outside of the National Capital Region, and more importantly, to create a greater awareness among tourists after they arrive. (1989, p.26)

Table 8.3 lists the range of promotional techniques used in community-run festivals in Ontario (Getz and Frisby, 1987). It is important to stress that publicity is an essential component of a successful event. Publicity 'is not a commodity to be measured by the yard or sold by the pound, but a function of good management. In the staging of a festival or special event, publicity should be all pervasive' (Canadian Government Office of Tourism, 1982, p.23). However, in many cases, particularly with larger-scale special events, the promotion of an event is not just concerned with the event but to convey images of the destination and region within which the event is located. This type of promotion is often one of the main objectives in hosting many hallmark events, as organisers and their municipal and private backers often recognise that media exposure may create interest in a destination in the marketplace and thereby attract future visitation and investment.

Table 8.3 Promotions and gimmicks used in community-run festivals in Ontario

Promotions	Yes	%	Gimmicks	Number of mentions
Newspaper Advertisements	48	92.3	Press Release	29
Radio Advertisements	46	88.5	Mascot	7
Posters	46	88.5	Souvenirs	5
Brochures	41	78.8	Flyers	4
Television Advertisements	30	57.7	'Freebies'	4
Roadsigns	28	53.8	Slogan	2
Other	14	26.9	Draw	1

Source: Getz and Frisby, 1987, p.24

For example, in addition to the direct media coverage of an event such as a motor-racing grand prix or a similar international sports event like the America's Cup or Olympic Games, indirect or incidental coverage of the destination will accrue to the host city (McCollum and McCollum, 1980). Indeed, in the case of certain mega-events such as the Olympics, just bidding for the event can be regarded as a form of destination promotion. As the Sydney Olympic Games Review Committee (1990) observed in their report to the State Premier as to whether or not Sydney should bid for the 2000 Summer Olympic Games, 'In terms of international marketing, the cost of bidding is regarded as a highly cost-effective method of promoting Sydney and Australia'.

Price

Although many events are 'free' in terms of entry costs, to many participants and visitors, particularly at community events, the issue of price is significant at all levels of event management and marketing. Prices, which are frequently called by other names such as fees, fare, collection, contribution, assessment and honorarium, may cover costs, maximise profits, subsidise all participants or certain market segments, encourage competition, or result in unanticipated consumer reaction (Gaedeke, 1977; Wanhill, 1989). Prices will be set according to a wide range of factors including past history, general economic conditions, ability to pay, revenue potential, costs, and the competition. Pricing may be used as a mechanism to appeal to particular markets. Rather than set a standard price to all entrants to an event, organisers may wish to lower price levels to certain demographic groups, such as children, in order to broaden the market base. For example, in 1985 the Calgary Stampede organisers provided discounted tickets for the youth age group when it discovered that only a small number of youths were attending the rodeo or evening show (Klassen, 1986). Pricing may also be linked with promotional strategies. For example, the Edmonton Klondike Days Exposition offered such promotions as:

• *Early Bird Admission* which offered half-price admission from gate opening at 11:00 a.m. to noon every day;

- *Advanced Gate Tickets* which offered a 25% reduction in the gate admission when purchased prior to Klondike days;
- *Klondike Family Day* on Sunday which gave free admission to all persons dressed in Klondike attire;
- *The Shell Canada Coupon*, a ticket for free admission which was received when 25 litres of gas were purchased from Edmonton-area Shell stations prior to Klondike Days. (Hughes, 1986, p.228)

All events have organisational costs that are borne by either the municipality, other public sector agencies, community groups, individuals, or the private sector. In the case of community events costs are recouped by charges to stall holders by organisers which are then passed on to consumers. Many management and infrastructure costs for events are completely borne or subsidised by government so as to enable events to be 'free' or at least have the price level kept to a minimum. In these instances, government may perceive the event to be in keeping with broader social and cultural objectives, as in the case of community-run events, celebrations, and festivals or, in the case of large scale events, government may perceive there to be major economic and promotional benefits (see Tourism South Australia, 1990b, for an example of a festivals assistance scheme). Either way, the costs of the event borne by government will eventually be passed on to the taxpayer through government charges and taxes.

To a great extent, price will be determined by whether or not event organisers are seeking to make a profit or simply cover their costs. The basic objectives for hosting an event will determine the pricing strategy. However, organisers must ensure that the cost of attending an event for the consumer does not price the event out of the market. Given the role of price in determining the relative attractiveness of an event, many event organisers are now seeking sponsorships in order to both directly subsidise the price of the event and/or to gain extra promotional channels. The increasing significance of sponsorships for event management and marketing is dealt with below.

Place and Methods of Distribution

The problem of efficient distribution is of vital importance in the delivery of products and services to customers. Despite the 'fixed' nature of the majority of events, distribution issues are also of significance to event managers. As noted above, the time and place in which events occur will be a major factor in determining the success of an event; questions of time and place are, in essence, about the most appropriate manner in which to 'distribute' the event product to its current and potential audience. Furthermore, issues of distribution will be tied up in the promotion of events. For instance, given a limited budget how can event organisers best distribute promotional materials such as fliers to the market that they have identified? Although direct mailing may be more efficient, it will probably be more costly than leaving fliers at set locations. In the case of art galleries which have a specific exhibition they wish to promote, having material available at the gallery will mean that the exhibition will be known to a certain number of their existing audience but, if they wish to broaden their audience, they will have to find additional means of distributing their promotional material to reach target markets.

The Four Additional Ps

Event tourism is often regarded as a distinct form of tourism product/service because of the emphasis on people. People are an integral part of hallmark events. In the case of carnivals, festivals, and community events, the interaction of people creates the atmosphere which makes the event a tourist attraction. Furthermore, the people element is made up not only of the customer but also the event staff. For example, in the case of many sporting events and expositions it is the volunteer staff, who participate because of their love for what the event represents, which helps to provide the special spirit and atmosphere which makes the event memorable for both host and guest.

Packaging and programming are related customer-oriented marketing and management techniques which are significant in their ability to match the supply of tourism product to demand. 'Packaging is the combination of related and complimentary services in a single-price offering' (Morrison, 1989, p.246). Event packages may consist of a selection of events which are sold together, for example a sporting event such as Wimbledon plus a cultural event such as a London theatre show, or an event plus transportation and accommodation.

Programming is the variation of service or product in order to increase customer spending and/or satisfaction, or to give extra appeal to an event or package. For example, many cultural festivals have a programme of successive acts and displays which are timed to follow and interrelate with each other. 'The weakness of festival programming is in trying to be "all things to all people" when the focus is lost or festivals just become a mish-mash of events without some coordinating theme or focus' (Wilkins, 1987, p.133).

The specific mix of performances which is developed may have the capacity to extend the interest of certain markets and hence, potentially, increase their level of satisfaction. Programming should consider such factors as the nature of the event venue and location, inclement weather options, and facilities for the disabled, the aged and young families, as well as providing quality experiential activities, a visually attractive event, balance within the choice of activities, and emphasis on the uniqueness of attractions (Tourism South Australia, 1990a).

Partnership refers to the cooperation that often develops between different tourism organisations and the mutual and/or shared benefits that may result. For example, different event organisers may band together to promote a number of events in a given region over a set period of time. Furthermore, sponsorship may be seen as a form of partnership in which the event and the sponsor/s seek a range of benefits from the sponsorship arrangement. During periods of recession or economic hardship this form of partnership takes on particular significance in the management and marketing of events. The nature and benefits of event sponsorship is discussed in greater detail later in this chapter.

Hallmark event marketing case studies   As noted above, marketing is an integral element of successful special art exhibitions and cultural events. For example, 'The Entombed Warriors' exhibition was carefully managed as a special arts event for the City of Edinburgh. The exhibition was held after the close of the Edinburgh Festival, thus filling a space in the cultural calendar devoid of other major arts events. Other features 'selling' this exhibition to the visiting public were low admission charges, extended opening hours, extensive newspaper coverage and free advertisements, involvement of the local Chinese community, media coverage of the opening, television advertising, a television documentary and staged 'stunts' (a free trip to China won by the 150,000th visitor) to maintain media interest. Constant publicity saw the number of visitors increase from 27,121 in the first week to 41,505 visitors by the seventh week (Coutts, 1986). Effective management of promotion and media coverage can thus provide a major marketing avenue for special art exhibitions.

Many European countries highlight cultural events as an essential part of their arts and heritage tourism marketing strategies (Thorburn, 1986, p.39). Heritage sites and historic buildings can also benefit from marketing strategies which incorporate the use of events and festivals. The marketing strategy implemented by English Heritage has substantially increased the level of visitation at many historic buildings around Britain. For example, at Audley End House, a Jacobean mansion with collections of furniture and paintings, the marketing emphasis shifted to promoting the landscaped surrounds. The gardens became a more popular aspect of the visit with the staging of various special events through the year, including concerts, arts and crafts and historic re-enactments. In the three years from 1984 to 1987 the implementation of the marketing strategy resulted in an increase of visitors (44,121 to 87,499), more 'repeat' visitors (33 to 37 per cent), vastly increased sales, greater per capita spending, and greater participation from middle class social groups (managerial: 14 per cent increase and skilled manual – 4 per cent increase). Six castles with a special programme of events also increased their visitation by 16 per cent from 1984 to 1987 (Eastaugh and Weiss, 1989). In 1987, some 928 British tourist attractions with an increase in visitor numbers reported that this was due to improved marketing (28 per cent), extra attractions or facilities (20 per cent) and more special events or exhibitions (10 per cent). Improved promotion was due to publicity on television or radio, press coverage, advertising in newspapers and magazines, poster advertising, wider brochure distribution and media exposure accompanying the presentation of national awards (British Tourist Authority/English Tourist Board, 1988). Effective marketing and event management can therefore act to reinforce and increase the visitor appeal of heritage properties.

Event Sponsorship

An American driver of any stature doesn't have much of a choice about Indianapolis; he has to be there. Usually he has an American sponsor, and so far as the sponsor is concerned, Indianapolis is the most important race in the world in terms of the promotion of his product. (Reed, 1980, in Rooney, 1988, p.97)

Sponsorships are a key element in the promotion and financial success of many hallmark events. However, there is an absence of an integrated and coherent body of research on event sponsorship (Hoek, *et al.*, 1990). As Shalofsky and di San Germano (1985, p.220) observed: 'compared with the mountainous heights scaled by research on advertising, sponsorship research has scarcely tackled the foothills'. Sponsorship was at one time virtually considered a form of philanthropy. Nevertheless, over the past three decades sponsorship has been recognised as a powerful promotional and marketing tool for both private industry and event organisers.

'Modern sponsorship is a mutually beneficial business arrangement between sponsor and sponsored to achieve defined objectives' (Head, 1981, p.2). Sponsorship may come in many forms: financial assistance, facilities, provision of event infrastructure, management skills and labour. Sponsors see events as a means of raising corporate profile, promoting particular products through enhanced profile and image, obtaining lower costs per impression than those achieved by advertising, improving sales, and being seen as good corporate citizens (Townley and Grayson, 1984; Beardsley, 1987; Gardner and Shuman, 1987; Mescon and Tilson, 1987; O'Neal, *et. al.*, 1987; Sneddon, 1987; Armstrong, 1988; Otker, 1988; Abratt and Grobler 1989; Hoek, *et al.*, 1990; Styles, 1990; Tourism South Australia, 1990a). Nevertheless, from the perspective of the event organisation and the host community it is essential that the potential sponsor be appropriate to the needs and image of the event. 'To the extent that sponsorship helps create and improve events as attractions and destination image-makers, tourism gains. But if sponsorship results in over-commercialized events and inauthentic images, the destination can suffer' (Getz, 1989a, p.306). Mismatching of events and sponsors will cause problems for both sponsor and the event. The perceived mismatch of sponsor and event is one of the central reasons why many countries and sporting organisations have ceased to accept the sponsorship of tobacco companies for major sporting events. In addition, it must be recognised that some sponsors will desire to influence the nature of the event while nearly all will expect a return of some description from their investment in the form of greater product and/or corporate recognition. It may even be the case that 'major sponsorships will cause changes in the event organization and its management' (Getz, 1989a, p.306).

Although sponsorships are a critical element in event development and promotion, the little evidence that is available suggests that sponsorship tends to be utilised by events that are more commercially oriented and/or which have an organisational structure which utilises professional promotion expertise on either a paid or volunteer basis. For example, in the survey of Ontario community-run festivals conducted by Getz and Frisby (1987, p.17), only 23 out of the 49 respondents reported gaining sponsorship for their festival, possibly reflecting 'a predominance of unsophisticated, small, volunteer efforts'. However, this situation may also be a reflection of a lack of potential sponsor interest in small, low-attendance events or events that do not appear to be 'professionally' organised.

In the United States the growth of non-traditional advertising and promotions, such as corporate sponsorship of sports and cultural events was estimated by Junker (1989) to be approximately 40 per cent between 1989 and the year 2000. In

1979 American corporations spent less than US$9 million on corporate sponsorship, in 1978 it was estimated as over half a billion dollars. However, as Junker went on to note: 'special events sponsorship is a niche market that allows companies to take greater advantage from sales and recognition standpoints – of their existing traditional advertising. In many cases, special events corporate sponsors are led into greater spending in traditional advertising through special event sponsorships' (1989, p.320).

Sponsorship can provide the financial input necessary to establish and organise new events. For example, Table 8.4 illustrates the involvement of New Zealand Breweries in one of New Zealand's more high profile events, the Speight's Coast to Coast from Christchurch on the east coast of the South Island to Kumara Junction on the west. The Coast to Coast is a one and two day event in which competitors have to run 26 kilometres, canoe 67 kilometres, and cycle 150 kilometres. The event started in 1983 as a joint effort between a private individual with interests in sporting events and two major sponsors. The value of the event to the sponsor is clearly demonstrated in the development of the event since 1983. The event generates substantial interest from visitors to New Zealand, provides substantial domestic and overseas publicity for the South Island of New Zealand, and produces substantial benefits for the major sponsor in terms of both brand imaging and direct sales. For example, 'the volume of Speights Beer consumed in the months before, during and after the event increased by 50 per cent and stayed at that level in the main target market (Christchurch)' (Harland, 1989, p.314).

Although sponsorship may be used to create or establish events, many sponsorships come about after a period in which events gain a profile through the activities of volunteers. For example, the Phoenix Fiesta Bowl was a non-profit, community based organisation which was set up in 1971. However, because of a perceived need by the organisation to stimulate the growth of the event, particularly the New Year's Day football game, the Bowl organisers set up a sponsorship with the Sunkist Growers citrus cooperative of California and Arizona in August of 1986.

The corporate sponsorship of what was now known as the Sunkist Fiesta Bowl had immediate benefits for the event, as the organisers were now able to attract two top college football teams to Phoenix because of the extra finance that was available to them. The first sponsored Bowl held in 1987 achieved two of the main objectives of hallmark events. First, the football game generated the most watched college game in household viewing terms in United States history, thereby generating significant public exposure and interest for both the event and the sponsor. Second, over 25,000 visitors were attracted to Arizona because of the game, and over US$70 million in new revenue, therefore generating the hoped-for economic input into the region (Junker, 1989).

Sponsorship may also be critical for cultural events. For example, in the case of the Te Haerenga Mai – the fourth Commonwealth arts festival held in conjunction with the 14th Commonwealth Games in Auckland in 1990 and the 150th anniversary of the signing of the Treaty of Waitangi, sponsorship was necessary because the majority of events at the cultural festival were to have free entry. In order to attract sponsorship the Trust which ran the festival developed specific sponsorship

Table 8.4   The changing nature of New Zealand Breweries (NZB)
sponsorship of the 'Coast to Coast' race

Product	Product characteristics	Event characteristics
Lion Brown 1983–85	high volume draught beer	Event called 'Coast to Coast' Event has only moderate profile; promotional efforts and product exposure limited (70 competitors in 1983, 140 in 1984)
Steinlager 1986–88	NZB's premium product Steinlager is NZB's most prestigious beer and enjoys international recognition through its association with the All Blacks rugby team and the Round the World Yacht races.	Event renamed 'Steinlager Coast to Coast'; NZB place Steinlager banners at strategic points in the race, and in order to maximise coverage of the event they pay Television New Zealand to make a documentary of the event and negotiate with airlines to cover the event. Attention of NZB over 1986–88 on the boosting of the event rather than the product because event not seen as appropriate to the quality image of Steinlager.
1987		Attracts 320 competitors. Three additional sponsors attracted. Changes to event included the introduction of the Steinlager Longest Day (1-day event) (45 entrants).
1988		Sponsors increased to 4 major sponsors (minimum of NZ$15,000 worth of products) and six associate sponsors (NZ$5,000 worth of products). Profile of the race further enhanced. NZB renegotiate sponsorship for a further three years.
Speights 1989–91	South Island (Dunedin) brewed beer, product strategy based on rugged outdoor image that reflects the nature of the event branding statement of 'Southern Man'	Steinlager replaced as product by Speights because of better matching of product with the event. NZB inject extra revenue into the event and the profile is further enhanced.
1989		Attracts 500 entries. The longest day event renamed the 'World Championship of Kayak, Cycle and Run' and entrants limited to 100 including overseas competitors. Major sponsors for the 1989 event also included Air New Zealand, Hertz, Beer Essentials, Helicopter Line, Alp Sports, and Suzuki.

Source: adapted from Harland, 1989

Table 8.5   Stages in the corporate sponsorship process

Stage	Characteristics
1. Research	Research to identify suitable company for event
2. Preparation	Preparation of sponsorship proposal which includes • details of specific event for which sponsorship is sought; • details of relationship of event to any broader festival or theme; • identification of potential benefits for sponsor; and • clearly identified set of legal, financial, managerial and marketing responsibilities for both event organisers and the sponsoring company.
3. Consideration	Consideration by potential sponsor • initial contact; • informal discussions with marketing manager/members of marketing division; • formal presentation to marketing manager/members of marketing division; and • if large sponsorship, formal presentation to company board.
4. Decision	If no, resume search, if yes proceed to next stage
5. Agreement	Legal agreement between corporate sponsor and event organisers detailing responsibilities of both parties
6. Implementation	Operationalise sponsorship through promotion and hosting of event
7. Evaluation and Feedback	Feedback to company which provides for evaluation of the success of the event and the event sponsorship, who will then decide to continue or discontinue sponsorship arrangements. Return to early stages of process

proposals which attempted to match events being run under the auspices of the festival to specific sponsors. However, as Harland (1989, p.317) observed: 'the difficulties faced in the early stages in attracting sponsorship vital to the actual implementation of the festival may have been avoided if it had been treated as a separate entity rather than as an add-on to the main event. The lack of clearly stated goals and inadequate funding arrangements limited the ability of the proposed festival to attract sponsorship'. Therefore, it is apparent that if sponsorship is to be successful, a clearly thought out strategy of attracting and satisfying sponsors needs to be developed.

Table 8.5 identifies the components of the corporate sponsorship process. Benefits from sponsorship can accrue to both sponsor and sponsored. It is essential that event organisers who are seeking sponsorship identify companies suitable for becoming involved in certain events. Organisers must also recognise that companies are seeking returns on their investments. Decisions about the suitability of an event for sponsorship are based on a number of criteria. Table 8.6 illustrates the decision criteria for sponsorship identified in a survey of New Zealand's top two hundred companies in 1991. Table 8.7 identifies those who are entrusted with the

Table 8.6 Decision-making criteria for corporate sponsorship

Decision criteria	per cent	Mean
The overall value for money represented by the sponsorship	92	3.5
The extent to which the sponsorship supports the company's image	92	3.4
The relevance of the cause for the company's customers	92	3.4
The extent to which the sponsorship enhances the good citizen role	88	3.1
The relevance of the cause to the community	90	2.8
The track record of the organisation seeking sponsorship	96	2.8
The extent to which the sponsorship provides a vehicle for corporate advertising	92	2.8
The amount of free publicity that can be generated for the company	92	2.7
The location where the sponsored activity takes place	94	2.7
The professionalism with which the sponsorship request is made	90	2.6
The relevance of the cause to the employees of the company	88	2.5
The extent to which the cause has been supported in the past	90	2.0
The personal interests of the chief executive officer	53	1.7
The personal interests of the members of the board	45	1.3

NOTE: The table above illustrates the percentage of respondents undertaking corporate sponsorship who used each criterion. Respondents were asked to rate the importance of each criterion on a scale of 1 to 4 (Very important = 4; Important = 3; Somewhat important = 2; Not particularly important = 1) thereby producing the mean. N=49.

Source: Adapted from New Zealand Marketing Magazine, 1991, p.34

Table 8.7 The sponsorship decision-makers (NZ$)

Decision-maker entrusted with authorisation	Over $100,000	$50,000 –$99,000	$10,000 –$49,000	Under $10,000
The board as a whole	30	25	22	12
Individual board members	2	2	8	5
Chief executive officer	47	47	45	42
Other person(s) in general management	17	17	28	45
Marketing	12	12	25	28
Consultants	0	0	0	0
Other	0	0	2	3

NOTE: Adds to more than 100 per cent because more than one response was possible. N=60.

Source: Adapted from New Zealand Marketing Magazine, 1991, p.36

authorisation to make sponsorship decisions. Corporate sponsorship is clearly dependent on the benefits the company will receive, while the size of the sponsorship will affect the level at which the sponsorship decision is made. However, regardless of the size of the sponsorship that is sought it is apparent that proposals must be detailed, professionally presented, and designed to meet company philosophies and objectives. In addition, the New Zealand survey indicated that corporate sponsorship programmes are closely linked with marketing activities, while 76 per cent of respondents indicated that they go through a formal cost-benefit analysis of all major sponsorships. Furthermore, 'many said that they require a significant input into the way in which sponsored organisations spend their money. A similar percentage said that they formally monitor the return on their sponsorships. The majority of companies also favour a range of smaller sponsorships to a single event' (New Zealand Marketing Magazine, 1991, p.36).

For the corporate sponsor the primary benefit from sponsorship is 'the ability to clearly target a specific region, a specific type of person, or a specific customer or client' (Junker, 1989, p.321) though clearly, because of the nature of events, for a defined period of time. Indeed, the same motivations which accrue to destinations in the hosting of events to overcome seasonal downturns may also be utilised by companies in the marketing of their products. In addition, corporate association with a popular event can create public goodwill towards the sponsor which then turns into greater sales of the sponsor's product. The potential pitfalls for the sponsor include the possible mismatch of product and event, and the failure of the event which may adversely reflect not only on the quality of a particular product but also the broader corporate image.

The evaluation of the success of event sponsorship relies, like advertising research, on surrogate measures of effectiveness, such as spontaneous and aided product or brand awareness, product recall, and aided and spontaneous association between a company, brand or product and the event that has been sponsored (Perlstein and Piquet, 1985). In addition, the attendance at an event and the size of the media audience may also give an indication of the success of any event sponsorship.

For the sponsored event, sponsorship can provide a number of financial and non-financial gains. For instance, the sponsorship of an event by prominent corporations may have flow-on effects in the form of greater recognition for the event and interest from other potential sponsors. However, the primary gain for the event from sponsorship is the stability that appropriate sponsorship can provide for event management, marketing and promotion. Nevertheless, it should be recognised that for the benefits of sponsorship to be maximised, sponsors should have the support of the community within which the event is being held otherwise negative reactions may result from potential supporters of the event.

Event sponsorship case study: World Cup skiing at Waterville Valley No North American ski resort has held as many World Cup ski events as Waterville Valley, New Hampshire. The gaining of media exposure and sponsorship provides one of the dominant rationales for the staging of World Cup events at Waterville Valley. Three primary mechanisms are utilised to assist in the gaining of media exposure. First, television exposure is gained internationally and nationally through the cable sports station ESPN. Each event is televised at least twice and up to five times. ESPN reach approximately fifty million American households 'and the resort feels that many potential vacationers in Waterville Valley are first exposed to the Valley through television' (Corcoran, 1988, p.101). Second, the name of the resort is prominently displayed in all the television coverage. Third, the resort 'invite the national ski press and set-up a fully staffed press room and provide TV newsclips of the events to stations in our region' with usually 'between 50 and 100 working press in attendance' (Corcoran, 1988, p.101).

Sponsorship is a critical element in the hosting of World Cup ski racing at Waterville. In order to make the events financially viable for the resort through the avoidance of 'out-of-pocket costs to the ski area' substantial sponsorship money has been attracted. Depending on the length of the event, each series costs between US$200,000 and $300,000 to run. As with the Speights Coast-to-Coast outlines above, World Cup skiing at Waterville will utilise a combination of principal and subsidiary sponsorship to make the event viable. According to Corcoran (1988, pp. 101–2), 'A major sponsor will typically provide anywhere from $1,000,000 to $200,000 in return for very prominent name exposure during the event, particularly on racing bibs and course banners in front of TV cameras'.

Hallmark Events as Imagemakers

As noted in the first chapter, hallmark events may be regarded as the imagemakers of modern tourism. Nations, regions, cities and corporations have used hallmark events to provide a favourable image in the international tourist and business marketplace (Ashworth and Goodall, 1988). According to the Mayor of Edmonton 'Major international events provide value well beyond the monetary-cost overruns, and deficits must be compared against the positive world image you create for a city through such events' (Decore, 1986, p.2). According to Hiller, hallmark or 'landmark' events have a 'showcase effect' which indicates that 'appearances are as important as essence' (1989, p.119; 1990).

> The emphasis on image is not meant to suggest that a false construction of reality is established but that the media transforms the sporting event into an urban 'happening' by exposing their audiences to numerous other facets of the city's non-sporting life, from cultural life to culinary activities and unique landmarks and traits. The attachment of the city's name to the event enhances not only global recognition but suggests that the success or failure of the global event itself reflects on the city. (Hiller, 1989, p.121)

For example, the 1988 Winter Olympics were seen as being crucial to improving the image of Calgary both for its own inhabitants but also so as to attract investment and tourism. Furthermore, events provide a 'visibility factor... which can be mobilised by event organisers and the local media to generate even larger support in the urban community' (Hiller, 1989, pp.121–2). Similarly, a visibility factor was clearly being sought by the Sydney Olympic Games Citizens' Council in their unsuccessful attempt at Australian Olympic Committee selection as a bidding city for the 1996 Summer Games:

> Sydney is a city of de Coubertin's vision. A city which has achieved much in a short time. A successful city of the new world. It is a place where people of all races, of all creeds, join together to perform at their highest level. It is a place where winning is infectious. A vibrant city of optimism, peace, achievement and vitality.

Table 8.8   European and American awareness of Calgary as a previous/
future Winter Games site

Region	Percentage of respondents			
	1986	1987	1988	1989
US	18.5	29.3	76.3	53.8
	(n=822)	(n=988)	(n=888)	(n=772)
Europe	36.2	38.7	39.8	40.2
	(n=857)	(n=807)	(n=927)	(n=562)

Source: Ritchie and Smith, 1991, p.8

Table 8.9   American respondents' images of Calgary, 1987-89

Image Expression	Percentage of respondents		
	1989	1988	1989
	(n=448)	(n=636)	(n=467)
Olympics	17.2	77.4	66.4
Stampede	25.7	10.8	8.4
Hockey	16.7	7.1	15.6
Cowboys, horses	5.6	4.7	3.2
Rodeo	11.4	4.4	6.2
Skiing	-	4.1	5.4
Mountains	2.2	3.5	6.0
Cold, snow	3.6	3.3	5.1
Western	4.2	3.2	3.0
Friendly	-	1.9	-
Oil	4.0	1.7	-
Beautiful	2.2	1.7	-
Football	2.2	-	-
Cattle ranching	2.0	-	-
American city	2.0	-	-
Total number of responses	626	929	652
Average number of responses per person	1.40	1.47	1.40

Source: Ritchie and Smith, 1991, p.7

Sydney and the Games of the XXVI Olympiad: a formidable combination. (Sydney Olympic Games Citizens' Council, 1988, p.3)

Probably the most detailed longitudinal study of the effect of hosting an event on the image of a city was a five-year study conducted by Ritchie and Smith (1991) on the 1988 Calgary Winter Olympics. The results of the study indicated that in addition to the greater awareness of Calgary as the host city (Table 8.8), the image of Calgary had changed in the minds of many respondents (Table 8.9), although this was followed by substantial image decay in the year after the hosting of the Games. Therefore, 'it would seem evident that municipal/tourism managers in a particular city must anticipate a certain (and as yet unknown) rate of awareness decay and take steps to counter it if they wish to remain visible and competitive in the international marketplace' (Ritchie and Smith, 1991, p.9).

The Olympic Games have also played a critical role in changing the image of certain nations. For example, in the 1964 Tokyo Summer Games and the 1972 Munich Summer Games the host countries sought to modify the images which were a legacy of the Second World War. Similarly, South Korea used the 1988 Seoul Summer Games to indicate its new-found economic position in the world (Jeong, 1988). Jeong's study revealed that the Olympics were perceived as a means to overcome the poor image of Korea in the international tourism market – particularly the United States – because of such factors as MASH (the highly popular television series based on the fictionalised exploits of an American field hospital during the Korean War), the devastation of the Korean War, the shooting down of Korean Airlines flight 007 in the early 1980s, and the ongoing political instability between North and South Korea.

In order to move away from the economic and political dimensions of popular Korean images, respondents to Jeong's (1988) survey indicated that Korea needed to use the Olympics in order to establish its own cultural identity, especially in the West where lack of knowledge of Korea has meant that Korean culture is often seen merely as an extension of Chinese or Japanese culture. Therefore, in order to strengthen the Korean cultural image, three strategies were utilised. First, the Korean Government focused media attention on Korean national holidays and festivals which occurred at the same time as the Olympics. As Jeong (1988, p.179) noted:

> If the Harvest Moon Festival is well-planned and orchestrated, it has a great potential to be promoted as a mega-event like Oktoberfest in Munich and Mardi Gras in New Orleans, through the Olympic publicity. Then, in long term perspective, the festival can become the powerful cultural attraction to induce a huge influx of tourists to the Korean cultural image every year to people around the world.

Second, the opening and closing ceremonies of the Games provided the opportunity for optimising the presentation of the Korean image to the world through folk dances and martial art performances that were a reflection of Korean culture. Third, promotional advertising for the Games also reflected Korean culture rather than just sports events or economic development. However, strategies for image development need to go beyond the immediacy of the event and should be framed for post-event strategies. In the case of Korea, Jeong (1988, p.180) argued that post-event strategies should include cultural events which built on the infrastructure and attractions already created by the staging of the Games, as 'on-going cultural or art festivals are more recommendable than sporting events to increase expenditure and enhance Korea's touristic image'. However, post-Asian Games (1986) and Olympic Games (1988) promotion suggests that, while cultural attractions are significant, the images of the events will be used by the Korea National Tourism Corporation for several years to come because of the idea of 'success' that has been attached to the Games in markets such as Japan (Breen, 1991).

Image and development Events are used to indicate phases of tourism develop-ment and each phase may be related to particular images. For example, the development of tourism in the City of Montreal has proceeded through four main stages, three of which correspond to the hosting of events (Labrie, 1988). The 1967 International Exposition represented the first stage of development which intro-duced Montreal to the international travel market and offered the image of Montreal as a modern city. The 1976 Olympics marked the second phase of development and provided the basis for mass media exposure and indicated the ability of the City to host major events. The third phase occurred in the 1980s with the opening of the City's convention centre, which in turn had built on the event base provided in the two previous phases. The fourth, and present phase, is the celebration of the 350th anniversary of Montreal in 1992 (which also ties in with the 125th anniversary of Canadian nationhood) and which takes advantage of the current interest in heritage and in expressions of the cultural and political indepen-dence of Quebec from the rest of Canada.

Sheffield's hosting of the World Student Games in 1991 was also an integral part of the city's attempt to improve its image and attract tourists and investment (Foley, 1991a, b; Roche, 1991). Hindered by its nineteenth century industrial image as the home of Sheffield steel, the city wanted to use the Games to raise its national and international profile and use the facilities established for the Games as a mechanism to attract more sports and cultural events to the region. However, Foley (1991a, pp.17-18) concluded with a note of caution about the economic and promotional benefits of the Games:

> In economic terms Sheffield will benefit from the World Student Games, but only to the extent that money was diverted from uses in other parts of Sheffield (or the UK for outside investment or visitor spending). If all the benefits in terms of job generation, improved sporting and cultural facilities, image improvement, and the feeling that enters the hearts of local residents as they see Sheffield on the television again are considered the expenditure of £174 million by the majority of politicians and the local community so be it.

Cities in the United States have also benefited from the appropriate develop-ment and promotion of cultural events. 'Baltimore, for instance, has used ethnic fairs, a city-wide festival and redevelopment of its theatre district as methods of improving the city's image among its own residents and then attracting tourists. Other cities such as San Antonio, Texas; San Francisco, and Boston have also used the arts as a means of promoting themselves as destinations' (Tighe, 1985, p.250). The cultural attractions of New York are strongly promoted as tourist drawcards (Zeppel and Hall, 1992). Tourist promotion of the city using the 'I love New York' marketing plan has, since 1977, focused on Broadway theatre and the arts. The success of the advertising campaign increased Broadway theatre attendances by 20 per cent in 1978 and a further 21 per cent during 1980–81. In 1983–84, 7.9 million people went to theatre performances on Broadway, with 2.2 million (37 per cent) from outside the New York metropolitan area and 700,000 (9 per cent) from overseas. Arts and tourism are closely linked industries in New York. An extensive visitor survey of New York's arts attractions in the early 1980s found that 'over half the visitors came to New York because of the arts (41.6 per cent) or extended their stay an average of two days because of them (15.6 per cent)' (Tighe, 1985, p.239).

The creation of a positive city image through the promotion of special events is also witnessed in the South Australian Department of Tourism's promotion of Adelaide as a prime cultural destination. Prior to the staging of the 16th biennial Adelaide Festival of Arts (1–18 March 1990), full colour advertisements appeared in major Australian magazines showing ballet dancers in a variety of cultural settings with the caption 'Adelaide. More culture per kilometre'. The text for this advertisement attempted to create an image of Adelaide as a desirable cultural destination by emphasising the city's historical architecture, sculpture, fine arts, galleries, museums, festivals, performing arts, Aboriginal culture, theatre, music and restaurants under the umbrella of the Festival. As Hiller (1989, p.119) observed, 'because of limitations on spectators and the short duration of the event, the media becomes the key in helping the city to redefine itself and to transmit that new image to the world'.

The record number of visitors at the 1990 Adelaide Festival and a national tourism award to Festival organisers for the best tourism marketing campaign in Australia both attest to the success of the marketing of this particular cultural event. Indeed, well directed marketing strategies have consistently enhanced the cultural reputation of the Adelaide Festival as a major international and local arts tourism event (Roeper, 1986; McDonald, 1988, 1990a) and the positioning of South Australia as the 'Festival State'. 'For South Australians, the Adelaide Festival provides the opportunity for a celebration of the arts which concentrates on presenting quality of product. It is a celebration for local people and is warranted for that alone but also presents the State with an event around which an image can be developed' (Hand, 1990, p.2). Therefore, the Adelaide Festival benefits Adelaide and the State as a whole by

• acting as the flagship for the state;
• positioning the state in people's perceptions both in Australia and overseas; and
• attracting visitors from outside the state.

The quality image which the Festival provides enhances the overall tourism image which the state is seeking and matches South Australia's tourism marketing and product development strategies. In a similar fashion, although with a substantially different theme, content and objectives, the Australian Formula One Grand Prix, which is also held in Adelaide, complements the high profile and quality image of the Adelaide Festival (Hand, 1990; McDonald, 1990a, b).

Maximising Events as a Tourism Marketing Tool

The event marketing process should consist not only of analysing market segments, planning a market entry strategy, and developing and implementing the

Table 8.10   Conclusions from a marketing audit of festivals in the National Capital Region (Ottawa, Canada)

- Contracting out of specific marketing functions, such as advertising and promotion, should be considered where budgets allow. This approach provides access to the required expertise and, through negotiations, forces a clear statement of responsibilities.
- Better marketing plans are required by most festivals. These plans help ensure better coordination of activities, more effective utilisation of resources, and less last minute problems.
- To help assess the effectiveness of the various marketing functions and the extent to which objectives are met, better information systems should be in place. Timely information should be collected on attendance, costs, revenues where applicable and responses to specific promotional efforts, e.g. sponsorship sales, direct mail promotions to tour operators and media relations.
- With better plans and information systems in place, priority should be given to promotional activities which have the greatest impact.
- Specific advertisements in well selected media appear to be more effective than expensive brochures.
- Joint marketing efforts should be considered, including securing support from major sponsors and undertaking promotions outside the region for festivals that lack a significant level of local non-participation.
- Sufficient resources should be allocated to permit good, effective, programmes, and to ensure that signage and guidebooks are available to assist visitors once they are here.
- Many festivals should exercise greater control on community events. This could include setting certain criteria which would have to be met for approval as a festival event and assigning liason responsibility to a specific festival staff member.
- A central location for major events permits greater control of logistics and provides a central focus for visitors.

Source: Coopers and Lybrand Consulting Group, 1989, p.29

marketing mix, but also of evaluating the marketing strategy in terms of its intrinsic success and in light of the broader objectives which determined the holding of the event in the first place. For example, the market audit which Coopers and Lybrand (1989, p.29) conducted on festivals in Ottawa were designed to

- describe the marketing organizations and systems;
- assess strategies, marketing plans and objectives;
- review communication efforts related to strategic plans; and
- comment on the success of the marketing efforts and to provide recommendations for the festivals

The conclusions which emerged from the marketing review are presented in Table 8.10

The results of the Event marketing also needs to be placed within the context of the broader marketing of a destination. For example, New Zealand is using events such as the Speight's Coast to Coast, the Kiwi Lager Ironman, and the Fletcher Challenge marathon, to attract the sport and fitness market segment to New

Table 8.11   Strategies to prolong the length of stay of Olympic tourists in Korea

Strategies	Actions
To develop various package tours	Pre/post Olympic tours focusing on historic relics and exotic scenery in local areas such as Kyongju and Jeju Island. Non-Olympic tours at discounted prices (promotional and educational programmes) about Korea and its culture.
To organise exotic cultural events	Traditional cultural events to demonstrate Korean folk customs which are quite different from other countries. Unique events sponsored by cultural organizations and companies.
To offer special discount for shopping goods	Shopping courses depending on tourist's taste. Expanded availability of tax-free shops. Post-Olympic shopping exhibitions offering discounted prices.

Source: Jeong, 1988, p.178

Zealand under the heading of 'New Zealand: The Ultimate Challenge' (New Zealand Tourism Department, 1991/92). The product 'is being promoted to a targeted group of endurance participants in selected overseas markets. The project is a joint venture involving the Tourism Board, Air New Zealand, event organisers and their sponsors, major sporting bodies and regional tourism organisations' (New Zealand Tourism Board, 1991, p.15). However, potential visitors are also encouraged to stay-on once the event is over, 'once you've put your body through hell, rest up in our little piece of paradise... the home of the Ultimate Challenge is also the Ultimate Destination for relaxation and fun' (New Zealand Tourism Department, 1991). Similarly, Jeong (1988) identified a number of marketing strategies to prolong the length of stay of Olympic tourists to Korea (Table 8.11), which could be applied to other destinations hosting events.

Events should not be seen as having an indefinite lifespan. Like all products, events go through a life cycle. The product life cycle idea suggests that a product will pass through four stages: introduction, growth, maturity and decline. Table 8.12 presents the relationship of strategic orientation and organisational characteristics of the event product to the various stages of the life cycle. Therefore, event organisers, marketers and boosters need to be aware of how their event and their destination may fall within a product or destination life cycle. Events may be one avenue to extend the life span of a destination (Hall and Selwood, 1989). Furthermore, it may be possible to rejuvenate an event, in the same way that a destination's attractiveness can be renewed by appealing to a different audience and through offering a different product (Butler, 1980). However, regardless of how an event is perceived, it is essential that events are seen within the broader strategic context of where the event and the destination is headed.

Table 8.12   The relationship between the strategic orientation and organisational characteristics of the event product, to the stages of the product life cycle

Stage	Strategic Orientation	Organisational Characteristics
Introduction	• Product oriented • New product development • Product testing by trying • Lack of long-term strategy	• Zealous volunteer participation • Community involvement and participation • No permanent staff • Little functional differentiation • Low budgets
Growth	• Product oriented • Emerging production orientation • Lack of long-term strategy	• Functional differentiation emerges • Incremental annual planning and budgeting • Promotion increases
Maturity	• Production oriented • Market oriented • Research orientation • Long-term strategy	• Functional differentiation • Specific marketing function • Full-time professional staff
Decline	• Production or market • Segmentation and response • Long-term strategy	• Staffing may fall • Functional differentiation • Tight budget control
Rejuvenation/ readjustment	• Product oriented • Market oriented • Research orientation • Long-term strategy	• Functional differentiation • Strategic planning • Professional staff working in conjunction with community and volunteers

Source: After Stewart, 1986

An effective marketing strategy will assist event organisers to reach the various stakeholder groups. As St-Onge (1991, p.53) observed, 'any well conceived and successfully produced festival or event has to achieve the purposes of its producers and sponsors; it also has to meet the needs of its clientele'. One of the primary mechanisms that managers can use to communicate with stakeholders is the development of a strategic marketing plan which contains the various elements of event marketing discussed in this chapter. Unfortunately, the development of marketing plans by event organisers and responsible government agencies may be 'rather crude, and often the only direction given to many tourism agencies is to promote growth' (Getz, 1991a, p.144). However, as discussed throughout this book, events have a far wider purpose than to merely promote growth. Indeed, as Shaw (1989, p.45) commented on the 1987 America's Cup, 'one of the salutory lessons immediately after the Cup extravaganza was that promotional rhetoric can only go so far towards creating consumer demand'. Therefore, it becomes essential for events to reach the broad spectrum of social, economic, and quality-of-life objectives that are tied into the hosting of events. Without the support of the local people marketing opportunities cannot be maximised. In order to achieve this goal it becomes essential that event organisers gain community support by addressing their needs, expectations and perceptions, and it is to this task that the final chapter will address itself.

9 Avoiding the Hangover: A Strategic Approach to Hosting Hallmark Events

> Despite the costs of growth the ideology of development possesses great appeal as the universal panacea for the ailments of society and is most often pursued with only minor concessions to those asked to pay for its local burdens. A narrow fix on pursuing growth chains local governments to the unquestioned acquisition of development projects, often of a spectacular nature such as football stadiums or world fairs, with limited payoffs to local areas. (Gottdeiner, 1987, p.18)

> Everyone hopes the party will be great, but many fear the hangover could be dreadful. (Kingston, 1987, p.3, commenting on the 1988 Brisbane Expo)

The final chapter will provide a strategy for tourism development through the hosting of hallmark events. The application of strategic quality management principles to the management and planning of hallmark events is regarded as one means to maximise returns to stakeholders. The strategy will emphasise the means to maximise the benefits of events and note the importance of community control of event planning and the need to integrate hallmark events within a long-term approach to tourism development.

Hallmark Events and Quality Tourism

Quality is an essential ingredient of tourism. However, substantial disagreement exists over the nature and meaning of quality tourism and the principles of how it should be applied. Nevertheless, a substantial body of literature is emerging which suggests that notions of quality in tourism are related to ideas of 'sustainable', 'appropriate', or 'ethical' tourism which seeks to harmonise economic, social, cultural and ecological interests (Association Internationale d'Experts Scientifiques du Tourisme, 1991; Dragicevic, 1991; Heritage Interpretation International, 1991; Hall and McArthur, 1991; Hall and Weiler, 1992; Weiler and Hall, 1992). For example, Kaspar (1991) has argued that quality tourism is borne by four pillars:

1. The quality of life of the local residents;
2. The well being of the guest (reception and items at his disposal);
3. Respect for the natural environment; and
4. Economic development, creation of jobs and incomes.

While demands for quality tourism are laudable and bare a close relationship to calls for community-oriented tourism planning (Murphy, 1985; Hall, 1991), relatively little attention has been paid to the quality management literature which may offer some guidance as to how the notion of quality tourism may be operationalised. The growth of service orientation in tourism economies has substantial implications not only for the economic returns from events but also for the manner in which management is conducted. As noted in Chapter 6, event managers need to utilise strategic analysis and evaluation to react and proact with the external environment in which he/she is operating. In particular, managers will need to be able to deal with the diverse demands which are placed on them from within the event organisation (such as employees and volunteers) and external to the organisation (for example, the market, the local community, social and environmental responsibility) regarding the event product. The following sections present a framework to help understand the relationship of the stakeholders to event management and describes how an understanding of the provision of service quality relates to the nature of the event product.

Quality

Quality in its simplest form can be defined as conforming to standards. The standards are set as part of the planning process and then operationalised and implemented as part of the control system so that deviations from these standards can be detected. Current performance is measured against the predetermined standards and deviations are then corrected (Pizam, 1991; Tweed and Hall, 1991).

At a more sophisticated level, true quality management must take a causal approach to determine the underlying reason why deviations from standards occur. At this level it is important to reduce the likelihood of further errors occurring for the same basic cause. Here quality management is concerned with reducing the potential for error. The methodology for this approach is an examination of the management system itself. Therefore, the key question becomes, what must be changed in the system to reduce the potential for error?

In service industries, such as tourism, this approach to quality management is particularly important as measurement of quality after the fact, i.e. after the service has been provided, is more difficult than for products. Fundamental shifts in the emphasis of measurement also occur when services are considered. The customer needs to be part of the standard setting process for both products and services, but the measurement of quality against standards differs. In manufacturing industries, products can be sampled and measured against standards while still in the domain of the firm, with relatively little or no input from the customer. In tourism, the quality of a service can really only be measured by the customer.

Quality in a Dynamic Environment

Operationalising quality as conforming to standards and removing the potential for error is relatively easy to conceptualise when the standards remain the same for long periods of time. In this situation the management system can be refined to the point that errors become extremely unlikely and standards are consistently achieved. However, the current operating environment for most events is in a state of flux because of increasing competition from other events and attractions, the changing demands that are made on events, and the growth of social and environmental concerns surrounding tourism development.

A dynamic environment poses far greater challenges for quality management than a relatively stable environment. Two management challenges arise from this situation. The first is that the standards by which quality is measured need constant reformulation, requiring regular input from the customers as to what the new standards should be. One of the implications of changing standards is that the management system will need to be redesigned or refocused in order to achieve the new standards. System adaptation may require fundamental and massive change. This is quite different to the relatively small incremental changes required in relatively stable environments to ensure that conformity to standards is achieved.

The second challenge arises from the impact of the changing environment on the system itself. Parts of the system that may have required no checking previously can become vulnerable to defects and error due to changes in the environment. In other words, it could be argued that non-critical areas have become critical, and that previously identified 'critical control points' in the service provision and delivery system have become non-critical or are not adequately functioning as indicators of quality achievement (Tweed and Hall, 1991). For example, event related rent increases and social dislocation which may once have been ignored by municipalities have now become substantial public concerns (Craik, 1988a; Hall, 1991).

The Dimensions of Quality

Quality has many dimensions depending on who it is for. Garratt (1987) promulgates a model of quality from the viewpoint of different stakeholder groups. Starting with what he termed the traditional thinking about management, including event management, as being concerned with finance, markets, people/production and the external environment (Figure 9.1), he then moved to refocus the model from the point of view of four stakeholder groups, namely the owners, the consumers, the providers and the public, a refocusing which parallels much of the shift towards community-oriented tourism (Murphy, 1985; Hall, 1991). A summary of this refocusing is provided in Table 9.1. The final form of this model is to provide a definition of the qualities that each stakeholder group seeks (Tweed and Hall, 1991). The four qualities are:

- the quality of business performance
- the quality of consumer service

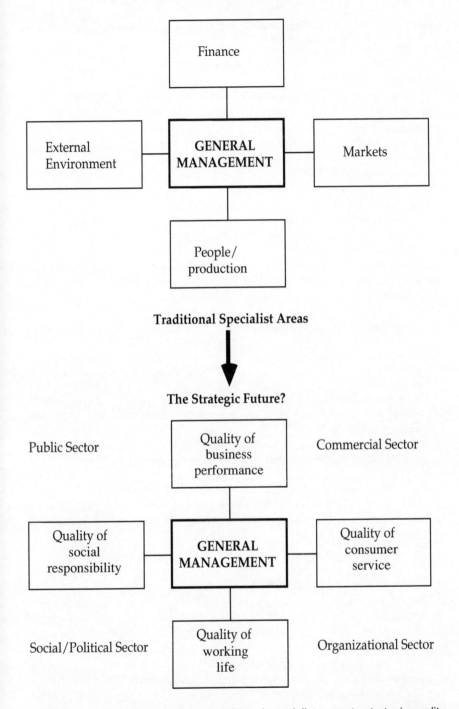

Figure 9.1   The transformation of traditional specialist areas to strategic quality
management concerns
Source: After Garratt, 1987, in Tweed and Hall, 1991

Table 9.1   The relationship between functional areas, stakeholder groups and definitions of quality

Functional area	Stakeholder group	Definition of quality
Marketing	Consumer	Consumer service
Finance	Owners	Business performance
People/production	Providers	Working life
External environment	Public	Social responsibility

Source: Tweed and Hall, 1991

- the quality of working life
- the quality of social responsibility

Similarly, Hand (1990, p.5) observed, that 'events clearly have social and economic objectives which are equally important' and argued that the value of events should be judged in relation to a number of stakeholders, an observation which parallels the definitions of quality outlined above.

- To the participant/visitor, value is judged by the quality of experience and the way the event satisfied their needs.
- To the organiser, value can be judged by the successful completion of the event by providing satisfying experiences to the visitors/participants and being financially viable.
- To the local community, value can be judged by reflected pride in a job well done, in enhanced image as a good place to visit and in the financial return or net return to business.
- To the State, value relates to the extent to which the event supports marketing efforts, leads to increased expenditure and ultimately increased employment. (Hand, 1990, p.5)

Therefore, from this perspective, issues of quality management take us back to what was identified in Chapter 1 as the most fundamental question which needs to be asked in the examination of hallmark events, for what and for who are the events being held?

Integrated Quality Management

According to Tweed and Hall (1991), an integrated model of quality management which examined quality within the service sector and views notions of quality from the perspective of four groups of stakeholders: customers, employees, owners and the public, would provide a better understanding of quality in all its dimensions. In particular, they stressed that notions of quality are determined by the questions 'Who is quality for?', while a second question which logically follows on from the first is 'How do they define quality?' Therefore, they argued that notions of quality should be seen within the context of a framework which identified the stakeholders in any particular event.

Event quality management is a process that needs to be implemented at three levels: the meta, macro and micro. The meta level examines the dynamic environment within which the event operates and sets the overall framework within which the business will operate. It determines which stakeholders will participate in the formulation of the standards by which quality will be measured and the process by which the appropriate standards will be identified. The macro level is concerned with the design and implementation, refinement and maintenance of the management system through which standards will be achieved. Day to day actions and responses operate at the micro level and provide the tactics for dealing with deviations from standards (Tweed and Hall, 1991).

This framework for analysing quality as a multi-dimensional concept is reproduced as Figure 9.2. The framework offers a conceptual tool to understand the processes by which quality is determined. In its broadest sense the model identifies levels, processes and outcomes. Policy, including the formulation of the objectives for which the event is being held, is the process used at the meta level and is used to determine the standards by which quality is to be measured. At the macro level, strategy is used to determine system design and decide how to meet the set objectives. Finally, tactics are used to determine day-to-day actions and responses in event management at the micro level. The outcomes of the higher levels become one of the inputs for the lower levels so that standards are input into and influence the system design, and system design becomes an input or determinant of the tactics that will be used (Tweed and Hall, 1991).

The model contains two feedback loops, one of which is provided by management and the other is provided by the relevant stakeholder group. However, it is the interaction between management and the various stakeholder groups which will in fact determine processes and outcomes at all levels of the organisation. The model recognises that quality cannot be defined in simple, rational, one dimen-

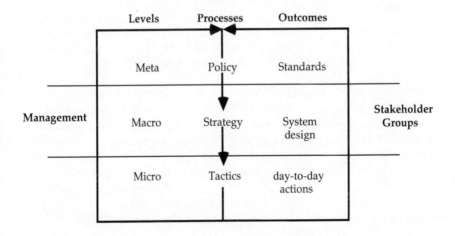

Figure 9.2 A model of integrated quality management
Source: Tweed and Hall, 1991

sional terms. Traditional concerns placed emphasis on the customers definition of quality as the dominant factor in the determining of standards. The new model emphasises that quality cannot be determined by one interest group at the expense of the others. This may be possible in the short term but will be detrimental to the survival of the event in the longer term or to the willingness of interest groups to allow similar events to be held again. Indeed, quality is the outcome of a complex negotiation process participated in by four different groups that have a mix of competing and complementary aims.

Where the objectives of the various groups are complementary and the organisation has the capacity to supply, the highest standards of quality are attainable for each stakeholder group. Where there are competing objectives then several alternatives are possible. One alternative is to negotiate standards that provide equal levels of satisfaction to each group. For example, to meet the public interest by ensuring that environmental and social standards are set and implemented (Tweed and Hall, 1991).

Another alternative is for one stakeholder group to dominate the others so that for example, owner (typically for larger events, government and associated business interests) definitions of quality are provided for at the expense of the public. Unfortunately, this definition of quality would appear typical of many large-scale events, such as World Fairs and the Olympic Games, which are hosted because of the interests of urban elites. Quality standards defined by owners in terms of promotional, political and economic return on investment could dominate with the effect that consumer satisfaction, quality of life, and level of social responsibility may decrease. These kinds of distortions are possible in the short term but become unsustainable in the medium and longer term (Tweed and Hall, 1991). As Heenan (1978, p.30) noted:

> Farsighted executives and city fathers find it useful to distinguish between viability and legitimacy. By viability, we mean the degree to which the financial objectives of the firm have been or will be satisfied... Legitimacy refers to stakeholder perceptions that the institution has a right to exist... Since legitimacy is confirmed not by management, but rather by outside or external stakeholders, the future of tourism in many parts of the world will be determined as much for legitimacy reasons as for viability.

In the case of the 1991 World Student Games in Sheffield, for example, Roche (1991, p.18) noted that the Games became 'political, controversial'and failed to win widespread community support because 'the fundamental problem as far as the political legitimacy of the Games goes is that the Labour leadership never asked the people of Sheffield directly (e.g. by a referendum) whether or not they actually wanted to stage a sporting mega-event or to build a new generation of prestige sport facilities, nor what they would be prepared to pay for them'. An indication of the need for legitimacy is to be found in the words of councillor Peter Duff who resigned from the city council partly in protest at the Games:

> The council has been dragged into the Thatcher myth that the future lies in tourism, leisure and recreation. We should be playing to the traditional strengths of a working class city not to the false future that Sheffield is a sports centre. We have partnerships

with the private sector which need properly defining, because at the moment we have politicians playing at being businessmen and businessmen playing at being politicians. The World Students Games sums it all up. (*Sheffield Star*, 18 January 1990, in Roche, 1991, p.20)

Integrated Quality Management: The Learning Event Organisation

The model of quality described above has a number of important benefits for event managers. In particular, it shows the three main areas in which learning is required about event organisation. The first is the learning required about the stakeholder groups, i.e. the 'who' of quality. According to this model, students of organisations should learn about the owners, the consumers, the providers and the public. In particular, the definitions that each group has of quality and how to measure it become important areas of study. The second area is in terms of the level or plane at which management should focus its attention and focuses on the 'how' of quality. It becomes important to understand the setting of policy and objectives, i.e. the standard setting process and the determinants of the standards that will be adopted. Strategy is the process by which appropriate management systems will be designed and implemented to ensure that the standards are complied with. The day-to-day actions and responses are determined by the tactics employed to ensure that deviations are corrected and prevented. The third area concentrates on the outcomes of combining the first two areas and considers the 'what' of quality. It requires the evaluation of standards, systems, and day-to-day actions in the manner discussed in Chapter 6. Furthermore, in order to maximise the interrelationships and contributions that stakeholders make to hallmark events, it is essential that greater attention is given to the role of the providers and the public in event management and planning.

Providers and Public: The Importance of Community Control of Event Planning

Owner and consumer perspectives on events have been relatively well covered in the event literature. Provider and public perspectives, particularly in terms of community and small scale events, have not been so well examined (the work of Frisby and Getz on Ontario festivals and events referred to throughout this book is a welcome exception to this situation). Nevertheless, the evidence that is available would appear to suggest that from provider and public perspectives, two points are central to the hosting of events: they must be unique and they must have community support.

Focusing on Uniqueness In order to be successful, hallmark events should focus on their uniqueness in order to carve out a niche in the visitor market. By concentrating on what is unique to the host community, event organisers can gain a competitive advantage over other events and tourist attractions. Armstrong, for example, argues that it is a myth to believe that what goes well in one place will go well in another and concludes that 'it is clear that a project designed uniquely to

Table 9.2   Events and the community: three attitudinal archetypes

Parameter	Type I	Type II	Type III
Underlying value	Locals, who live here, set the tone. Outsiders considered second best.	Outsiders are more interesting and valuable to event and community. Locals considered second-best.	Success and continuity demand equal sharing by outsiders and locals.
Primary theme	Usually always local or indigenous. May build on ethnic, religious, or historical theme peculiar to the community.	May be either local or international, but is intended for outside audience.	May be either local or international, but attempts to integrate both dimensions.
Target market	Local visitors. Outsiders really not welcome.	Outside visitors. Locals given only incidental consideration.	Mix of outside and local visitors.
Organisation and leadership	Key role reserved for locals, who alone have sensitivity to manage event. Outsiders hired only for specialised technical areas.	Key role reserved for outsiders, who are considered to have superior skills. Locals may have secondary roles.	Best-person approach – using combination of outside and local managers.
Financial support	Local public and private funding critical. Little solicitation of outside funds. Best to go-it-alone.	Active outside support solicited. Linkages to external corporate support; television revenues essential. Minimal local support	Success depends on attracting substantial outside and local financial support. Shared approach considered best.

Source: After Heenan, 1978, p.31

meet specific needs in a unique community fares much better than imitations' (1986, p.23). Similarly, the Canadian Government Office of Tourism (1982, p.5) identified four criteria which appear basic to the successful hosting of hallmark events and festivals. Events must

- be conceived with imagination;
- have a strong focal point of interest;
- be unique and entertaining, not a carbon copy of similar projects held in neighbouring communities; and
- capture local interest and enthusiasm from the moment it is first proposed.

Maximisation of Benefits to the Host Community Events reflect the central character of a community (Heenan, 1978), they express the social structures, power relationships, and social boundaries. From this perspective three archetypal representations of the values, themes, target markets, organisation and financial support for events can be established (Heenan, 1978) (Table 9.2). Type I reflects exclusively local themes and values that typically occur at the community level and are often characterised by the folk and religious festivals and celebrations discussed in Chapter 2. Type II is dominated by xenophilia, the love of things foreign, which

Heenan argues may be either a manifestation of cultural inferiority or simply a reflection of economic reality or, alternatively, may occur because of the perceptions of one set of stakeholders, the owners, at the expense of others. Type III 'integrates the positive features of the xenophobic and xenophilic approaches. Here, outside investors and community groups agree that a comprehensive appeal to both insiders and outsiders will best insure a program's viability' in a collaborative manner which 'underscores the community's involvement with the outside world' (1978, p.32).

Heenan's categorisation of events, albeit idealised, presents a fundamental maxim to the event organisers, 'The first job of event planners is to get in touch with people at the grassroots' (St-Onge, 1991, p.60). Without the support of the host community sustainable forms of event tourism cannot be established. For many years, the support of communities for large-scale events was either assumed to be automatic or was ignored. However, social and environmental concerns, and a desire for community consultation in event planning has changed all that. As Nancarrow (1989, p.x) observed, 'any city hosting a hallmark event should consider the residents and their needs and expectations, where perhaps previously they have been overlooked in favour of the economic and political justification'. Furthermore, the involvement of government in the management and planning of nearly all types and levels of hallmark events 'is subject to certain special considerations, not the least of which is responsibility to the tax-payer – who just happens to be both sponsor and client of the event' (St-Onge, 1991, p.53). Therefore, in order to examine the ways in which the benefits of event tourism can be maximised for the residents, the next section discusses the importance of integrating events within a long-term approach to tourism development.

The Need to Integrate Hallmark Events Within a Long-Term Approach to Tourism Development

Hallmark events do not occur in isolation from their economic, social and environmental milieux. As noted in the first chapter, events both influence and are products of the society in which they are located. Similarly, the use of events to attract tourists should not be separated from the broader scope of tourism development (Ahn, 1987; Hall, 1989b). The lessons of an integrated quality management approach to events can be applied to tourism in general. The existence of a wealth of tourist infrastructure and 'ready-made' tourist attractions does not ensure the long-term future of event hosts as a major tourist destination. As Butler (1980, p. 10) observed:

> The assumption that tourist areas will always remain tourist areas and be attractive to tourists appears to be implicit in tourism planning. Public and private agencies, rarely, if ever, refer to the anticipated life span of a tourist area or its attractions. Rather, because tourism has shown, as yet, an unlimited potential for growth, despite economic recessions, it is taken for granted that numbers of visitors will continue to increase.

Events should be managed to meet the needs of all stakeholders and should be incorporated within broader tourism development strategies. However, the benefits of event tourism will clearly not be maximised unless they have community support and are appropriate to local needs and circumstances. As Huxley (1991, p.151) stated, 'in the long term, the question of the economic and social viability of strategies based on tourism must be carefully reassessed. Rather than "making cities fun" for some people, we should be making them sustainable and convivial for all of us'. Similarly, Frisby and Getz (1989, p.11) argued:

> Tourism agencies should not focus on turning all festivals into tourist attractions; rather they should foster high quality event management and products. Overemphasizing tourism could cause serious problems for volunteer managers who have a primary responsibility to the community. Well run and authentic community celebrations will automatically have appeal to tourists.

'We do know that the Olympics, The World Cup and myriad other contests attract hordes. International and intercontinental movements are the rule where these powerful travel lures are concerned. But still we have no systematic database and no valid means of judging the variable effects of different types of mega-events' (Rooney, 1988, p.94). Armstrong (1986) has argued that international sporting events often do not have a net positive impact on tourism. Furthermore, in a study of the five Olympic Games in Europe between 1960 and 1984, Schulmeister has criticised the assumption that holding a Summer or Winter Olympics will automatically have a positive effect on attracting tourists to a city or region and found that

- Before and during an Olympiad, there was an increase in demand for expensive accommodation, but [a] sharp decline for lower cost hotels.
- People changed their travel patterns, staying away by the thousands; local vacationers go elsewhere. (in Armstrong, 1986, p.24)

Furthermore, substantial doubts may be raised as to the benefits of mega-events as an employment generating device. In the case of the Calgary Winter Olympics labour demand was expected to build up from 700 person-years in 1984 to a pre-Games peak of 3,600 in 1987 as the construction phase neared completion. During the Games year of 1988, total labour demand was expected to be approximately 6,800 person-years (DPA Group, 1985). However, it was also noted that 'labour demand is expected to drop off rapidly after the Games and governments should investigate means of reducing this impact through innovative scheduling of capital projects or events which would absorb some of this surplus labour' (DPA Group, 1985, p.vi). In the case of the 1991 World Student Games in Sheffield, Foley (1991a, p.17) argued that 'in total nearly 1,980 jobs will be directly created by the Games at an average cost of £82,370 per job. This figure is certainly high… If an equivalent amount of money was spent on factories or offices there would be far more jobs created (or accommodated) in the buildings provided'.

One of the main reasons for the fascination of urban elites with events is their perceived economic, commercial, promotional and political benefits. Smaller events, with correspondingly lower costs and less social dislocation may be more effective in attracting tourists, utilising existing facilities and meeting community needs and concerns. However, they do not meet the interests of elites nor, often, of government. As Crenson (1971, p.181) recognised, pluralism is 'no guarantee of political openness or popular sovereignty', and 'neither the study of [overt] decision-making' nor the existence of 'visible diversity' will tell us anything about 'those groups and issues which may have been shut out of a town's... life'.

'An event should be a unique and innovative response to a particular situation, set of problems or a goal achievement strategy for a particular location' (Armstrong, 1986, p.35), it should not be regarded as a universal panacea for failed economic development policies. As Slade, Picard and Blackorby (1986, p.252) commented in the case of the Vancouver Expo:

> Perhaps the most enduring lesson of Expo 86 is that something is seriously wrong with the province's strategy of economic development through megaprojects. The government has shown a disturbing tendency to drop vast amounts of public funds into megaprojects like Expo 86 which are deficient in terms of both hard-headed sense of business profitability and economic desirability for the province as a whole.

Events should be community specific and developed in and out of the particular set of economic, social and environmental circumstances of the host. However, events do present a dilemma 'because the strategy for getting the maximum local benefit will not necessarily generate the maximum national benefit' (Marris, 1987, p.4). It may well be possible to find an appropriate balance between local, regional and national demands, yet in many cases, it will not. Decisions therefore have to be made about exactly why, how and for who, events are being held. I for one will place my bets. If clichés are what people want then clichés they will get. If communities lose their identity, if they stop doing the things that make that community unique, that have a local style, that are authentic to host and guest and are real for that community, then we won't have a tourism industry at all.

References

Abratt, R., Grobler, P.S., 1989, The evaluation of sports sponsorship, *International Journal of Advertising*, 8: 351–62

Ahn, J-Y., 1987, The role and impact of mega-events and attractions on tourism development in Asia, 133–186 in Association Internationale d'Experts Scientifiques du Tourisme, *The role and impact of mega-events on regional and national tourism development*, Association Internationale d'Experts Scientifiques du Tourisme, St. Gallen

Albertsen, N., 1988, Postmodernism, post-Fordism and critical social theory, *Society and Space*, 6: 339–66

Allix, A., 1922, The geography of fairs: illustrated by Old-World examples, *Geographical Review*, 12: 332–69

Allwood, J., 1977, *The great exhibitions*, Studio Vista, London

America's Cup Defence Tenancy Working Party, 1985, *Final Report of the America's Cup defence tenancy working party*, America's Cup Defence Tenancy Working Party, Perth

America's Cup Information Centre, 1985, *Government participation and responsibility*, America's Cup Information Centre, Fremantle

America's Cup Information Centre, 1987, *America's Cup... government involvement in retrospect*, America's Cup Information Centre, Fremantle

America's Cup Support Group, 1984, *America's Cup defence 1987: the Commonwealth's response*, America's Cup Support Group, Fremantle

Anderson, R., Wachtel, E., 1986, Introduction, 1–17 in R. Anderson and E. Wachtel, eds, *The Expo story*, Harbour Publishing, Madiera Park

Andressen, B., 1981, *Planning for the social impacts of tourism: The Spray Lake Resort, the Winter Olympics, and Canmore*, unpublished MA thesis, University of Waterloo, Waterloo

Archer, B.H., 1977, *Tourism multipliers: the state of the art*, Bangor Occasional Papers in Economics No.11, University of Wales Press, Bangor

Archer, B.H., 1980, Forecasting demand: quantitative and intuitive techniques, *International Journal of Tourism Management*, 1: 5–12

Archer, B.H., 1982, The value of multipliers and their policy implications, *Tourism Management*, 3: 236–41

Archer, B.H., 1986, Demand forecasting and estimation, 77–85 in J.R.B. Ritchie and C.R. Goeldner, eds, *Travel, tourism and hospitality research*, John Wiley,

New York

Armstrong, C., 1988, Sports sponsorship: a case study approach to measuring its effectiveness, *European Research*, 16: 97–103

Armstrong, J., 1984, *Contemporary prestige centres for art and culture, exhibitions, sports and conferences: an international survey*, unpublished doctoral theses, Centre for Urban and Regional Studies, University of Birmingham, Birmingham, England

Armstrong, J., 1986, International events and popular myths, 7–37 in Travel and Tourism Research Association (Canadian Chapter), *International events: the real tourism impact, proceedings of the 1985 Canada chapter conference*, Travel and Tourism Research Association (Canadian Chapter), Edmonton

Arnold, A., Fischer, A., Hatch, J., Paix, B., 1989, The Grand Prix – road accidents and the philosophy of hallmark events, 186–94 in G.J. Syme, B.J. Shaw, D.M. Fenton, W.S. Mueller, eds, *The planning and evaluation of hallmark events*, Avebury, Aldershot

Ascher, F., 1985, *Transnational corporations and cultural identities*, UNESCO, Paris

Ashworth, G., Goodall, B., 1988, Tourist images: marketing considerations, 213–38 in B. Goodall and G. Ashworth, eds, *Marketing in the tourism industry: the promotion of destination regions*, Croom Helm, London

Asian Coalition for Housing Rights, 1989, Evictions in Seoul, South Korea, *Environment and Urbanization* 1: 89–94

Association Internationale d'Experts Scientifiques du Tourisme, 1991, *Quality tourism: concept of a sustainable tourism development, harmonising economical, social and ecological interests*, Association Internationale d'Experts Scientifiques du Tourisme, St. Gallen

Auf der Maur, N., 1976, *The billion-dollar game: Jean Drapeau and the 1976 Olympics*, James Lorimer and Company, Toronto

Australian Federal Police, 1986, *Australian Federal Police Annual Report 1985–86*, Parliamentary Paper No. 416/1986, Australian Government Publishing Service, Canberra

Badger, R.R., 1979, *The great American fair: the World's Columbian Exposition and American culture*, Nelson-Hall, Chicago

Badmin, P., Coombs, M., Rayner, G., 1988, *Leisure operational management Volume 1: facilities*, Longman/ILAM Leisure Management Series, Longman, Harlow

Bailey, P., 1987, *Leisure and class in Victorian England: rational recreation and the contest for control, 1830–1885*, Methuen, London

BarOn, R.R., 1975, *Seasonality in tourism*, Economist Intelligence Unit, London

Beardsley, P., 1987, Priorities of small budget event sponsors, 151–3 in Department of Sport and Recreation, *Marketing sport and recreation events in country regions, Proceedings of a two day seminar 'special event marketing', 15th and 16th July, Warrnambool Performing Arts Centre*, Department of Sport and Recreation, Melbourne

Bendix, R., 1989, Tourism and cultural displays: inventing traditions for whom? *Journal of American Folklore*, 10(2): 131–46

Benedict, B., 1983, The anthropology of World Fairs, 1–65 in B. Benedict, ed., *The anthropology of world fairs*, Scolar Press, London

Benedict, B., ed., 1983, *The anthropology of world fairs*, Scolar Press, London

Bentick B.L., 1986, The role of the Grand Prix in promoting South Australian entrepreneurship, exports and the terms of trade, 169–85 in J.P.A. Mules, J.H. Hatch and T.L. Mules, eds, *The Adelaide Grand Prix: the impact of a special event*, The Centre for South Australian Economic Studies, Adelaide

Berman, R.A., 1987, The routinization of charismatic modernism and the problem of post-modernity, *Cultural Critique*, 5: 49–68

Berry, M., 1988: The impact of mega-projects on metropolitan development: the case of Darling Harbour, *Planner*, 7 (3): 7–14

Blake, C., McDowall, S., Devlen, J., 1979, *The 1978 Open Championship at St. Andrews: an economic impact study*, Academic Press, Edinburgh

Bodewes, T., 1981, Development of advanced tourism studies in Holland, *Annals of Tourism Research*, 8(1): 35–51

Bonnemaison, S., 1990, City policies and cyclical events, 24–32 in *Celebrations: urban spaces transformed, Design Quarterly 147*, Massachusets Institute of Technology for the Walker Art Center, Cambridge

Bonnemaison, S., Macy, C., 1990, The RamLila in Ramnagar, 2–23 in *Celebrations: urban spaces transformed, Design Quarterly 147*, Massachusets Institute of Technology for the Walker Art Center, Cambridge

Boorstin, D.J., 1973, *The image: a guide to pseudo-events in America*, Atheneum, New York.

Bos, H., van der Kamp, C., Zom, A., 1987, Events in Holland, *Revue de Tourisme*, 4: 16–19

Bratton, B., 1991, Tourism: the role of volunteers at events and attractions, 597–8 in R.D. Bratton, F.M. Go, and J.R.B. Ritchie, eds, *New Horizons in Tourism and Hospitality Education, Training and Research* , World Tourism Education and Research Centre, University of Calgary, Calgary

Breen, M., 1991, By leaps and bounds, *Asia Travel Trade*, June: 41–2

Brissenden, C., 1987, Expo 86 – scenario for success, *Tourism Management*, 8(1): 49–53

British Tourist Authority/English Tourist Board, 1988, *Sightseeing in 1987*, British Tourist Authority/English Tourist Board Research Services, London

Britton, S., 1990, The role of services in production, *Progress in Human Geography*, 14: 529–46

Britton, S., forthcoming a, Services and national accumulation, *International Journal of Urban and Regional Research*

Britton, S., forthcoming b, Tourism, capital and place: towards a critical geography of tourism, *Environment and Planning D, Society and Space*

Buck, R.C., 1977, Making good business better: a second look at staged tourist attractions, *Journal of Travel Research* 15(3): 30–2

Bull, A., 1991, *The economics of travel and tourism*, Longman Cheshire, South Melbourne

Burns, J.P.A., 1987, Analysing 'special events' with illustrations from the 1985 Adelaide Grand Prix, 1–14 in *The impact and marketing of special events, papers of the Australian Travel Research Workshop, Mt. Buffalo Chalet, Victoria, 12–14 November, 1986*, Australian Standing Committee on Tourism, Canberra

Burns, J.P.A., Hatch, J.H., Mules, F.J., eds, 1986, *The Adelaide Grand Prix: the impact of a special event*, The Centre for South Australian Economic Studies, Adelaide

Burns, J.P.A., Mules, T.J., 1986, A framework for the analysis of major special events, 5–38 in J.P.A. Mules, J.H. Hatch and T.L. Mules, eds, *The Adelaide Grand Prix: the impact of a special event*, The Centre for South Australian Economic Studies, Adelaide

Burns, J.P.A., Mules, T.J., 1989, An economic evaluation of the Adelaide Grand Prix, 172–85 in G.J. Syme, B.J. Shaw, D.M. Fenton, W.S. Mueller, eds, *The planning and evaluation of hallmark events*, Avebury, Aldershot

Butler, R.W., 1980, The concept of a tourist area cycle of evolution, implications for the management of resources, *Canadian Geographer*, 24 (1): 5–12

Butler, R.W., 1990, Alternative tourism: pious hope or trojan horse, *Journal of Travel Research*, 28 (3): 40–45

Butler, R.W., Grigg, J.M., 1989, The hallmark event that got away: the case of the 1991 Pan American Games and London, Ontario, 142–53 in G.J. Syme, B.J. Shaw, D.M. Fenton, W.S. Mueller, eds, *The planning and evaluation of hallmark events*, Avebury, Aldershot

Butler, R.W., Smale, B.J.A., 1991, Geographic perspectives on festivals in Ontario, *Journal of Applied Recreation Research*, 16(1): 3–23

Camacho, J.A., 1979, *Festivals, commemorations and anniversaries*, rev. ed., British Tourist Authority, London

Cameron, C., 1989, Cultural tourism and urban revitalization, *Tourism Recreation Research*, 14(1): 23–32

Canadian Government Office of Tourism, 1982, *Planning festivals and events*, Canadian Government Office of Tourism, Ottawa

Canan, P., Hennessy, M., 1989, The growth machine, tourism and the selling of culture, *Sociological Perspectives*, 32 (2): 227–43

Carroll, P., Donohue, K., 1991, Special events and tourism, 129–40 in P. Carroll, K. Donohue, M. McGovern, J. McMillen, eds, *Tourism in Australia*, Harcourt Brace Jovanich, Sydney

Carroll, P., 1989, The origins of EXPO 88, *Australian Journal of Public Administration*, 48 (1): 41–52

Carter, J., 1986, Potential impact of a one-off event: the America's Cup, 3–9 in Australia Council, *Tourism and the arts*, Policy and Planning Division, Australia Council, North Sydney

Cawelti, J., 1968, America on display, 1876, 1893, 1933, 316–63 in F.C. Jaher, ed., *America in the age of industrialism*, Free Press, New York

Centre for Applied and Business Research, 1985, *Visitor numbers study: America's Cup defence series, 1986/87*, Centre for Applied and Business Research, Nedlands

Centre for Applied and Business Research, 1987, *America's Cup defence series, 1986/87, impact on the community*, Centre for Applied Business Research,

University of Western Australia, Nedlands

Chaffee, E.E., 1985, Three models of strategy, *Academy of Management Review*, 10 (1): 89–96

Chang, P.C., Singh, K.K., 1990, Risk management for mega-events: the 1988 Olympic Winter Games, *Tourism Management*, 11 (1): 45–52

Chesneaux, J., 1978, *Pasts and futures, or what is history for?*, Thames and Hudson, London

Chick, C., 1983, Tourism Canada, *Recreation Canada*, 42 (5): 24–5

China Travel Press, 1989, Asian Games centre to become meetings venue, *China Travel Press*, 3 (9): 6

Coates, A.W., 1964, American scholarship comes of age: the Louisiana purchase exposition of 1904, *Journal of the History of Ideas*, 22: 404–17

Cohen, A., 1980, Drama and politics in the development of a London carnival, *Man* (n.s), 15: 65–87

Cohen, A., 1982, A polyethnic London carnival as a contested cultural performance, *Ethnic and Racial Studies*, 5 (1): 23–41

Cohen, E., 1979, Rethinking the sociology of tourism, *Annals of Tourism Research*, 6 (1): 8–35

Collins, R.E., 1983, Tourism and heritage conservation – the Pacific experience, *Heritage Australia*, 2 (2): 58–9

Commissioner of Police, 1986, *Annual Report of the Commissioner of Police for the year ended June 30, 1986, 52198-1*, Government Printer, Perth

Cooke, K., 1982, Guidelines for socially appropriate tourism development in British Columbia, *Journal of Travel Research*, 21 (1): 22–8

Coopers and Lybrand Consulting Group, 1989, National Capital Region 1988 festivals study, *Recreation Canada*, 47(4): 24–9

Coppock, J.T., 1977, Tourism as a tool for regional development, 1.2–1.15 in B.S. Duffield, ed., *Tourism: a tool for regional development*, Tourism and Recreation Research Unit, University of Edinburgh, Edinburgh

Corcoran, T., 1988, Advantages and considerations in staging a major sporting event: World Cup skiing competitions at Waterville Valley, New Hampshire, 101–2 in *Tourism research: expanding boundaries*, Travel and Tourism Research Association, Nineteenth Annual Conference, Montreal, Quebec, Canada, 19–23 June 1988, Bureau of Economic and Business Research, Graduate School of Business, University of Utah, Salt Lake City

Corporation of the City of Melbourne, 1989, *Tourism development plan, part 1, the Corporation's position statement on tourism*, Corporation of the City of Melbourne, Melbourne

Coubertin, P. de, 1967, *The Olympic idea: discourses and essays*, Stuttgart

Cousineau, C., 1991, Festivals and events: a fertile ground for leisure research, *Journal of Applied Recreation Research*, 16 (1): 1–2

Coutts, H., 1986, Profile of a blockbuster, *Museums Journal*, 86 (1): 23–6

Cowie, I., 1986, Housing policy options in relation to the America's Cup, *Urban Policy and Research*, 3 (2): 40–1

Cowie, I., 1987, The role of country sport in regional development: prospects and current issues, 31–57 in Department of Sport and Recreation, *Marketing sport* and recreation events in country regions, Proceedings of a two day seminar 'special event marketing', 15th and 16th July, Warrnambool Performing Arts Centre, Department of Sport and Recreation, Melbourne

Cowie, I., 1989, Possible measure to protect private tenants from any impact associated with hallmark events with special reference to the America's Cup defence in Perth, 81–91 in G.J. Syme, B.J. Shaw, D.M. Fenton, W.S. Mueller, eds, The planning and evaluation of hallmark events, Avebury, Aldershot

Craik, J., 1988a, The social impacts of tourism, 17–31 in B. Faulkner and M. Fagence, eds, Frontiers in Australian tourism: the search for new perspectives in policy development and research, Bureau of Tourism Research, Canberra

Craik, J., 1988b, Showing the world: the politics of Expo 88, paper delivered to Australasian Political Studies Association Conference, 26–8 August, University of New England, Armidale

Craik, J., 1988c, The site of EXPO or the art of savoir faire, paper delivered to the Conference on Genre, ASPACLS, 4–8 July, University of Queensland, St. Lucia

Craik, J., 1989, The Expo experience: the politics of expositions, Australian–Canadian Studies, 7 (1–2): 95–112

Crenson, M.A., 1971, The un politics of air pollution: a study of non-decisionmaking in the cities, The John Hopkins Press, Baltimore

Cribb, M., 1984, The political impact of the Games III, 49–52 in The 1982 Commonwealth Games: a retrospect, Australian Studies Centre, University of Queensland, Brisbane

Cunneen, C., Findlay, M., Lynch, R., Tupper, V., 1989, Dynamics of collective conflict: riots at the Bathhurst 'bike races, The Law Book Company, Sydney

Cunneen, C., Lynch, R., 1988a, The socio-historical roots of conflict in riots at the Bathurst 'bike races, Australian and New Zealand Journal of Sociology, 24 (1): 5–31

Cunneen, C., Lynch, R., 1988b, The social meanings of conflict in riots at the Australian Grand Prix Motorcycle Races, Leisure Studies, 7 (1): 1–19

Curti, M., 1950, America at the World's Fairs, 1851–1893, American Historical Review, 55: 833–56

Da Matta, R., 1977, Constraint and license: a preliminary study of two Brazilian national rituals, in S.F. Moore and B. Myerhoff, eds, Secular ritual, Van Gorcum, Amsterdam

Da Matta, R., 1984, Carnival in multiple planes, 208–40 in J.J. MacAloon, ed., Rite, drama, festival, spectacle: rehearsals toward a theory of cultural performance, Institute for the Study of Human issues, Philadelphia

Davidson, G., 1982/83, Exhibitions, Australian Cultural History, 2: 5–21

Davidson, G., 1988, Festivals of nationhood: the international expositions, in S.L. Goldberg and F.B. Smith, eds, Australian cultural history, Cambridge University Press, Cambridge

Davidson, L.S., Schaffer, W.A., 1980, A discussion of methods employed in analysing the impact of short-term entertainment events, Journal of Travel Research, 18 (3): 12–16

Dawson, D., 1991, Panem et circenses? A critical analysis of ethnic and multicultural festivals, *Journal of Applied Recreation Research*, 16(1): 35–52

Day, P., 1988, *The big party syndrome a study of the impact of special events and inner urban change in Brisbane*, Department of Social Work, University of Queensland, St. Lucia

Debord, G., 1973, *Society of the spectacle*, Black and Red, Detroit

Decore, L., 1986, Introduction, 2–3 in Travel and Tourism Research Association (Canadian Chapter), *International events: the real tourism impact, proceedings of the 1985 Canada chapter conference*, Travel and Tourism Research Association (Canadian Chapter), Edmonton

Della Bitta, A.J., Loudon, D.L., Booth, G.G., Weeks, R.R., 1977, Estimating the economic impact of a short-term tourist event, *Journal of Travel Research*, 16 (Fall): 10–15

Department of Sport, Recreation and Tourism, 1986, *Department of Sport, Recreation and Tourism Annual Report 1985–86*, Parliamentary Paper No. 413/ 1986, Australian Government Publishing Service, Canberra

Derek Murray Consulting Associates, 1985, *A study to determine the impact of events on local economies*, Saskatchewan Tourism and Small Business, Regina

Diffendererfer, P., 1989, The economic expenditure of fans attending cactus league games in Scottsdale, Arizona, *Visions in Leisure and Business: An International Journal of Personal Services, Programming and Administration*, 8 (3): 61–75

Dixon, O.F., 1982, *Report on action taken by police regarding allegations of graft and corruption in the Police Force, Western Australia*, Government Printer, Perth

Dobkin, M.M., 1983, A twenty-five-million dollar mirage, 66–93 in B. Benedict, ed., *The Anthropology of World Fairs*, Scolar Press, London

Doenecke, J.D., 1972, Myths, machines, and markets: the Columbian Exposition of 1893, *Journal of Popular Culture*, 6: 535–44

Douglas, W.L., 1984, An event of place, *Landscape Architecture*, July/August: 48–55

Dovey, K., 1989, Old Scabs/new scars: the hallmark event and the everyday environment, 73–80 in G.J. Syme, B.J. Shaw, D.M. Fenton, W.S. Mueller, eds, *The planning and evaluation of hallmark events*, Avebury, Aldershot

DPA Group in association with Pannell Kerr Forster, 1985, *Economic impacts of the XV Olympic Winter Games*, prepared for the City of Calgary and Alberta Tourism and Small Business, DPA Group in association with Pannell Kerr Forster, Calgary

Dragicevic, M., 1991, Towards sustainable tourism, 29–62 in Association Internationale d'Experts Scientifiques du Tourisme, *Quality tourism: concept of a sustainable tourism development, harmonising economical, social and ecological interests*, Association Internationale d'Experts Scientifiques du Tourisme, St. Gallen

Dryden, P.F., 1987, Assessing economic impacts of regional short term events, 70–84 in Department of Sport and Recreation, *Marketing sport and recreation events in country regions, Proceedings of a two day seminar 'special event marketing', 15th and 16th July, Warrnambool Performing Arts Centre*, Department of Sport and Recreation, Melbourne

Duffy, M., 1991/92, The Olympics: Greiner's lost race, *The Independent Monthly*, 3 (6): 12

Dungan, Jr., T., 1984, How cities plan special events, *The Cornell Hotel and Restaurant Administration Quarterly*, 25 (1): 83–9

Dunstan, D., 1986, Packaging the developing arts for an increase in tourist trade, 18–23 in Australia Council, *Tourism and the arts*, Policy and Planning Division, Australia Council, North Sydney

Dutton, I., Hall, C.M., 1989, Making tourism sustainable: the policy/practice conundrum, in *Proceedings of the Environment Institute of Australia second national conference*, Melbourne, 9–11 October

Duvignaud, J., 1976, Festivals: a sociological approach, *Cultures*, 3: 15–25

Dyck, N., 1979, Powwow and the expressions of community in Western Canada, *Ethnos*, 44(1–2): 78–98

Dyck, N., 1983, Political powwow: the rise and fall of an urban native festival, 165–84 in F.E. Manning, ed., *The celebration of society: perspectives on contemporary cultural performance*, Bowling Green University Popular Press, Bowling Green

Eastaugh, A., Weiss, N., 1989, Broadening the market, 58–67 in Uzzell, D.L., ed., *Heritage interpretation, vol. 2, The visitor experience*, Belhaven Press, London

Economic Impact Resources Consulting, 1989, *1996 Melbourne Olympic Games: a preliminary social impact assessment*, a report for the Social Impact Assessment Steering Committee prepared by Economic Impact Resources Consulting, Melbourne

Edgely, C., 1987, Beer, speed and real men: Indianapolis during the month of May, *Sport Place*, 1 (1): 20–6

Edmonson, M.S., 1956, Carnival in New Orleans, *Caribbean Quarterly*, 4 (3–4): 233–45

Edwards, H., 1984, The free enterprise Olympics, *Journal of Sport and Social Issues*, 8 (2): i–iv

Edwards, J., 1986, *Prostitution and human rights: a Western Australian case study*, Discussion Paper No. 8, Human Rights Commission, Canberra

Evans, M., 1982, Planning for the World's Fair: how to house five million guests, *The Cornell Hotel and Restaurant Administration Quarterly*, 23 (1): 31–4

Falassi, A., ed., 1987, *Time out of time: essays on the festival*, University of New Mexico Press, Albuquerque

Farber, C., 1983, High, healthy and happy: Ontario mythology on parade, 33–50 in F. Manning, ed., *The celebration of society: perspectives on contemporary cultural performance*, Bowling Green Popular Press, Bowling Green

Fawcett, B., 1986, Why the carnival came to town: the politics of Expo 86, *The Canadian Forum*, May: 10–15

Fischer, A., Hatch, J., Paix, B., 1986, Road accidents and the Grand Prix, 151–68 in J.P.A. Burns, J.H. Hatch, and T.J. Mules, eds, *The Adelaide Grand Prix – the impact of a special event*, Centre for South Australian Economic Studies, Adelaide

Fleming, W.R., Toepper, L., 1990, Economic impact studies: relating the positive and negative impacts to tourism development, *Journal of Travel Research*, 29 (1): 35–42

Fletcher, J., Snee, H., 1989, Input-output analysis, 223-6 in S.F. Witt and L. Moutinho, eds, *Tourism marketing and management handbook*, Prentice Hall, Hemel Hempstead

Foley, P., 1991a, The impact of the World Student Games on Sheffield, paper presented to the cities of spectacle session, Institute of British Geographers Conference, Sheffield, 4 January

Foley, P., 1991b, The impact of major events: a case study of the World Student Games and Sheffield, *Environmental and Planning C: Government and Policy*, 9 (1): 65–79

Frechtling, D.C., 1987, Assessing the impacts of travel and tourism – introduction to travel impact estimation, 325–31 in J.R.B. Ritchie and C.R. Goeldner, eds, *Travel, tourism and hospitality research; a handbook for managers and researchers*, John Wiley and Sons, New York

Friedmann, M., 1990, Editor's notes, in *Celebrations urban spaces transformed*, *Design Quarterly 147*, Massachusets Institute of Technology for the Walker Art Center, Cambridge.

Fremantle Focus, 25 August 1986

Fremantle Gazette, 1986, Life after the Cup, 14 October: 23

Frisby, W., Getz, D., 1989, Festival management: a case study perspective, *Journal of Travel Research*, 28 (1): 7–11

Gaedeke, R.M., 1977, *Marketing in private and public nonprofit organizations: perspectives and illustrations*, Goodyear Publishing Company, Santa Monica

Gardner, M.P., Shuman, P.J., 1987, Sponsorship: an important component of the promotions mix, *Journal of Advertising*, 16: 11–17

Garnsey, J.M., 1984, Queensland and Brisbane as a focus for advertising strategies and the Games, 19–23 in *The 1982 Commonwealth Games: a retrospect*, Australian Studies Centre, University of Queensland, Brisbane

Garratt, B., 1987, *The learning organisation*, Fontana, London

Gartner, W.C., Holecek, D.F., 1983, Economic impact of an annual tourism industry exposition, *Annals of Tourism Research*, 10 (2): 199–212

Geddert, R.L., Semple, R.K., 1985, Locating a major hockey league franchise: regional considerations, *Regional Science Perspectives*, 15: 13–29

Getz, D., 1977, The impact of tourism on host communities a research approach, 9.1–9.3 in B.S. Duffield, ed., *Tourism: a tool for regional development*, Tourism and Recreation Research Unit, University of Edinburgh, Edinburgh

Getz, D., 1984, Tourism, community organisation and the social multiplier, 85–100 in J. Long, R. Hecock, eds, *Leisure, tourism and social change*, Centre for Leisure Research, Dunfermline College of Physical Education

Getz, D., 1986, Models in tourism planning towards integration of theory and practice, *Tourism Management*, 7 (1): 21–32

Getz, D., 1989a, Festival and special event sponsorship: a systems approach, 305–7 in *Travel research: globalization the Pacific Rim and beyond*, The Travel and Tourism Research Association, Honolulu, Hawaii, Twentieth Annual Conference, 11–15 June, 1989, Bureau of Economic and Business Research, Graduate School of Business, University of Utah, Salt Lake City

Getz, D., 1989b, Special events defining the product, *Tourism Management*, June: 125–37

Getz, D., 1991a, *Festivals, special events, and tourism*, Van Nostrand Reinhold, New York

Getz, D., 1991b, Assessing the economic impacts of festivals and events: research issues, *Journal of Applied Recreation Research*, 16 (1): 61–77

Getz, D., Frisby, W., 1987, *Report on a survey of community-run festivals in Ontario*, Department of Recreation and Leisure Studies, University of Waterloo, Waterloo

Getz, D., Frisby, W., 1988, Evaluating management effectiveness in community-run festivals, *Journal of Travel Research*, 27(1): 22–7

Gillespie, A., 1987, Folk festival and festival folk in twentieth century America, 153–61 in A. Falassi, ed., *Time out of time: essays on the festival*, University of New Mexico Press, Albuquerque

Gilmore, D., 1975, Carnival in Fuenmayor: class conflict and social cohesion in an Andulusian town, *Journal of Anthropological Research*, 31 (4): 331–49

Goeldner, C., Long, P., 1987, The role and impact of mega-events and attractions on tourist development in North America, 119–31 in Association Internationale d'Experts Scientifiques du Tourisme, *The role and impact of mega-events on regional and national tourism development*, Association Internationale d'Experts Scientifiques du Tourisme, St. Gallen

Gonzalez, N.L., 1970, Social functions of carnival in a Dominican city, *Southwestern Journal of Anthropology*, 26 (4): 328–42

Gottdeiner, E., 1987, *The decline of urban politics: political theory and the crisis of the local state*, Sage Publications, Newbury Park

Government of Victoria, 1984, Victoria. *The next step: economic initiatives and opportunities for the 1980's*, Government of Victoria, Melbourne

Government of Victoria, 1987, *People and opportunities: Victoria's social justice strategy*, Government of Victoria, Melbourne

Gray, J., Mistele, M., Hamilton, S., Somersan, Z., Kessenich, T., 1988, *A peek into the 1988 Wisconsin State Fair, Wisconsin State Fair, August 4–14, 1988*, UWEX Cooperative Extension Service, Recreation Resource Center, University of Wisconsin-Extension, Madison

Greenhalgh, P., 1988, *Ephemeral vistas: the expositions universelles, great exhibitions and world fairs, 1851–1939*, Manchester University Press, Manchester

Greenwood, D.J., 1976, Tourism as an agent of change: a Spanish Basque case, *Annals of Tourism Research*, 3: 128–42

Greenwood, D.J., 1977, Culture by the pound, in V.L. Smith, ed., *Hosts and guests*, University of Pennsylvania, Philadelphia

Groussard, S., 1975, *The blood of Israel*, New York

Groves, D.L., 1985a, Expectations, outcomes, and impacts – a perspective, *Visions in Leisure and Business*, 4 (1): 60–69

Groves, D.L., 1985b, Analysis of the Louisiana World Exposition: a consumer perspective, *Visions in Leisure and Business*, 4 (1): 70–89

Gunn, C.A., 1977, Industry pragmatism vs tourism planning, *Leisure Sciences*, 1(1): 85–94

Gunn, C.A., 1988, *Tourism planning*, 2nd edn, Taylor and Francis, New York

Gusfield, J.R., Michalowicz, J., 1984, Secular symbolism: studies of ritual, ceremony and the symbolic order in modern life, *Annual Review of Sociology*, 10: 417–35

Gutowski, J., 1978, The protofestival: local guide to American folk behaviour, *Journal of Folklore Institute*, 15: 113–31

Gutstein, D., 1986, The impact of Expo on Vancouver, 65–99 in R. Anderson and E. Wachtel, eds, *The Expo story*, Harbour Publishing, Madiera Park

Hall, C.M., 1987, The effects of hallmark events on cities, *Journal of Travel Research*, Fall: 44–5

Hall, C.M., 1988a, Expos 86 and 88: a comparison, *Expo 88 Seminar*, Faculty of Business, Queensland Institute of Technology, Brisbane

Hall, C.M., 1988b, Broadening the scope of tourism research in Australia, 329–40 in B. Faulkner and M. Fagence, eds, Frontiers in Australian tourism: the search for new perspectives in policy development and research, Bureau of Tourism Research, Canberra

Hall, C.M., 1988c, The future of tourism in Australia: counting the pennies without counting the cost, *Recreation Australia*, 7 (4): 2–11, 20

Hall, C.M., 1989a, Hallmark tourist events: analysis, definition, methodology and review, 3–19 in G.J. Syme, B.J. Shaw, D.M. Fenton, W.S. Mueller, eds, *The planning and evaluation of hallmark events*, Avebury, Aldershot

Hall, C.M., 1989b, Hallmark events and the planning process, 20–39 in Syme, G.J., Shaw, B.J., Fenton, D.M., Mueller, W.S., eds, *The planning and evaluation of hallmark events*, Avebury, Aldershot

Hall, C.M., 1989c, The politics of hallmark events, 219–41 in Syme, G.J., Shaw, B.J., Fenton, D.M., Mueller, W.S., eds, *The planning and evaluation of hallmark events*, Avebury, Aldershot

Hall, C.M., 1989d, The definition and analysis of hallmark events, *Geojournal*, 19(3): 263–8

Hall, C.M., 1989e, The impacts of the 1987 America's Cup on Fremantle, Western Australia: implications for the hosting of hallmark events, 74–80 in R. Welch, ed., *Geography in action*, Department of Geography, University of Otago, Dunedin

Hall, C.M., 1991, *Introduction to tourism in Australia: impacts, planning and development*, Longman Cheshire, South Melbourne

Hall, C.M., McArthur, S., 1991, Whose heritage, whose interpretation, and whose quality tourism?: perspectives on the politics and sustainability of heritage tourism, in Heritage Interpretation International, *Joining hands for quality tourism: interpretation, preservation and the travel industry, the third global congress of heritage interpretation international*, University of Hawaii, Honolulu

Hall, C.M., Selwood, H.J., 1987. Cup gained, paradise lost? a case study of the 1987 America's Cup as a hallmark event, 267–74 in R. Le Heron, M. Roche, M. Shepherd, eds, *Geography and Society in a Global Context*, Department of

Geography, Massey University, Palmerston North

Hall, C.M., Selwood, H.J., 1988, The political impact of hallmark tourist events: the case of the Australian bicentennial, Canadian Association of Geographer's Conference, Halifax, June

Hall, C.M., Selwood, H.J., 1989, America's Cup lost, paradise retained? The dynamics of a hallmark tourist event, 103–18 in Syme, G.J., Shaw, B.J., Fenton, D.M., Mueller, W.S., eds, *The planning and evaluation of hallmark events*, Avebury, Aldershot

Hall, C.M., Weiler, B., 1992, Introduction: what's special about special interest tourism?, 1–14 in B. Weiler and C.M. Hall, eds, *Special interest tourism*, Belhaven Press, London

Hall, C.M., Zeppel, H., 1990a, Cultural and heritage tourism: the new grand tour?, ✗ *Historic Environment*, 7 (3/4): 86–98

Hall, C.M., Zeppel, H., 1990b, History, architecture, environment: cultural heritage and tourism, *Journal of Travel Research*, 24 (2): 54–5

Hall, P., 1970, *Theory and practice of regional planning*, Pemberton Books, London

Hamilton, D., Steadward, B., 1986, Keys to success: volunteerism and major events, 170–3 in Travel and Tourism Research Association (Canadian Chapter), *International events: the real tourism impact, proceedings of the 1985 Canada chapter conference*, Travel and Tourism Research Association (Canadian Chapter), Edmonton

Hand, R., 1990, What represents tourism value in festivals and special events?, in Tourism South Australia, *Seminar for organisers of festivals and special events: speakers notes*, Tourism South Australia, Adelaide

Handley, P., 1991, Thailand: tarting up for company, *Far Eastern Economic Review*, 26 September: 32

Hardy, D., 1988, Historical geography and heritage studies, *Area*, 20: 333–8

Harland, J., 1989, Festival and special event sponsorships case studies from New Zealand, 309–18 in *Travel research: globalization the Pacific Rim and beyond*, The Travel and Tourism Research Association, Honolulu, Hawaii, Twentieth Annual Conference, 11–15 June 1989, Bureau of Economic and Business Research, Graduate School of Business, University of Utah, Salt Lake City

Harris, S., 1972, *Political football: the Springbok tour of Australia, 1971*, Gold Star Publications, Melbourne

Harrison, H., ed., 1980, *Dawn of a new day: the New York World's Fair, 1939/40*, The Queens Museum/New York University Press, New York

Harvey, D., 1979, Monument and myth, *Annals, Association of American Geographers*, 69: 362–81

Harvey, D., 1987, Flexible accumulation through urbanization: reflections on 'post-modernism' in the American city, *Antipode*, 19: 260–86

Harvey, D., 1988, *The condition of postmodernity: an enquiry into the origins of cultural change*, Basil Blackwell, Oxford

Harvey, D., 1990, Between space and time: reflections on the geographical imagination, *Annals of the Association of American Geographers*, 80 (3): 418–34

Haug, W.F., 1987, *Commodity aesthetics, ideology and culture*, International General, New York

Head, V., 1981, *Sponsorship: the newest marketing skill*, Woodhead–Faulkner, London

Heenan, D., 1978, Tourism and the community, a drama in three acts, *Journal of Travel Research*, 16 (4): 30–2

Heinich, N., 1988, The Pompidou Centre and its public: the limits of a utopian site, 199–212 in R. Lumley, ed., *The museum time machine: putting cultures on display*, Routledge, London and New York

Heritage Interpretation International, 1991, *Joining hands for quality tourism: interpretation, preservation and the travel industry, the third global congress of heritage interpretation international*, University of Hawaii, Honolulu

Hewison, R., 1987, *The heritage industry: Britain in a climate of decline*, Methuen, London

Hewison, R., 1988, *In anger: culture in the cold war 1945–60*, Methuen, London

Hiller, H.H., 1989, Impact and image: the convergence of urban factors in preparing for the 1988 Calgary Winter Olympics, 119–31 in G.J. Syme, B.J. Shaw, D.M. Fenton, W.S. Mueller, eds, *The planning and evaluation of hallmark events*, Avebury, Aldershot

Hiller, H.H., 1990, The urban transformation of a landmark event: the 1988 Calgary Winter Olympics, *Urban Affairs Quarterly*, 26 (1): 118–37

Hillman, S., 1986, Special events as a tool for tourism development, *Special Events Report*, 5 (16): 4–5

Hipkins, M., 1987, Making better use of urban space in Fremantle, in *People and physical environment research conference, the effects of hallmark events on cities*, Centre for Urban Research, University of Western Australia, Nedlands

Hipkins, M., 1989, How Fremantle coped with the challenge, 59–72 in G.J. Syme, B.J. Shaw, D.M. Fenton, W.S. Mueller, eds, 1989, *The planning and evaluation of hallmark events*, Avebury, Aldershot

Hirschfield, C., 1957, America on exhibition: the New York Crystal Palace, *American Quarterly*, 9: 101–16

Hoek, J.A., Gendall, P.J., West, R.D., 1990, The role of sponsorship in marketing: planning selected New Zealand companies, *New Zealand Journal of Business*, 12: 87–95

Howarth and Howarth, 1987, Strategy for growth: Australian tourism five to ten years on – release and discussion on ATIA's strategy document, identification of the principal elements of a national tourism strategy, *Tourism Towards 2000 Conference*, Western Australian Tourism Industry Association, Perth, 25 February

Hughes, C.G., 1982, The employment and economic effects of tourism reappraised, *Tourism Management*, 3 (3): 167–76

Hughes, G., 1986, Edmonton Klondike Days exposition, 223–32 in Travel and Tourism Research Association (Canadian Chapter), *International events: the real tourism impact, proceedings of the 1985 Canada chapter conference*, Travel and Tourism Research Association (Canadian Chapter), Edmonton

Hughes, H.L., 1987, Culture as a tourist resource – a theoretical consideration, *Tourism Management*, 8 (3): 205–16

Hughes, R., 1980, *The shock of the new: art and the century of change*, British Broadcasting Corporation, London

Humphreys, J.S., Walmsley, D.J., 1991, Locational conflict in metropolitan areas: Melbourne and Sydney, 1989, *Australian Geographical Studies*, 29 (2): 313–28

Hunt, J.D., 1975, Image as a factor in tourism development, *Journal of Travel Research*, 13 (Winter): 1–7

Huxley, M., 1991, Making cities fun: Darling Harbour and the immobilisation of the spectacle, 141–52 in P. Carroll, K. Donohue, M. McGovern, J. McMillen, eds, *Tourism in Australia*, Harcourt Brace Jovanich, Sydney

Huxley, M., Kerkin, K., 1988, What price the bicentennial? A political economy of the Darling Harbour project, Australasian Political Studies Association Conference, University of New England, Armidale, August

International Bureau of Exhibitions, 1989, *The International Bureau of Exhibitions and regulations respecting international exhibitions*, International Bureau of Exhibitions, Paris

Isar, R.F., 1976, Culture and the arts festival of the twentieth century, *Cultures*, 3 (2): 125–45

Jackson, J.B., 1984, *Discovering the vernacular landscape*, Yale University Press, New Haven and London

Jafari, J., 1977, Editor's page, *Annals of Tourism Research*, 5: 6–11.

Jafari, J., 1988, Tourism mega-events, *Annals of Tourism Research*, 15 (2): 272–3

Janiskee, R.L., 1979, Harvest and food festivals in South Carolina: rural delights for daytripping urbanites, paper presented at the special session on the cultural and behavioral aspects of recreation and sport, annual meeting of the Association of American Geographers, Philadelphia, April

Janiskee, B., 1980, South Carolina's harvest festivals: rural delights for day tripping urbanites, *Journal of Geography*, October: 96–104

Jeong, G-H., 1988, Tourism expectations on the 1988 Seoul Olympics: a Korean perspective, 175–82 in *Tourism research: expanding boundaries*, Travel and Tourism Research Association, Nineteenth Annual Conference, Montreal, Quebec, Canada, 19–23 June 1988, Bureau of Economic and Business Research, Graduate School of Business, University of Utah, Salt Lake City

Jones, R., 1986, Historic places and historic events; the townscape of Fremantle and the 1986–87 America's Cup defence, *Sixth International Conference of Historical Geographers*, Louisiana State University, Baton Rouge

Junker, J., 1989, Experience with major corporate sponsorship, 319–21 in *Travel research: globalization, the Pacific Rim and beyond*, The Travel and Tourism Research Association, Honolulu, Hawaii, Twentieth Annual Conference, 11–15 June 1989, Bureau of Economic and Business Research, Graduate School of Business, University of Utah, Salt Lake City

Kanin, D.B., 1980, The Olympic boycott in diplomatic context, *Journal of Sport and Social Issues*, 4 (1): 1–24

Kapferer, B., 1979, Entertaining demons: comedy, interaction and meaning in a Sinhalese healing ritual, *Social Analysis*, 1: 108–52

Kapferer, B., 1984, The ritual process and the problem of reflexivity in Sinhalese demon Exorcisms, 179–207 in J.J. MacAloon, ed., *Rite, drama, festival, spectacle: rehearsals toward a theory of cultural performance*, Institute for the Study of Human Issues, Philadelphia

Kaspar, C., 1991, Quality tourism: concept of a sustainable tourism development, harmonising economical, social and ecological interests, 21–5 in Association Internationale d'Experts Scientifiques du Tourisme, *Quality tourism: concept of a sustainable tourism development, harmonising economical, social and ecological interests*, Association Internationale d'Experts Scientifiques du Tourisme, St. Gallen

Katz, A., 1981, Self-help and mutual aid: an emerging social movement, *Annual Review of Sociology*, 129–55

Katz, D., Kahn, R.L., 1966, *The social psychology of organisations*, John Wiley and Sons, New York

Kaufmann, H., 1964, Organisational theory and political theory, *American Political Science Review*, 51: 5–14

Keller, C.P., 1984, Centre-periphery tourism development and control, 77–84 in J. Long and R. Hecock, eds, *Leisure, tourism and social change*, Centre for Leisure Research, Dunfermline College of Physical Education, Dunfermline

Kelly, I., 1989, The architecture and town planning associated with a hallmark event, 263–73 in G.J. Syme, B.J. Shaw, D.M. Fenton, W.S. Mueller, eds, 1989, *The planning and evaluation of hallmark events*, Avebury, Aldershot

Kelly, M., 1986, The Regina Exhibition, 186–205 in Travel and Tourism Research Association (Canadian Chapter), *International events: the real tourism impact, proceedings of the 1985 Canada chapter conference*, Travel and Tourism Research Association (Canadian Chapter), Edmonton

Kemp. S., 1984, Estimating the size of sports crowds, *Perceptual and Motor Skills*, 59: 723–29

Kingston, M., 1987, Llew's Expo auction: eight bid for Brisbane's heart, *Times on Sunday*, 19 July: 1,3

Klassen, J., 1986, The Calgary Exhibition and Stampede, 215–22 in Travel and Tourism Research Association (Canadian Chapter), *International events: the real tourism impact, proceedings of the 1985 Canada chapter conference*, Travel and Tourism Research Association (Canadian Chapter), Edmonton

Knack, R.E., 1982, Knoxville's redevelopment ploy, *Planning*, 48 (7): 8–12

Knipp, S., 1990, A long hard march ahead, *PATA Travel News*, October: 22–3

Kolsun, J., 1988, The Calgary Olympic visitor study, *The Operational Geographer*, 16: 15–17

Kotler, P., 1972, A generic concept of marketing, *Journal of Marketing*, 36: 46–54.

Kotler, P., Levy, S.J., 1969, Broadening the concept of marketing, *Journal of Marketing*, 33 (January): 10–15.

Krippendorf, J., 1987, *The holiday makers: understanding the impact of leisure and travel*, Heinemann Professional Publishing, Oxford

Kusamitsu, T., 1980, Great exhibitions before 1851, *History Workshop Journal*, 9: 70–89

Labrie, P., 1988, The long term tourism and economic impact of major sports events: Montreal and the 1976 Olympics – a love story, 103–5 in *Tourism research: expanding boundaries*, Travel and Tourism Research Association, Nineteenth Annual Conference, Montreal, Quebec, Canada, 19–23 June 1988, Bureau of Economic and Business Research, Graduate School of Business, University of Utah, Salt Lake City

Lavenda, R., Lauer, M., Norwood, J., Nelson, C., Evenson, A., 1984, Festivals and organization of meaning, in B. Sutton-Smith and D. Kelly-Byrne, eds, *The masks of play*, Leisure Press, New York

Lavenda, R.H., 1980, The festival of progress: the globalizing world-system and the transformation of the Caracas carnival, *Journal of Popular Culture*, 14(3): 465–75

Law, C.M., 1985, *Urban tourism: selected British case studies*, Urban tourism project working paper no.1, Department of Geography, University of Salford, Salford

Law, C.M., 1987, Conferences and exhibition tourism, *Built Environment*, 13(2): 85–95

Lawrence, P., Rosenthal, L., 1990, Employment experiences following the Stoke on Trent Garden Festival, *Local Economy*, 5(2): 154–8

Lederer, F.L., 1973, Competition for the World's Columbian Exposition: the Chicago campaign, *Journal of the Illinois State Historical Society*, 45: 365–81

Lee, J., 1984, *Capitalising on sports events*, British Columbia Recreation and Sport, Vancouver

Leiper, N., 1981, Towards a cohesive curriculum in tourism: the case for a distinct discipline, *Annals of Tourism Research*, 8 (1): 69–74

Lenngren, E., 1987, *The America's Cup – it's impact on property values in Fremantle, Western Australia*, unpublished M.Sc. in Surveying Research Project, Department of Real Estate Economics, Royal Institute of Technology, Stockholm

Ley, D., Olds, K., 1988, Landscape as spectacle: world's fairs and the culture of heroic consumption, *Environment and Planning D: Society and Space*, 6: 191–212

Lin, S.G, Patnaik, N., 1982, Migrant labor at Asiad '82 construction sites in New Delhi, *Bulletin of Concerned Asian Scholars*, 14 (3): 23–31

Lipsitz, G., 1984, Sports stadia and urban development: a tale of three cities, *Journal of Sport and Social Issues*, 8 (2): 1–18

Lloyd, B., 1987, The South West Games: an overview, 105–120 in Department of Sport and Recreation, *Marketing sport and recreation events in country regions, Proceedings of a two day seminar 'special event marketing', 15th and 16th July, Warrnambool Performing Arts Centre*, Department of Sport and Recreation, Melbourne

Long, P.T., Perdue, R.R., 1990, The economic impact of rural festivals and special events: assessing the spatial distribution of expenditures, *Journal of Travel Research*, 28 (4): 10–14

Long, P.T., Perdue, R.R., Behm, J., 1987, *1986 Carbondale Mountain Fair visitor survey: an evaluation of nonresident expenditures*, Center for Rural Recreation Development, University of Colorado, Boulder

Louviere, J.J., Hensher, D.A., 1983, Using discrete choice models with experimental design data to forecast consumer demand for a unique cultural event, *Journal of Consumer Research*, 10: 348–61

Low, T., 1983, Métis heritage days, *Recreation Canada*, 41 (5): 26–9

Lowenthal, D., 1977, The bicentennial landscape: a mirror held up to the past, *Geographical Review*, 67: 249–67

Lowi, T.A., 1972, Four systems of policy, politics and choice, *Public Administration Review*, 32 (4): 298–310

Lynch, P.G., Jensen, R.C., 1984, The economic impact of the XII Commonwealth Games on the Brisbane region, *Urban Policy and Research*, 2 (3): 11–14

MacAloon, J.J., 1978, Religious themes and structures in the Olympic movement and the Olympic Games, in F. Landry and W.A.R. Orban, eds, *Philosophy, theology and history of sport and of physical activity*, Miami

MacAloon, J.J., 1981, *This great symbol: Pierre de Coubertin and the origins of the modern Olympic Games*, Chicago

MacAloon, J.J., 1984a, Olympic Games and the theory of spectacle in modern societies, 241–80 in J.J. MacAloon, ed., *Rite, drama, festival, spectacle: rehearsals toward a theory of cultural performance*, Institute for the Study of Human issues, Philadelphia

MacAloon, J.J., 1984b, Introduction: cultural performances, cultural theory, 1–15 in J.J. MacAloon, ed., *Rite, drama, festival, spectacle: rehearsals toward a theory of cultural performance*, Institute for the Study of Human issues, Philadelphia

MacCannell, D., 1973, Staged authenticity: arrangements of social space in tourist settings, American Journal of Sociology, 79 (3): 357–61

MacCannell, D., 1976., *The tourist: a new theory of the leisure class*, Schocken, New York

Maher, M., 1986, Pressure on coastal resources: America's Cup, 207–11 in *Australian environmental council coastal management conference proceedings*, Queensland Institute of Technology, Brisbane

Mandell, R.D., 1967, *Paris 1900*, University of Toronto Press, Toronto

Manning, F.E., ed., 1983a, *The celebration of society: perspectives on contemporary cultural performance*, Bowling Green University Popular Press, Bowling Green

Manning, F.E., 1983b, Cosmos and chaos: celebration in the modern world, 3–30 in F.E. Manning, ed., *The celebration of society: perspectives on contemporary cultural performance*, Bowling Green University Popular Press, Bowling Green

Manning, F.E., 1989, Carnival in the city: the Caribbeanization of urban landscapes, *Urban Resources*, 5 (3): 3–43

Manquis, R., 1989, Parades, parodies and paradigms: the bicentennial of the French revolution, *Environment and Planning D: Society and Space*, 7: 363–5

Marris, T., 1987, The role and impact of mega-events and attractions on regional and national tourism development: resolutions, *Revue de Tourisme*, 4: 3–10

Marsh, J.S., 1984, The economic impact of a small city annual sporting event: an initial case study of the Peterborough Church League Hockey Tournament,

Recreation Research Review, 11: 48–55

Mashiach, A., 1977, A study to determine the factors which influenced American spectators to go see the Summer Olympic Games in Montreal, 1976, Ohio State University, *Dissertation Abstracts International*, 38A, DA77–31931

Mathieson, A., Wall, G., 1982, *Tourism: economic, physical and social impacts*, Longman, London and New York

Matthews, H., 1978, *International tourism: a political and social analysis*, Schenkman Publishing, Cambridge

Mazitelli, D., 1989, Major sports events in Australia – some economic, tourism and sports-related effects, 195–202 in G.J. Syme, B.J. Shaw, D.M. Fenton, W.S. Mueller, eds, *The planning and evaluation of hallmark events*, Avebury, Aldershot

McCloud, P., Syme, J., 1987, Forecasting the economic impact of the America's Cup, 44–74 in *The impact and marketing of special events, papers of the Australian Travel Research Workshop, Mt. Buffalo Chalet, Victoria, 12–14 November, 1986*, Australian Standing Committee on Tourism, Canberra

McCollum, R.H., McCollum, D.F., 1980, Analysis of ABC–TV coverage of the 21st Olympiad Games, Montreal, *Journal of Sport and Social Issues*, 4(1): 25–33

McDonald, M.J., Wheeler, W.B., 1983, *Knoxville, Tennessee: continuity and change in an Appalachian city*, The University of Tennessee Press, Knoxville

McDonald, S., 1988, *The 1988 Adelaide festival: an economic impact study*, Centre for South Australian Economic Studies, University of Adelaide, Adelaide

McDonald, S., 1990a, *The 1990 Adelaide Festival the economic impact, vol.I, Summary*, Tourism South Australia, Adelaide

McDonald, S., 1990b, *The 1990 Adelaide Festival the economic impact, vol.II, methodology and results: details*, Tourism South Australia, Adelaide

McDougall, L., 1986, Two major events in 1984 – a national perspective, 147–68 in Travel and Tourism Research Association (Canadian Chapter), *International events: the real tourism impact, proceedings of the 1985 Canada chapter conference*, Travel and Tourism Research Association (Canadian Chapter), Edmonton

McGeoch, R., 1991, What a Sydney Olympics 2000 could mean for Australian tourism, Tourism '91 conference, Sydney, 27 August.

McGregor, A., 1984, The Games v. land rights as a media event, 9–12 in *The 1982 Commonwealth Games: a retrospect*, Australian Studies Centre, University of Queensland, Brisbane

McKinnon, A., 1987, Warrnambool playing to win: the social and economic benefits of regional events, 58–69 in Department of Sport and Recreation, *Marketing sport and recreation events in country regions, Proceedings of a two day seminar 'special event marketing', 15th and 16th July, Warrnambool Performing Arts Centre*, Department of Sport and Recreation, Melbourne

Melamed, A., Schaecter, J., Emo, M., 1984, The effects of forced location in Montreal, *Habitat*, 27 (4): 29–36

Melbourne Olympic Candidature 1996, 1990, Panel examines social impact of Games, *Melbourne 1996*, June: 2

Mescon, T.S., Tilson, D.J., 1987, Corporate philanthropy: a strategic approach to the bottom line, *California Management Review*, 29: 49–60

Mills, S., 1990, Disney and the promotion of synthetic worlds, *American Studies International*, 28 (2): 66–79

Mills, S., 1991, Spectacle in the city: from the Great Exhibition to the Glasgow Garden Festival, Paper presented at the Institute of British Geographers Conference, Sheffield, January

Mings, R.C., 1978, The importance of more research on the impacts of tourism, *Annals of Tourism Research*, 5: 340–44

Minnikin, R.N., 1987, World Expo 88 – an economic impact study, in *The effects of hallmark events on cities, conference on people and physical environment research, Perth, 15–19 June, 1987*, Centre for Urban Research, University of Western Australia, Nedlands

Mitchell, C., Wall, G., 1986, Impacts of cultural festivals on Ontario communities, *Recreation Research Review*, 13 (1): 28–37

Mommaas, H., van der Poel, H., 1989, Changes in economy, politics and lifestyles: an essay on the restructuring of urban leisure, 254–76 in P. Bramham, I. Henry, H. Mommaas, H. van der Poel, eds, *Leisure and urban processes*, Routledge, London and New York

Montgomery, R., 1968, Hemisfair 68: prologue to renewal, *Architectural Forum*, October: 85–8

Morgan, G., 1986, *Images of organization*, Sage Publications, Newbury Park

Morrison, A.M., 1989, *Hospitality and travel marketing*, Delmar Publishers, Albany

Morrison, J., 1987, Perth leads increase in housing rents, *The Weekend Australian*, 28–9 March: 35

Mulgrew, I., 1984a, B.C. union workers stripped of contract rights at Expo, *Globe and Mail*, 27 August: 8

Mulgrew, I., 1984b, World's fair will go on, Bennett says, *Globe and Mail*, 14 April: 1,2

Mulgrew, I., 1984c, Financial horror returns to haunt fair, *Globe and Mail*, 13 April: 1,4

Murphy, P., 1985, *Tourism: a community approach*, Methuen, New York and London

Murphy, P., Carmichael, B.A., 1991, Assessing the tourism benefits of an open access sports tournament: the 1989 B.C. Winter Games, *Journal of Travel Research*, 29 (3): 32–6

Nancarrow, B., 1989, Foreword, ix–x in G.J. Syme, B.J. Shaw, D.M. Fenton, W.S. Mueller, eds, 1989, *The planning and evaluation of hallmark events*, Avebury, Aldershot.

New South Wales Treasury, 1990, *Economic assessment of Eastern Creek Raceway*, New South Wales Treasury, Sydney

New Zealand Marketing Magazine, 1991, Sponsors demand tangible returns, *New Zealand Marketing Magazine*, 10 (7): 33–4, 36

New Zealand Tourism Board, 1991, *Tourism in New Zealand a strategy for growth*, New Zealand Tourism Board, Wellington

New Zealand Tourism Department, 1991, *New Zealand. Some say it's beautiful, others say it's paradise... You'll say 'It's tough!'* (brochure), New Zealand Tourism Department, Wellington

New Zealand Tourism Department, 1991/92, *New Zealand: the ultimate challenge*, Dow Publishing, Auckland

Newman, P., 1988, Fremantle and the America's Cup: Avoiding the autocratic trap, *Architecture Australia*, 72 (2): 72–7

Newman, P., 1989, The impact of the America's Cup on Fremantle – an insider's view, 46–58 in G.J. Syme, B.J. Shaw, D.M. Fenton, W.S. Mueller, eds, *The planning and evaluation of hallmark events*, Avebury, Aldershot

Noblet, A., 1986, Consolidating this profitable partnership, 24–8 in Australia Council, *Tourism and the arts*, Policy and Planning Division, Australia Council, North Sydney

O'Brien, D., 1991, The bicentennial affair: the inside story of Australia's 'birthday bash', Australian Broadcasting Commission Enterprises, Crows Nest

O'Connell, C.J., 1985, Meeting the challenges of Olympic traffic, *Public Works*, 116 (4): 52–62

O'Gorman, T., 1984, The political impact of the Games II, 43–8 in *The 1982 Commonwealth Games: a retrospect*, Australian Studies Centre, University of Queensland, Brisbane

O'Hara, J., 1986, The grand design of a world's fair: special report/Expo 86. *Macleans*, 99, 17 March: 16–23

O'Neal, M., Finch, P., Hamilton, J.O.C., Hammonds, K., 1987, Nothing sells like sports, *Business Week*, August 31: 48–53

O'Reilly, A., 1987, The impact of cultural hallmark/mega-events on national tourism development in selected West Indian countries, *Revue de Tourisme*, 4: 26–9

Oakes, A.F., 1986, The Canadian National Exhibition (CNE), 206–14 in Travel and Tourism Research Association (Canadian Chapter), *International events: the real tourism impact, proceedings of the 1985 Canada chapter conference*, Travel and Tourism Research Association (Canadian Chapter), Edmonton

Oakley, A., 1987, Glenelg Games: a model for Victoria, 89–95 in Department of Sport and Recreation, *Marketing sport and recreation events in country regions, Proceedings of a two day seminar 'special event marketing', 15th and 16th July, Warrnambool Performing Arts Centre*, Department of Sport and Recreation, Melbourne

Okner, B.A., 1974, Subsidies of stadiums and arenas, 325–48 in R.G. Noll, ed., *Government and the sports business*, The Brookings Institution, Washington D.C.

Okrant, M.J., 1988, Sporting events: an untapped market share for travel and tourism, 91 in *Tourism research: expanding boundaries*, Travel and Tourism Research Association, Nineteenth Annual Conference, Montreal, Quebec, Canada, 19–23 June 1988, Bureau of Economic and Business Research, Graduate School of Business, University of Utah, Salt Lake City

Olds, K., 1988, *Planning for the housing impacts of a hallmark event: a case study of Expo 1986*, unpublished MA thesis, School of Community and Regional Planning, University of British Columbia, Vancouver

Olds, K., 1989, Mass evictions in Vancouver: the human toll of Expo '86, *Canadian Housing*, 6 (1): 49–53

Olsen, M.E., Merwin, D.J., 1977, Toward a methodology for conducting social impact assessments using quality of social life indicators, 43–63 in K. Finsterbusch and C.P. Wolf, eds, *Methodology of social impact assessment*, Dowden, Hutchinson and Ross, Stroudsburg

Olympic Games Social Impact Assessment Steering Committee, 1989, *Social impact assessment Olympic Games bid Melbourne 1996*, report to: Victorian Government, City of Melbourne, Olympic Games Social Impact Assessment Steering Committee, Melbourne

Otker, T., 1988, Exploitation: the key to sponsorship success, *European Research*, 16: 77–86.

Palmer, P., 1989, Attracting major tournaments, the Saint John experience, *Recreation Canada*, 47(4): 44–6

Papson, S., 1981, Spuriousness and tourism: politics of two Canadian provincial government, *Annals of Tourism Research*, 8: 220–35

Park, D., Feros, V., 1985, Planning for World Expo 88, *Australian Planner*, June: 11–15

Patterson, D., 1987, Opening address, 1–6 in Department of Sport and Recreation, *Marketing sport and recreation events in country regions, Proceedings of a two day seminar 'special event marketing', 15th and 16th July, Warrnambool Performing Arts Centre*, Department of Sport and Recreation, Melbourne

Patterson, E., Hagan, J., 1988, *First Australian Masters Games: analysis appraisal*, Tasmanian Department of Sport and Tourism, Hobart

Pearce, D.G., 1989, *Tourism development*, 2nd edn, Longman Scientific and Technical, Harlow

Pearce, J.A., Robinson, R.B., Jr, 1989, *Management*, McGraw-Hill Book Company, New York

Pearce II, J.A., 1980, Host community acceptance of foreign tourists: strategic considerations, *Annals of Tourism Research*, 7: 224–33

Pearse, A., 1956, Carnival in nineteenth century Trinidad, *Caribbean Quarterly*, 4 (3–4): 175–93

Pennington, J., 1987, Country sport and the bicentennial celebrations, 85–8 in Department of Sport and Recreation, *Marketing sport and recreation events in country regions, Proceedings of a two day seminar 'special event marketing', 15th and 16th July, Warrnambool Performing Arts Centre*, Department of Sport and Recreation, Melbourne

Perdue, R.R., Coughlin, A.S., Valerius, L., 1988, Tourism and commercial recreation, 161–74 in L.A. Barnett, ed., *Research about leisure: past, present and future*, Sagamore Publishing, Champaign

Perelman, R.B., ed., 1985, *Olympic retrospective: the Games of Los Angeles*, Los Angeles Olympic Organizing Committee, Los Angeles

Perlstein, J., Piquet, S., 1985, Sponsorship and donation: action evaluation and control, *ESOMAR Weisbarden*, 493–510.

Peters, J., 1982, After the fair: what expos have done for their cities, *Planning*, 18 (7): 13–19

Phillips, J., 1984, Commentary on Macnaught's "mass tourism and the dilemmas of modernization, *Annals of Tourism Research*, 11: 299–302

Pizam, A., 1991, The management of quality tourism destinations, 79–88 in Association Internationale d'Experts Scientifiques du Tourisme, *Quality tourism: concept of a sustainable tourism development, harmonising economical, social and ecological interests*, Association Internationale d'Experts Scientifiques du Tourisme, St. Gallen

Powrie, B.E., 1956, The changing attitudes of coloured middle class towards carnival, *Caribbean Quarterly*, 4 (3–4): 224–32

Preshing, B., 1986, The 1984 papal visit – a research opportunity missed, 141–6 in Travel and Tourism Research Association (Canadian Chapter), *International events: the real tourism impact, proceedings of the 1985 Canada chapter conference*, Travel and Tourism Research Association (Canadian Chapter), Edmonton

Pyo, S., Cook, R., Howell, R.L., 1988, Summer Olympic tourist market – learning from the past, *Tourism Management*, 9(2): 137–44

Pyo, S., Uysal, M., Howell, R., 1988, 1988 Seoul Olympics – visitor preferences, *Tourism Management*, 9(1): 68–72

Queensland Tourist and Travel Corporation, 1989, *Expo 88 impact: the impact of World Expo 88 on Queensland's tourism industry*, prepared by the National Centre for Studies in Travel and Tourism, James Cook University, Queensland Tourist and Travel Corporation, Brisbane

Queensland, 1990a, *South Bank Corporation Area Approved Development Plan, part A*, Government Printer, Brisbane

Queensland, 1990b, *South Bank Corporation Area Approved Development Plan, part B – supporting information*, Government Printer, Brisbane

Quekkett, M., O'Connor, S., 1987, Why Perth has the biggest rent rises, *The West Australian*, 23 March: 6

Redman, M.B., 1983, Economic impact of a short-term tourism industry exposition: a comment, *Annals of Tourism Research*, 10 (3): 434–5

Reed, T., 1980, *Indy: race and ritual*, Presideo Press, San Rafael

Reichert, A., 1978, Three Rivers Festival economic impact study, *Indian Business Review*, March–April: 5–9

Reiss, S.A., 1981, Power without authority: Los Angeles elites and the construction of the coliseum, *Journal of Sport History*, 8 (1): 50–65

Reiss, S.A., 1989, *City games the evolution of American urban society and the rise of sports*, University of Illinois Press, Urbana

Rey, P., 1987, Economic impact of special events using examples of World Cup Athletics, Canberra, 35–43 in *The impact and marketing of special events, papers of the Australian Travel Research Workshop, Mt. Buffalo Chalet, Victoria, 12–14 November, 1986*, Australian Standing Committee on Tourism, Canberra

Richardson, B., Richardson, R., 1989, *Business planning: an approach to strategic management*, Pitman, London

Richter, G., McGeough, P., 1987, A birthday with a $6 billion present – maybe. *Times on Sunday*, 19 July: 6

Richter, L.K., 1983, Tourism and political science: a case of not so benign neglect. *Annals of Tourism Research*, 10: 313–15

Richter, L.K., 1984, A search for missing answers to questions never asked: reply to Kosters, *Annals of Tourism Research*, 11: 613–15

Richter, L.K., 1989, *The politics of tourism in Asia*, University of Hawaii Press, Honolulu

Ritchie, J.R.B., 1984, Assessing the impact of hallmark events: conceptual and research issues, *Journal of Travel Research*, 23 (1): 2–11

Ritchie, J.R.B., Aitken, C.E., 1984, Assessing the impacts of the 1988 Olympic Winter Games: the research program and initial results, *Journal of Travel Research*, 22 (3): 17–25

Ritchie, J.R.B., Aitken, C.E., 1985, OLYMPULSE II – evolving resident attitudes towards the 1988 Olympic Winter Games, *Journal of Travel Research*, 23 (Winter): 28–33

Ritchie, J.R.B., Beliveau, D., 1974, Hallmark events: an evaluation of a strategic response to seasonality in the travel market, *Journal of Travel Research*, 14 (Fall): 14–20

Ritchie, J.R.B., Hu, Y., 1987, The role and impact of mega-events and attractions on national and regional tourism: a conceptual and methodological overview, Paper presented at the 37th Annual Congress of the International Association of Scientific Experts in Tourism (AIEST), Calgary, Canada, August

Ritchie, J.R.B., Lyons, M.M., 1987, OLYMPULSE III/IV: a mid-term report on resident attitudes concerning the 1988 Olympic Winter Games, *Journal of Travel Research*, 26 (Summer): 18–26

Ritchie, J.R.B., Lyons, M.M., 1990, OLYMPULSE VI: a post-event assessment of resident reaction to the XV Olympic Winter Games, *Journal of Travel Research*, 28 (3): 14–23

Ritchie, J.R.B., Smith, B.H., 1991, The impact of a mega-event on host region awareness: a longitudinal study, *Journal of Travel Research*, 30 (1): 3–10

Roberts, E.J., McLeod, P.B., 1989, The economics of a hallmark event, 242–9 in G.J. Syme, B.J. Shaw, D.M. Fenton, W.S. Mueller, eds, *The planning and evaluation of hallmark events*, Avebury, Aldershot

Robinson, A., Noël, J-G., 1991, Research needs for festivals: a management perspective, *Journal of Applied Recreation Research*, 16 (1): 78–88

Roche, M., 1988, *Mega-events and multipliers: issues for the sociology of tourism*, Policy Studies Centre, University of Sheffield, Sheffield

Roche, M., 1990, *Mega-events and micro-modernization: on the sociology of the new urban tourism*, Policy Studies Centre, University of Sheffield, Sheffield

Roche, M., 1991, *Mega-events and urban policy: a study of Sheffields World Student Games 1991*, Policy Studies Centre, University of Sheffield, Sheffield

Roeper, J. de., 1986, The Adelaide Festival as a tourist attraction, 13–17 in Australia Council, *Tourism and the arts*, Policy and Planning Division, Australia Council, Sydney

Rooney, J.F., 1988, Mega-Sports events as tourist attractions: a geographical analysis, 93–9 in *Tourism research: expanding boundaries, Travel and Tourism Research Association, Nineteenth Annual Conference, Montreal, Quebec,*

Canada, June 19–23, 1988, Bureau of Economic and Business Research, Graduate School of Business, University of Utah, Salt Lake City

Runyan, D., Wu, C–T., 1979, Assessing tourism's more complex consequences, *Annals of Tourism Research*, 6: 448–63

Ryan, L., 1984, Griffith University, land rights and the Games, 5–8 in *The 1982 Commonwealth Games: a retrospect*, Australian Studies Centre, University of Queensland, Brisbane

Rydell, R.W., 1978, The World's Columbian Exposition of 1893: racist underpinnings of a utopian artifact, *Journal of American Culture*, 1: 253–75

Rydell, R.W., 1981, The Trans-Mississippi and International Exposition: 'to work out the problem of universal civilization', *American Quarterly*, 33: 587–607

Rydell, R.W., 1983, Visions of empire: international expositions in Portland and Seattle, *Pacific Historical Review*, 52: 37–65

Rydell, R.W., 1984, *All the world's a fair*, The University of Chicago Press, Chicago

Sack, R.D., 1988, The consumer's world; place as context, *Annals, Association of American Geographers*, 78: 642–65

Saeniger, D., 1987, Mass participation and tourism: North Queensland Regional Games, 121–8 in Department of Sport and Recreation, *Marketing sport and recreation events in country regions, Proceedings of a two day seminar 'special event marketing', 15th and 16th July, Warrnambool Performing Arts Centre*, Department of Sport and Recreation, Melbourne

Sawicki, D.S., 1989, The festival marketplace as public policy, *Journal of the American Planning Association*, 55: 347–61

Selwood, H.J., Hall, C., 1986, The America's Cup: a hallmark tourist event, 67–82 in J. Marsh, ed., *Canadian studies of parks, recreation and tourism in foreign lands*, Occasional Paper 11, Department of Geography, Trent University, Peterborough

Selwood, H.J., Hall, C.M., 1988, The hidden underbelly: some observations on the unpublicized impacts of the America's Cup, Canadian Association of Geographer's Annual Conference, St. Mary's University, Halifax

Seth, P., 1990, Along the right lines, *Asia Travel Trade*, 22 (January): 30–36.

Shalofsky, I., di San Germano, N., 1985, Sponsorship impact and how to read it – the need for research, *ESOMAR Milan*: 217–28

Shaw, B.J., 1985, *Fremantle W.A. and the America's Cup the impact of a hallmark event*, Working Paper No. 11, Australian Studies Centre, Institute for Commonwealth Studies, University of London, London

Shaw, B.J., 1986, Fremantle and the America's Cup... the spectre of development?, *Urban Policy and Research*, 3 (2): 38–40

Shaw, B.J., 1989, The 'auld mug' and the 'vintage port' – papers dealing with the effect of the America's Cup defence upon Fremantle, W.A.: an introduction, 43–5 in G.J. Syme, B.J. Shaw, D.M. Fenton, W.S. Mueller, eds, *The planning and evaluation of hallmark events*, Avebury, Aldershot

Sheldon, P.J., Var, T., 1985, Tourism forecasting: a review of empirical research, *Journal of Forecasting*, 4 (2): 183–95

Shephard, D., 1982, *Community organisations and hallmark events, a case study of the Wellesley Apple Butter and Cheese Festival*, Unpublished undergraduate honours research project, Department of Recreation, University of Waterloo, Waterloo

Shinnick, P.K., 1982, Progressive resistance to nationalism and the 1980 boycott of the Moscow Olympics, *Journal of Sport and Social Issues*, 6 (2): 13–21

Shire of Bright, 1988, Hosting a world championship, *Local Government Management*, 22 (6): 8–10

Silverman, D.L., 1978, The 1889 Exhibition: the crisis of bourgeois individualism, *Oppositions*, 8: 71–91

Singer, M., ed., 1959, *Traditional India: structure and change*, Philadelphia

Slade, M., Picard, R., Blackorby, C., 1986, The macroeconomic consequences of Expo, 231–56 in R. Anderson and E. Wachtel, eds, *The Expo story*, Harbour Publishing, Madeira Park

Smith, E., 1987, Marketing techniques for hallmark events (the first Australian defence of the America's Cup, 75–96 in *The impact and marketing of special events, papers of the Australian Travel Research Workshop, Mt. Buffalo Chalet, Victoria, 12–14 November, 1986*, Australian Standing Committee on Tourism, Canberra

Smith, V., ed., 1977, *Hosts and guests: the anthropology of tourism*, University of Pennsylvania Press, Philadelphia

Smith, M.P., Keller, M., 1983, '"Managed growth" and the politics of uneven development in New Orleans', 126–66 in N. Fainstein and S. Fainstein, eds, *Restructuring of the city: the political economy of urban redevelopment*, Longman, New York

Sneddon, R., 1987, Sponsorship: what's it all about? Why do companies sponsor, 142–50 in Department of Sport and Recreation, *Marketing sport and recreation events in country regions, Proceedings of a two day seminar 'special event marketing', 15th and 16th July, Warrnambool Performing Arts Centre*, Department of Sport and Recreation, Melbourne

Socher, K., 1987, Economic impacts of Olympic Winter Games, *Revue de Tourisme*, 2: 24

Socher, K., Tschurtschenthaler, P., 1987, The role and impact of mega-events: economic perspectives – the case of the Winter Olympic Games 1964 and 1976 at Innsbruck, 103–17 in Association Internationale d'Experts Scientifiques du Tourisme, *The role and impact of mega–events on regional and national tourism development*, Association Internationale d'Experts Scientifiques du Tourisme, St. Gallen

Soutar, G.N., McLeod, P., 1989, The impact of the America's Cup on Fremantle residents: some empirical evidence, 92–102 in G.J. Syme, B.J. Shaw, D.M. Fenton, W.S. Mueller, eds, *The planning and evaluation of hallmark events*, Avebury, Aldershot

Sparrow, M., 1989, A tourism planning model for hallmark events, 250–262 in G.J. Syme, B.J. Shaw, D.M. Fenton, W.S. Mueller, eds, *The planning and evaluation of hallmark events*, Avebury, Aldershot

St–Onge, T., 1991, Canada's 125th anniversary: an example of public participation, *Journal of Applied Recreation Research*, 16 (1): 53–60

Stansfield, C.A., 1991, Book review: festivals, special events, and tourism, *Annals of Tourism Research*, 18 (2): 350–3

Stewart, J.K., 1986, Strategy and organization for annual events: introduction, 180–5 in Travel and Tourism Research Association (Canadian Chapter), *International events: the real tourism impact, proceedings of the 1985 Canada chapter conference*, Travel and Tourism Research Association (Canadian Chapter), Edmonton

Stoddard, R.H., 1982, *Field techniques and research methods in geography*, Kendall Hunt, Dubuque

Styles, P., 1990, Attracting sponsorship for your event, in Tourism South Australia, *Seminar for organisers of festivals and special events: speakers notes*, Tourism South Australia, Adelaide

Susman, W.I., 1980, The people's fair: cultural contradictions of a consumer society, 17–28 in H. Harrison, ed., *Dawn of a new day: the New York World's Fair, 1939/40*, The Queens Museum/New York University Press, New York

Sutton, R., 1984, On being the host broadcaster: producing the Games, 13–18 in *The 1982 Commonwealth Games: a retrospect*, Australian Studies Centre, University of Queensland, Brisbane

Sydney Olympic Games Citizens' Council, 1988, Executive summary of submission to the Australian Olympic Federation, 31 August, Appendix B in Sydney Olympic Games Review Committee, 1990, *Report to the Premier of New South Wales*, 11 December, Sydney Olympic Games Review Committee, Sydney

Sydney Olympic Games Review Committee, 1990, *Report to the Premier of New South Wales*, 11 December, Sydney Olympic Games Review Committee, Sydney

Taylor, P., Gratton, C., 1988, The Olympic Games: an economic analysis, *Leisure Management*, 8 (3): 32–4

Telecom Australia, Royal Perth Yacht Club, Western Australian Tourism Commission, 1986, *The Official America's Cup directory, a visitor's guide*, Government Printing Office of Western Australia, Perth

The Australian, 2 May 1984: 13

The West Australian, 10 October 1986

The West Australian, 14 May 1987: 4

The West Australian, 1987, Rumours hurt WA, says tourism body, *The West Australian*, 20 July: 32

Thomas, A., 1984, The spirit of '76?: Calgary, site of the 1988 Winter Games, is showing symptoms of 'Montreal disease' – the scandal and debt that followed in the wake of the Montreal Olympics, *Saturday Night*, 99 (3): 67–8

Thomason, P.S., Perdue, R.R., 1987, Festivals and special events, *Leisure Today, Journal of Physical Education, Recreation and Dance*, 58: 54–6

Thorburn, A., 1986, Marketing cultural heritage: does it work in Europe?, *Travel and Tourism Analyst*, Decenber: 39–48

Thorne, R., Munro–Clark, M., 1989, Hallmark events as an excuse for autocracy in urban planning: a case history, 154–71 in G.J. Syme, B.J. Shaw, D.M. Fenton, W.S. Mueller, eds, *The planning and evaluation of hallmark events*, Avebury, Aldershot

Thorne, R., Munro-Clark, M., Boers, J., 1987, Hallmark events as an excuse for autocracy in urban planning: a case history, in *The effects of hallmark events on cities*, Centre for Urban Research, University of Western Australia, Nedlands

Thrift, N., Forbes, D., 1983, Review essay. A landscape with figures: political geography with human conflict, *Political Geography Quarterly*, 2: 247–63

Thurot, J.M., Thurot, G., 1983, The ideology and class of tourism: confronting the discourse of advertising, *Annals of Tourism Research*, 10: 173–89

Tighe, A.J., 1985, Cultural tourism in the USA, *Tourism Management*, 6 (4): 234–51

Tomlinson, A., Whannel, G., eds, 1984, *Five ring circus: money, power and politics at the Olympic Games*, Pluto Press, London

Tourism South Australia, 1990a, *Planning of festivals and special events*, Planning and Development Division, Tourism South Australia, Adelaide

Tourism South Australia, 1990b, Notes on the Tourism South Australia festivals assistance scheme, in Tourism South Australia, *Seminar for organisers of festivals and special events: speakers notes*, Tourism South Australia, Adelaide

Townley, S., Grayson, E., 1984, *Sponsorship of sport, arts and leisure*, Sweet and Maxwell, London

Travis, A.S., Croizé, J-C., 1987, The role and impact of mega-events and attractions on tourist development in Europe, 59–78 in Association Internationale d'Experts Scientifiques du Tourisme, *The role and impact of mega-events on regional and national tourism development*, Association Internationale d'Experts Scientifiques du Tourisme, St. Gallen

Tuppen, J.N., 1985, *Urban tourism in France – a preliminary assessment*, Urban tourism project working paper no.3, Department of Geography, University of Salford, Salford

Turner, V., 1957, *Schism and continuity*, Manchester

Turner, V., 1974, *Dramas, fields and metaphors*, Ithaca

Turner, V., 1984, Liminality and the performative genres, 19–41 in J.J. MacAloon, ed., *Rite, drama, festival, spectacle: rehearsals toward a theory of cultural performance*, Institute for the Study of Human Issues, Philadelphia

Turner, V., ed., 1982, *Celebration: studies in festivity and ritual*, Smithsonian Institution Press, Washington D.C.

Turner, V., 1983, Carnival in Rio: Dionysian drama in an industrializing society, 103-24 in Manning, F.E., ed., *The celebration of society: perspectives on contemporary cultural performance*, Bowling Green University Popular Press, Bowling Green

Tweed, D.M., Hall, C.M., 1991, The management of quality in the service sector: an end in itself or a means to an end? in *Australian and New Zealand Association of Management Educators conference proceedings*, Bond University, Queensland

Ueberroth, P., 1985, *Made in America: his own story*, William Morrow, New York

United States Department of Housing and Urban Development, 1981, *The urban fair: how cities celebrate themselves*, Office of Public Affairs, United States Department of Housing and Urban Development, Washington D.C.

Unsworth, B.J., 1984, New Darling Harbour Authority Bill, *NSW parliamentary debates*, Legislative Council, 26 November: 1485–9

Uysal, M., Backman, K.F., Backman, S.J., Potts, T.D., 1991, An examination of event tourism motivations and activities, pp.203–18 in R.D. Bratton, F.M. Go, and J.R.B. Ritchie, eds, *New horizons in tourism and hospitality education, training and research*, World Tourism Education and Research Centre, University of Calgary, Calgary

Uysal, M., Crompton, J.L., 1985, An overview of approaches used to forecast tourism demand, *Journal of Travel Research*, 23: 7–15.

Uzzell, D., 1984, An alternative structuralist approach to the psychology of tourism marketing, *Annals of Tourism Research*, 11: 79–99

Van Der Lee, P., 1987, The Adelaide Grand Prix and tourism, 15–34 in *The impact and marketing of special events, papers of the Australian Travel Research Workshop, Mt. Buffalo Chalet, Victoria, 12–14 November, 1986*, Australian Standing Committee on Tourism, Canberra

Van Der Lee, P., Williams, J., 1986, The Grand Prix and tourism, 124–50 in J.P.A. Mules, J.H. Hatch and T.L. Mules, eds, *The Adelaide Grand Prix: the impact of a special event*, The Centre for South Australian Economic Studies, Adelaide

Vanhove, N., Witt, S.F., 1987, Report of the English-speaking group on the Conference theme, *Revue de Tourisme*, 4: 10–12

Vaughan, D.R., 1977, *The economic impact of the Edinburgh Festival, 1976*, Scottish Tourism Board, Edinburgh

Wachtel, E., 1986, Expo 86 and the World's Fairs, 19–44 in R. Anderson and E. Wachtel, eds, *The Expo story*, Harbour Publishing, Madiera Park

Waites, J., 1991/92, Gay crossover, *The Independent Monthly*, 3(6): 18–22

Wall, G., Guzzi, J., 1987, *Socio-economic analyses of the 1980 and 1988 Winter Olympics* (draft), University of Waterloo, Waterloo

Wall, G., Hutchinson, J., 1978, Community festivals in Canada and the anatomy of one of the most popular, Oktoberfest, *Recreation Canada*, 36 (6): 21–4

Wall, G., Knapper, C., 1981, *Tutankhamun in Toronto*, Department of Geography Publication Series, 17, University of Waterloo, Waterloo

Wall, G., Mitchell, C., 1989, Cultural festivals as economic stimuli and catalysts of functional change, 132–41 in G.J. Syme, B.J. Shaw, D.M. Fenton, W.S. Mueller, eds, *The planning and evaluation of hallmark events*, Avebury, Aldershot

Wallis–Smith., 1989, Major international sporting events – characteristics and criteria for selection: a South Australian viewpoint, 203–13 in G.J. Syme, B.J. Shaw, D.M. Fenton, W.S. Mueller, eds, *The planning and evaluation of hallmark events*, Avebury, Aldershot

Wang, P., Gitelson, R., 1988a, Economic limitations of festivals and other hallmark events, *Leisure Industry Report*, August: 4–5

Wang, P., Gitelson, R., 1988b, Limitations with the economic benefits of short-term events, 257-61 in *Tourism research: expanding boundaries, proceedings of the 19th Travel and Tourism Research Association Conference, Montreal, Quebec*, Travel and Tourism Research Association, Boulder

Wanhill, S.R.C., 1989, Pricing for event catering, *International Journal of Hospitality Management*, 8 (4): 299–308

Wardlaw, D., 1990, Barossa Valley Vintage Festival – why is it successful?, in Tourism South Australia, *Seminar for organisers of festivals and special events: speakers notes*, Tourism South Australia, Adelaide

Warhurst, J., 1987, The politics and management of Australia's bicentennary Year, *Politics*, 22: 8–18

Warhurst, J., 1988, Politial studies and the monarchy, *Politics*, 23: 1–7

Warnock, J.W., 1987, Politics in lotusland: Jimmy Pattison and the making of carnival '86, *Newest Review*, 12 (7): 10–11

Watson, L., 1984, The land rights movement after the Games, 1–4 in *The 1982 Commonwealth Games: a retrospect*, Australian Studies Centre, University of Queensland, Brisbane

Weber, M., 1968, *Economy and society*, Free Press, New York

Weiler, B., Hall, C., 1992, Conclusion. Special interest tourism: in search of an alternative, 199–204 in B. Weiler and C.M. Hall, eds, *Special interest tourism*, Belhaven, London

Wells, J., Dunn, J., 1991, Marketing research for a hallmark event to maximise tourism benefits, paper presented at the Costs and Benefits of Tourism Conference, University of Newcastle, Newcastle (NSW, Australia)

Western Australia, Legislative Assembly, 1986, *Hansard*, 18 November 1986: 4381–2

Western Australian Police Department, 1986, *America's Cup defence operational orders*, America's Cup Division, Western Australian Police Department, Perth

Western Australian Police Department, 1987, *America's Cup Division De-Briefing Report*, America's Cup Division, Western Australian Police Department, Perth

White, C.A., 1986, Evictions: no room at the inn, *Canada and the World*, 51: 4

White, P., 1991, Games and circuses: the state and the creation of spectacle in Paris, paper presented to the session of 'Cities of Spectacle', Institute of British Geographers Conference, 4 January

Wilkins, B.W., 1987, Special events – what works and what doesn't, 133 in Department of Sport and Recreation, *Marketing sport and recreation events in country regions, Proceedings of a two day seminar 'special event marketing', 15th and 16th July, Warrnambool Performing Arts Centre*, Department of Sport and Recreation, Melbourne

Willens, M., 1978, Selling of a spartan spectacle, 1984: The three scenarios for the LA Olympic Games, *California Journal*, 9: 41–4

Willis, J., 1987, Bicentenary launch set for Sunday, *Times on Sunday*, 19 July: 6

Wilson, J., Udall, L., 1982, *Folk festivals: a handbook for organisation and management*, University of Tennessee Press, Knoxville

Witt, S.F., 1988, Mega-events and mega-attractions, *Tourism Management*, 9(1): 76–7

Witt, S.F., 1989a, Forecasting international tourism demand: the econometric approach, 163–9 in S.F. Witt and L. Moutinho, eds, *Tourism marketing and management handbook*, Prentice Hall, Hemel Hempstead

Witt, S.F., 1989b, Forecasting international tourism demand: univariate time series methods (noncausal quantitative techniques), 169–74 in S.F. Witt and L. Moutinho, eds, *Tourism marketing and management handbook*, Prentice Hall, Hemel Hempstead

Witt, S.F., Martin, C.A., 1987, International tourism demand models – inclusion of marketing variables, *Tourism Management*, 8 (1): 33–40

Wolch, J., Law, R., 1989, Social reproduction in a post–Fordist era, *Society and Space*, 7: 249–52

World Tourism Organisation, 1985, *The state's role in protecting and promoting culture as a factor of tourism development and the proper use and exploitation of the national cultural heritage of sites and monuments for tourism*, World Tourism Organisation, Madrid

Yake, G.A., 1974, Expo 74 sparks city's downtown renewal, *The American City*, November: 55–6

Young, L., 1988, The Sydney International Exposition: 1879, Australia's first expo, *Heritage*, 7(2): 25–9

Zauhar, J., Kurtzman, J., 1991, Professional preparation for the management of festival events, 363–74 in R.D. Bratton, F.M. Go, and J.R.B. Ritchie, eds, *New horizons in tourism and hospitality education, training and research*, World Tourism Education and Research Centre, University of Calgary, Calgary.

Zeppel, H., 1992, Case study: the Festival of Pacific Arts: an emerging special interest tourism event, 69–82 in B. Weiler and C.M. Hall, eds, *Special interest tourism*, Belhaven Press, London

Zeppel, H., Hall, C.M., 1991, Selling art and history: cultural heritage and tourism, *Journal of Tourism Studies*, 1 (3): 29–45

Zeppel, H., Hall, C.M., 1992, Review: art and heritage tourism, 46–68 in Weiler, B. and Hall, C.M., eds, *Special Interest Tourism*, Belhaven Press, London

Zimmerman, L., 1974, The seven eras of world's fairs – 1851–1976, *Progressive Architecture*, 8: 64–9

Zukin, S., 1987, Gentrification: culture and capital in the urban core, *Annual Review of Sociology*, 13: 129–47

Zwolak, R., 1987, Economic impacts of hallmark events, 7–30 in Department of Sport and Recreation, *Marketing sport and recreation events in country regions, Proceedings of a two day seminar 'special event marketing', 15th and 16th July, Warrnambool Performing Arts Centre*, Department of Sport and Recreation, Melbourne

Name Index

Place Index

Subject Index